COLD WARS

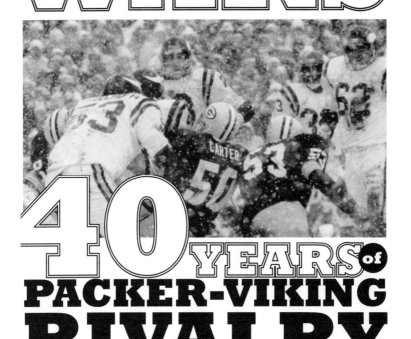

40 YEARS of PACKER-VIKING RIVALRY

TODD MISHLER

Prairie Oak Press
A division of Trails Media Group, Inc.
Black Earth, WI

Library of Congress Control Number: 2002107959
ISBN: 1-931599-16-5

Editor: Jerry Minnich
Designer: Colin Harrington
Cover Designer: John Huston
Cover Photo: Vernon J. Biever

Printed in the United States of America by McNaughton & Gunn.
07 06 05 04 03 02   6 5 4 3 2 1

Prairie Oak Press, a division of Trails Media Group, Inc.
P.O. Box 317 • Black Earth, WI 53515
(800) 236-8088 • e-mail: books@wistrails.com
www.trailsbooks.com

DEDICATION

To my family and friends for their love and support throughout the years. To my wife, Carol, who believed in me even when I didn't; my kids, Trevor and Rachel, the two best things I've co-authored; and to my mother-in-law, Sue, and brother-in-law, Val, who as Viking fans inspired this project more than they know.

ACKNOWLEDGMENTS

TO THE FOOT SOLDIERS who've been involved in these border wars since 1961: the players, coaches, fans, and media members, especially those who took the time for interviews and to share their perspectives.

Also to the Packers and Vikings public relations staffs for the information they provided. And to Penny Paris of Children's Hospital in Appleton, Wisconsin, and Corinne Beavers of the NFL's Retired Players Association, for their help in tracking down many of the former gladiators.

TABLE OF CONTENTS

FOREWORD
by Stu Voigt, Former Minnesota Vikings Tight End

ALTHOUGH IT ISN'T THE longest rivalry in sports, you wouldn't know it by the intensity and passion involved in a Viking-Packer game, whether it was in 1961 or 2001. As a player and then a broadcaster, I have been around most of those games.

My recollections are still clear, which further indicates that as a Viking we took the rivalry very seriously.

It is important to note that in the 40-year time span that the teams have played, dominance has shifted back and forth without affecting the quality or significance.

I'm sure the geographical closeness of the teams has played a role, as has the great support that the teams' fans give the players. Throw in the fact that many of the games have been played during inclement weather only enhances the vivid memories everyone has.

They have been called border battles, which is appropriate because of the bragging rights that Wisconsin and Minnesota fans claim and relish with every win "they" achieve. I have known of many families that have been strained as Packer and Viking fans are forced to get along during the football season.

When I was playing with the Vikings and going back to work on my master's degree at the University of Wisconsin, I felt that even though I was a hometown boy that many still thought of me as the enemy. My parents remained Green Bay fans even though I spent 11 years as a Viking tight end.

My memories of the rivalry are special. Whenever I caught a touchdown pass or was on the winning end of the score, it meant more than the normal NFL contest. The guys I played alongside, as well as those I competed against, are greatly respected. I'm proud when honors or recognition have been bestowed upon Viking or Packer players.

A Madison native, I was a huge Packer fan during the glory years of Vince Lombardi. It really inspired me to want to emulate my boyhood heroes. Since playing and then living in the Twin Cities since 1970, I have fallen in love with Minnesota, too. I look at the rivalry a little differently, which is understandable. Regardless, at least twice a year I watch my two favorite teams battle it out. In my mind, that creates even better memories.

FOREWORD

by Blaise Winter, Former Green Bay Packers Defensive Lineman

I SPENT 11 YEARS IN the National Football League, losing parts of my mind and body while playing in the trenches of some amazing games. Be it in the AFC or NFC, the NFL was a rush: the best coaches, players, and competition the sport has to offer.

Winning gives you the right to talk with pride. To know that control comes to those who win is a thrill. To control a region and possibly a country with the mind-set that you are better than everybody else is what competitors live for. This relentless search for excellence brings about classic match-ups with special meaning. The Packer-Viking games have that appeal.

The obvious regional/divisional placement creates the friction necessary to start the fire. States being side-by-side with loyal fans reminded players like me about the importance of dominance. It's not good enough to win. You must win, win, and win again so you can express superiority for years to come. The Packer-Viking rivalry has a rich history, one that causes the level of intensity to rise to new heights within many people.

To realize you'll be a part of that history makes efforts extraordinary. Being a football player with the Packers was nothing but electrifying because, like the Packers-Vikings, it makes you realize how tough you must be to play the game.

But toughness takes on a new meaning when it's close to home. The games are played with the same rules, but not in the same way. It's bone-jarring and mind-blowing because it always seems to have a playoff atmosphere. To know that these two games (one home, one away) can determine your fate when it comes to reaching the Super Bowl adds even more to the emotional pull of the moment.

It's like a family feud. You're part of one family, you know each other well (past and present) and live in the same neighborhood. But boy do you dislike each other the more you get to know one another.

Since my retirement from playing football and the emergence of my career as a motivational speaker, I thought the Packer-Viking conversations would fade. Was I ever wrong. When you're a part of something so big, even for players like me, it never goes away.

So, let this book touch you by reminding you how great the Packers-Vikings games are. It truly shows how big America's love is for this game, these two teams and the NFL.

INTRODUCTION:
NORSEMEN COMETH

Dave "Hawg" Hanner (79) and other Packer defenders chased Minnesota running back Hugh McElhenny around in 1961–62. McElhenny was named to the National Football League's Hall of Fame in 1970.

IN THE YEAR 845, the infamous raider Ragnar and his Danish flotilla of 120 ships sailed for Paris. Ragnar's fleet approached by mid-March, forcing Charles the Bald, king of the West Franks, to conscript an army. However, he foolishly divided it in two to guard opposite banks of the Seine River.

The Vikings took 111 prisoners in trouncing the inept monarch's outnumbered ranks. Then, as the other group watched in horror, Ragnar sacrificed his Frankish captives, hanging them on makeshift gallows. Needless to say, Ragnar met with no more resistance.

On Easter Sunday, he moved onward and ravaged Paris. Charles offered the Danes the awesome sum of 7,000 pounds of silver to induce them to mercifully leave, and they accepted. So it was that Ragnar departed, clutching his souvenir, a bar taken from the Paris city gate.

The hefty ransom was the first of many so-called danegelds, or Danish money, surrendered to Viking raiders during the coming years as fiefdoms of Western Europe sought relief from the endless barrage of assaults.

Move west one hemisphere and fast-forward 1,115 years to January 1960. A group of marauders, including such aptly named leaders as H.P. Skoglund and Ole Haugsrud, invaded the kingdom known as the National Football League.

Within a few months, they hired Bert Rose as general manager. One of his first maneuvers was to recommend a nickname for this new breed of battlers, a symbol that represented an aggressive person who exuded the will to win and expressed the Nordic tradition of the region.

Thus, the Minnesota Vikings were born, a band of purple-and-gold-clad warriors who've continued to pillage their neighbors on a battlefield called the gridiron and in an arena appropriately described as the Black and Blue Division.

Unlike the surprise attacks that their distant ancestors faced from the dreaded soldiers of the North, combatants in such places as Green Bay, Chicago, and Detroit have known the enemy was coming, often welcoming the annual invasions because they always got to return the favor.

And none of the confrontations has been more fierce and competitive than the border wars fought between the Minnesota Vikings and the Green Bay Packers.

Sports writer Jim Klobuchar chronicled most of the Twin Cities franchise's conquests and defeats since its inception, and this entry from his most recent book, *Knights and Knaves: 40 Years of Pro Football and the Minnesota Vikings*, characterizes the series so well.

Klobuchar wrote: "The Viking rosters, even their earliest years, were dappled with players of distinction, won then or later in their careers. Fran Tarkenton, Hugh McElhenny, Tommy Mason, Grady Alderman, Mick Tingelhoff, Jim Marshall, Bill Brown, Ed Sharockman, and more. But the personification of the team for the six years he coached it was [Norm] Van Brocklin. He engulfed the team and gave it its waterfront mentality.

"Vince Lombardi hated to play the Vikings. He had a football team with stars, discipline, and championships, and in the early years Green Bay whipped the Vikings in all venues. But Lombardi was convinced that somehow Van Brocklin was schooling designated thugs on his team to maim his players. It was a suspicion that festered with special furies after Jerry Kramer, one of his best linemen, suffered a leg fracture in a game against Minnesota.

"None of the Vikings ever corroborated Lombardi's private charges in the years that followed, which simply proves there are symptoms of paranoia in all coaches. Van Brocklin's last pregame orders to his brawling mediocrities were to 'go get yourself a jockstrap,' meaning 'hit somebody.' It's a code to which practically all football coaches subscribe. But it was heard with particular attention by the Viking warriors of the early 1960s because not hitting somebody usually meant adios for the timid soul (if he was lucky) or consignment to the kickoff team (if he wasn't)."

Such has been the backdrop for a rivalry that's only intensified with each season, each game, and each blow, physical or verbal. So much so that it is being mentioned in the same breath with the Green and Gold's celebrated feud with the Bears, and that's saying something. Actually, that speaks volumes.

Bob Harlan joined the Green Bay organization in 1971 and has been at the forefront in keeping the franchise viable and vibrant. Named president and chief executive officer in 1989, the Iowa native and Marquette University graduate also witnessed the down times before he hired General Manager Ron Wolf, a move that signaled a rebirth in Titletown in the 1990s.

But throughout the Packers' struggles, one thing that emerged from the rubble was their series against the Vikings.

"The most significant thing when I first came here was that there was no doubt that our rivalry with the Chicago Bears was at the top," Harlan said via phone interview from his Lombardi Avenue office. "But the success that the Vikings had has made them the hottest ticket in town and made this a very intense rivalry. A lot of people in Minnesota were Packer fans before they came around and have continued to support the Packers, and that's obvious by the huge following we have when we play at the Metrodome."

Harlan, whose steadying but aggressive leadership has earned him kudos around the state and throughout the league, said the Minnesota–Green Bay matchup is arguably the best series in the NFL.

"This goes back to when the Vikings had Bud Grant and Fran Tarkenton. They were a very, very strong team," Harlan said. "Now, when they played outside at old Met Stadium it was very difficult, and today we have no tougher places to play than in the Metrodome and at Pontiac [the Silverdome, home of the Detroit Lions].

"But this border rivalry has grown and grown; just ask anybody in our ticket offices," Harlan added. "It's become a heated rivalry, and that's why sweeping them in 2000 was so big for us, particularly winning over there in December, when we won all four games against division teams. And the fact that that victory was our 100th for Ron Wolf only added to the significance.

"These two organizations want to beat each other at everything, but they respect us and we respect them."

Minnesota and Green Bay have squared off 81 times since 1961; they played only once during the 1982 strike season. The Vikings entered the NFL as an expansion team, beginning their existence under the late Van Brocklin, who coached them through the 1966 season.

Heading into 2002, the series amazingly is tied, each team having won 40 games. There also has been one tie, a 10-10 overtime standoff played in Green Bay in 1978. Along the way, five other games have been decided in sudden death, the Vikings prevailing 27-21 in 1979 and 13-10 in 1994, both at home, and 20-17 in 1983 and 23-20 in 1992 in Green Bay. The Packers' first and only overtime victory came in 2000 on wide receiver Antonio Freeman's miraculous catch at Lambeau Field for a 26-20 decision.

Another surprising fact is how well the teams have played at each other's stadiums: The Vikings are 21-19 at home after losing their first seven on friendly turf and are 19-21-1 away, including 6-9 at Milwaukee and 13-12-1 at Lambeau. The Vikings won four times on the road before claiming their first home victory (1968) and won 11 of their first 17 tries in Green Bay or Milwaukee. The teams have split home-and-home series 17 times, and during eight of those seasons, the visitors have won all of the games, all from 1964–83.

One person who walked the sidelines for 26 years worth of those games was Jerry Burns, the colorful and lovable character who was a secondary coach for Green Bay's Super Bowl I and II teams before working with the Vikings from 1968–91, the final six as head coach.

"Burnsie" led the team to three straight playoff berths before 6-10 and 8-8 campaigns issued in the Dennis Green era. He said the fans from both sides have stoked the flames in this series from the beginning.

"When I think about Green Bay and Minnesota, I see snow-covered fields and stands and people dressed up in snowmobile suits, lots of cold-weather games and situations," said Burns via telephone from his Twin Cities area home. "But the thing that stands out the most is the fans. It was always more intense because of the Green Bay fans, particularly when the Packers came over here. This was Green Bay territory before Minnesota became a solid entrant in the league. And the success they had under Vince Lombardi, and then the Vikings had under Bud Grant, only added to it.

"Good or bad, they were hard-fought games," Burns added. "In their heyday, the Packers had trouble with the Vikings, and the same thing happened with Minnesota."

Burns, who coached at the University of Iowa for 12 years and worked with Grant in the Canadian Football League, said every contest in the Central Division was a slugfest. However, the atmosphere surrounding the Viking-Packer games set them apart.

"Because of being neighboring states, you had people intermingling because of families and business, so it was bigger with the fans than it was for us as coaches," he said. "All of the parties prior to the games and the cooking at the stadiums, especially at the old Met and Lambeau. The Packer fans couldn't be nicer win or lose, but the rivalry was definitely fueled by the fans."

And that continued regardless of which team enjoyed the upper hand.

Minnesota's longest winning streak in the series was seven games from 1975 until the tie in 1978; it's also won four in a row three times. Green Bay's best string is six, the first six games in the series. It also won five straight from 1983–85. Green Bay won nine of the first 10 meetings, with its only loss being by one point in 1964.

The Vikings' biggest winning margin was 35 points, 42-7 in 1986. Green Bay's largest victory was by 29, 42-13 in 1964. The Packers also earned 28-point triumphs twice (45-17 in 1984 and 38-10 in 1996). Thirty of the games, counting the tie, have been decided by a touchdown or less, including 11 of 18 from 1992 through 2000.

Longtime Milwaukee sports journalist Bud Lea opened his article in the Nov. 2–8, 2000, issue of the *Journal-Sentinel's Packer Plus* magazine with this statement: "The Minnesota Vikings have been the moment of truth for the Green Bay Packers over the past eight years."

Much of that can be attributed to Mike Holmgren taking control in the league's smallest city and Dennis Green grabbing the reins in Minnesota. Both men joined the NFL head coaching fraternity in 1992 after learning the ropes under the Bill Walsh–George Seifert regime in San Francisco.

So, whether Holmgren or Green would admit it, the rivalry automatically became more significant because of their shared backgrounds, forceful personalities, and leadership abilities.

And those intangibles quickly permeated the locker rooms and spilled onto the playing fields twice every season, often escalating into gamesmanship at its best.

Classic examples have included Minnesota wide receiver Cris Carter head-butting Green Bay safety Darren Sharper, Packer center Frank Winters and Viking defensive lineman John Randle showing off their kicking talents, Minnesota cornerback Corey Fuller poking Winters in the eye because he accused Winters of hitting after the whistle, and Green Bay quarterback Brett Favre grabbing Viking middle linebacker Jeff Brady's facemask while exchanging pleasantries.

However, many of these heated and colorful incidents would easily have slipped into people's subconscious had both teams not been so successful.

Minnesota and Green Bay combined to win seven of the nine Central Division titles from 1992 through 2000, with the Vikings making the playoffs eight times and the Packers six.

This rivalry has become the biggest in the Midwest and has dramatically climbed the ladder in league importance, illustrated by the fact that one of their matchups was booked for coveted "Monday Night Football" coverage four straight seasons starting in 1997.

And even though most of their showdowns have been instrumental in determining postseason positioning, the bizarre plays and unpredictable endings have pushed this series into the national spotlight.

Who can forget the Terrell Buckley and T.J. Rubley snafus that turned almost certain Green Bay victories into crushing setbacks? Or the dumbfounded expressions of the Packer defensive backs after Randall Cunningham and Randy Moss repeatedly sliced and diced them up to end the second-longest regular-season home winning streak in league history? Or the ESPY Award–winning catch that Freeman made to give Green Bay the thrilling victory in 2000?

So, while Detroit and Tampa Bay have been far from pushovers, those tussles have never attained the level of the Packers vs. the Vikings, at least not over the long haul. And although rabid Packer and Bear fans might have legitimate arguments, Green Bay vs. Chicago wasn't much of a rivalry for a long time before the 2001 contests, both Packer victories. Green Bay has won 14 of its last 16 meetings with the team from the Windy City, taking much of the luster off that series. Chicago held an 11-7 advantage in the 1980s, which was one of the most intense periods in that or any rivalry's history.

But even that was often a personal battle of wills between coaches Forrest Gregg of the Packers and Mike Ditka of the Bears, as Chicago was a division contender while Green Bay plodded through another decade of losing. Although they played close games, the Bears and Packers were usually terrible in the 1970s. And in the 1960s, the perennial champion Packers swatted away the Monsters of the Midway by a 15-5 margin, with 1963 being the last time these two foes really played a late-season contest with playoff ramifications for both teams until 2001.

The Packers and Vikings have gone through peaks and valleys, too.

Green Bay dominated the early going, but Minnesota often provided the Packers with many frustrating and nerve-wracking games in the 1960s, pulling upsets in '64, '66, and '67 against some of Lombardi's best lineups. And despite controlling the Central during the 1970s, Grant's Super Bowl contenders seldom had an easy time with the Packers. In the 1980s, both squads often earned middle-of-the-pack status, but explosive offenses and porous defenses usually created entertaining encounters.

Wild and wacky finishes haven't been relegated to the 1990s. What about the 1964 get-together at Green Bay in which Tarkenton and the Vikings overcame a fourth-and-22 situation to set up the game-clinching field goal for the visitors' first win in the series?

Then there was the dreadful 1971 affair in which Minnesota triumphed 3-0 despite registering team records for fewest first downs (5) and yards gained (87) because the Packers' generosity featured fumbles, interceptions, and failed short-yardage plays deep in Viking territory.

And the Sept. 23, 1979, contest that Minnesota tied at 21 late before winning it in overtime when Tommy Kramer hooked up with Green Bay nemesis Ahmad Rashad on a 50-yard scoring pass in overtime.

Or the 1987 strike replacement game at the Metrodome in which Jim Bob Morris' interception at the goal line made him a hero and Minnesota quarterback Tony Adams the goat in securing Green Bay's 23-16 decision.

This series, although more civil than the Packer-Bear free-for-alls of the 1980s and the bygone days of the '40s through mid-'50s, has featured its share of extracurricular activities and offbeat characters.

Remember the October 1978 game in which Grant and the Minnesota bench wanted to lynch Green Bay defensive tackle Dave Roller for hitting Tarkenton late on the Viking sidelines? Roller was penalized and booted out of the game because of his action against his former New York Giant teammate.

The Bears weren't the only ones Gregg had his run-ins against, as illustrated by the 1969 grudge match against the Vikings at the University of Minnesota in which he got kicked out after an altercation with former Packer teammate Dale Hackbart, an incident that so incensed the All-Pro offensive tackle that he wanted to continue the discussion afterward in the parking lot.

Viking defensive tackle Keith Millard was considered one of the most off-the-wall players around, making his hand-to-hand battles against Green Bay guard Rich Moran, who attended the same California high school, as intense as any in the series.

Then there was pass-rushing linebacker Tim Harris, Green Bay's earlier equivalent of Minnesota's John Randle. Harris' constant trash talking and post-sack six-shooter routine irritated opposing blockers to no end, while Randle's painted face, comments about their mothers, and dog barking antics has gotten inside the head of more than one Green Bay offensive lineman.

And who could forget fiery Minnesota signal-caller Joe Kapp, who according to one former Green Bay television reporter gave the Packers the finger after turning in a big play to beat them in the late 1960s. And then there were the tirades of Van Brocklin and Lombardi, two men whose tempers often erupted close to each other because both benches were on the same side of the field at Metropolitan and County stadiums.

While fans have witnessed numerous plot twists in this storied rivalry during the past four decades, it may never have taken place if not for a series of events during 1922–1923.

Green Bay was struggling financially when a second major rainstorm during the 1922 season threatened to cancel the Packers' contest against Duluth. If they played, the expected low crowd turnout wouldn't be enough to pay the guarantees they owed the visiting team.

Green Bay Press-Gazette business manager Andrew B. Turnbull convinced cofounders Curly Lambeau, the coach, and George Calhoun, the newspaper's sports editor, that they had to play the game if they wanted to keep professional football alive in the small northeastern Wisconsin city. Turnbull paid the advance and also spearheaded an effort to round up investors for a stock sale to finance the next season, which provided the basic foundation of the team's corporate structure that remains intact today, an arrangement unique in the NFL.

The Minnesota angle to the story doesn't pick up again until after World War II. Green Bay played exhibition games in the Twin Cities in 1948, 1951–54, and 1957–59, competing for crowds ranging from 15,000 to 21,000.

Minneapolis was scheduled to become one of eight charter members of the American Football League but was lured away by a promise of a team in the senior professional league for 1961. The team that became known as the Vikings was replaced in the AFL lineup by the Oakland Raiders.

So, the Packers and their beloved faithful followers have blessed and cursed that geographical and competitive change in fortune ever since. And as the series has ebbed and flowed, fans from both sides of the mighty Mississippi River, many because they live and/or work in "enemy territory," have suffered and rejoiced accordingly.

The depth to which they bleed, no matter if it's green or purple, is something to behold. Take this letter to the editor that was published in the Sunday, November 12, 2000, edition of the *Minneapolis Star-Tribune*. Eau Claire, Wisconsin, resident Steve Flaten's comments after the Packers' upset and unbelievable 26-20 win were titled, 'I demand a re-kick.'

"I am outraged by the outcome of last Monday night's game between the Green Bay Packers and the Minnesota Vikings. American football fans should also be outraged at the unfair advantage afforded the Packers.

"At the end of regulation play the Vikings were attempting a field goal that would have assured victory, but because of weather irregularities, the wet ball was mishandled and we did not get the three points we rightfully had coming to us.

"In Minnesota, you see, we play in a dome. We don't have to worry about rain, snow or wind. It is unfair that we should lose this game because of Green Bay's lousy weather. After all, we've scored more points than the Packers so far this season. For crying out loud, we have a better record!

"I have called upon Jesse Jackson to come to Green Bay and hold a rally to demand that the Vikings be allowed to re-kick the ill-fated field goal in the Metrodome. Our governor, the honorable Jesse Ventura, will monitor the kick and make sure that the outcome is fair and unbiased."

Many Viking fans and players have grown soft since moving indoors, a fact lamented by those graybeards from the 1960s and '70s from both organizations. But that doesn't negate what Flaten and his brethren go through after circling two dates on their calendars when the NFL schedule is announced every April.

At this point, we won't get into what these fans, these masters of the tailgate party, have done to—or put inside—their bodies before, during, and after these games. Suffice it to say, they know how to celebrate or drown their sorrows better than most, and Packer and Viking fans will go to great lengths to display their loyalties.

Take Everett "Hub" Meeds. He liked his Minnesota team so much that he became one of the Vikings, or should we say, The Viking. Meeds became Ragnar, the team's mascot, the guy every opponent loved to hate. He strolled the Viking sidelines or beyond the end zone for 22 years (1970–92). The Stillwater native taunted opposing players and fans while titillating his fellow gold-braided disciples. His life as a true weekend warrior began innocently enough, although it occurred on professional football's biggest stage, the Super Bowl.

"My brother and I went down to the game in New Orleans," Meeds said of the Vikings' eventual 23-7 setback to Kansas City in Super Bowl IV on January 11, 1970. "We rented some Viking costumes, went into the stadium around where the players come out and nobody said a word to us or asked for tickets or anything. So we got to see the whole game from down on the field.

"That spring, I wrote a letter to the team and told them what we had done and asked them about doing it for their home games," Meeds added. "I got my picture in the paper with Bud Grant and everything. They didn't have anybody doing it, and eventually I got to go to all of the away games. I only missed one preseason game in all of those years."

Amazing, especially considering he was originally a Green Bay fan.

"I was a Packer fan for quite a few years and even for the first three or four years that the Vikings were around," said Meeds from his St. Paul residence. "The Packers were all we had in those days."

Meeds, who earned his nickname from his brother as a youngster, looked much more imposing in his Viking regalia than he actually was.

"I was 5-foot-11 and 210 pounds," said Meeds. "TV always makes you look bigger than you really are."

Like this series and many fellow Viking and Packers fans, Meeds was larger than life. But he enjoyed every minute of being his alter ego.

"It was always more fun when they played outside, even when it was cold," Meeds said. "Being indoors was more like you were on a stage. People take their coats off and you had to get them warmed up. When they played at the Met, everybody tailgated. It was one big party. But we couldn't do that when they moved downtown."

A host of things have changed since the Vikings left Bloomington, except for the hordes of those known lovingly or despisingly as Cheeseheads, the same ones who make themselves feel right at home inside the thunderous Metrodome once every season.

Minnesota players have expressed respect and contempt for such devotion. *Minneapolis Star-Tribune* columnist Patrick Reusse observed both sides in his commentary that was published in *Packer Plus* after the Vikings remained unbeaten (4-0) and knocked the rolling Packers (3-1) down a notch in their first meeting in 1996, which was before Green Bay picked up steam en route to its victory in Super Bowl XXXI in New Orleans.

Vikings' free safety Orlando Thomas couldn't believe the sea of cheese despite Minnesota's victory.

"It was 50-50 out there with the fans," Thomas said after Minnesota's 30-21 victory. "When the Packers made some plays early, it sounded like we were playing on the road, in Miami or someplace."

In the same article, teammate Derrick Alexander talked about how he finally had had enough after gazing at the myriad banners that zealous Packer-backers had brought with them. And the second-year defensive end said Green Bay wide receiver Robert Brooks rubbed salt in the wound when he tried to do one of his trademark Lambeau leaps into the stands.

"I didn't think Brooks should have done that in our stadium," the Florida State graduate said. "I don't think we would go to Green Bay and do something like that (Randy Moss has feigned the Lambeau leap several times since then). And I don't think those banners belonged in our stadium. Before the game, a couple of us said, 'We're going to get those things after we win.'"

A later target of Alexander's rage was one that read, "Hey diddle, diddle, Koonce in the middle," in reference to Packer middle linebacker George Koonce, who then returned a Warren Moon interception 75 yards for a score, pressing the football against the banner when he arrived at pay dirt.

Koonce's score had put the visitors ahead 21-17, but the Vikings rallied, and then Alexander headed for the south end zone. He ripped up the Koonce banner one diddle at a time and disposed of several others before finishing his tirade. "I had to do it," Alexander said. "We shouldn't have to see that in our stadium."

No player represents the emotions of these engagements more than former veteran Viking wideout Cris Carter, who never met an opposing defensive back he couldn't antagonize, a teammate he didn't yell at if necessary, or a first down he failed to signal for.

Carter displayed that fiery attitude after Corey Bradford's TD catch rallied the Packers past Minnesota, 23-20, at Lambeau in 1999, a game in which Carter also kicked one of the Packers' defensive backs.

"It's a football game," Carter told the *Journal-Sentinel*. "Did you come to a ballet or a football game? That's what a football game is about when you play your rival."

Poetically spoken by an artist whose dancing toes around the sidelines only Mikhail Baryshnikov could appreciate. However, the latter doesn't have hands like the acrobatic Ohio State product, who has more than backed up his words and antics with on-field results.

But in this rivalry, words have often spoken louder than actions; unless you've seen the national television commercial in which former Minnesota defensive lineman Randle is shown chasing a chicken that's wearing a No. 4 Favre jersey. While members of PETA weren't laughing, Randle got his bird, and fans have eaten up everything to do with these teams.

Whether they're waving Purple Pride or Titletown towels, this matchup has evoked the best and worst from the fans and the teams. Win or lose, players know these contests are a whole new ball game.

Take Viking running back Robert Smith, who surprised friend and foe alike with his retirement shortly after the 2000 season. He got a close-up look at just how much love Packer fans had for him when Minnesota visited Lambeau in September 1997.

The speedy Ohio State product said it was the first time in his professional career that he looked up and saw somebody in the stands with his No. 26 doll hanging in effigy, which in his mind meant that he had finally arrived, because the fans really hated him.

Even the staunchest Green Bay fans, if they truly appreciate the competitive nature of the sport and their skirmishes with the Vikings, had to be saddened by Smith's exit during the prime of his career.

Meanwhile, these games have become a spectacle that won't fade, and the friendly and not-so-friendly fire won't die.

Odin, the Norse god of battle, still joyously feasts with his compatriots in Valhalla, the mythological hall where he receives great warriors after their deaths.

The ghosts of stars past and present continue to glide across the frozen tundra the same as always, and because of realignment beginning in 2002, they'll be playing in a division even more appropriately named, the NFC North.

The *Journal-Sentinel*'s Lea hit the proverbial nail on the head in a September 1998 column in *Packer Plus* when he wrote this about the rivalry: "It's not a game, it's a mania. Packers vs. Vikings. It's hate. It's fear. It's anger. It's joy. It's memories."

So, here's a salute to 40 more years of games, mania, hate, fear, anger, joy and memories.

CHAPTER ONE

THE 1960s TITLETOWN AND THE UPSTARTS

Guard Gale Gillingham (68) provides the protection for quarterback Bart Starr in
Green Bay's 9-7 loss to Minnesota in November 1969 at Milwaukee's County Stadium.

DAVE ROBINSON was an All-American end at Penn State University who became one of the best pass-defending linebackers in the National Football League with Green Bay.

The team's No. 1 draft pick in 1963 registered 21 interceptions during his 10 seasons with the Packers, including five in 1966. One of his first thefts stands out, at least the part about the play he can remember, and it happened against the Vikings.

"Most of the players from Minnesota were great guys. Some I got to know from playing in the Pro Bowl and some that I developed friendships with over the years," said Robinson, who was named All-Pro from 1967–69 before playing his final two seasons with the Washington Redskins in 1973–74. "I think there was only one guy I didn't like and that was a tight end named Hal Bedsole.

"In my senior year in college, Pat Richter (from Wisconsin), me and Bedsole (from Southern California) made the *Look* magazine All-America team and were going to be on the Johnny Carson show. Well, I hear Bedsole asking Richter, 'How did Robinson ever make the team? He never caught any passes.' I walk over and tell him that's because we hardly ever threw the ball, but I played both ways and he was the first one they snatched off the field.

"Well, it so happens that he gets drafted (No. 2) by the Vikings and we're playing them," added Robinson, who was inducted into the Packer Hall of Fame in 1982. "I grab an interception over my shoulder in the end zone and I see a flash. He hit me so hard I went out like a light. Ray Nitschke picks me up and hauls me to the sidelines. I decided I was going to systematically get him and beat him up.

"Sometime in the fourth quarter, Herb Adderley sees the blood on my jersey and asks me how I'm feeling. I told him the blood must be Bedsole's, and Herb tells me that Bedsole isn't No. 89, he's No. 86. I guess I had gotten my revenge on the wrong guy."

Like many players from both teams, Robinson recalled his first game against Minnesota, the one in which Hank Gremminger raced 80 yards after Adderley blocked a field goal to secure a 37-28 victory in 1963, and his last, the Packers' division-clinching 23-7 win at Metropolitan Stadium in December 1972. Robinson said the teams engaged in many classic and sometimes wacky battles.

"Bill Brown was quite a ball carrier," said Robinson, who also recovered eight fumbles in his Green Bay career. "I think it was my rookie year and he beat Dan Currie on that pattern where he would go out and then down the sideline. Dan was a good cover guy, but Brown beat him on that one, so I was always worried about that because he was such a great receiver.

"And I always thought Dave Osborn was one of the best running backs in the league. After he got hurt he wasn't quite the same player, but I had great respect for him.

"And Fran Tarkenton always gave us fits," Robinson said from his former Ohio business office. "We had a drill where one of our faster, younger players would run around, and Willie Davis, Henry Jordan, and the other defensive linemen had to chase him. By Friday they had it down. Then on Sunday it looked like they had forgotten everything they learned. Sometimes it seemed like Fran had eyes in the back of his head and was always running for his life. But many people don't remember how well he threw on the run, and that's what made him so effective."

And as always is the case with any good rivalry, the two combatants' records weren't indicative of how their encounters came out.

"We played many tight ball games against Minnesota," Robinson said. "I remember the first time I went up to Met Stadium and we got a bigger applause than they did, and I'm sure that didn't sit too well with them. They wanted to prove that they belonged in the NFL. They were all big games. Besides, who wanted to come back home with Vince Lombardi after a loss?"

Robinson and the Packers didn't have to worry about that too often, especially early in the series. Green Bay survived victorious nine of the first 10 games from 1961–65.

However, the Vikings weren't alone as Green Bay dominated most teams during its great run, compiling the best record in football in the 1960s at 96-37-5. The Packers won NFL titles in 1961, '62, '65, '66, and '67 after claiming a Western Conference championship in 1960, losing 17-13 to Philadelphia in the title contest.

The Packers also finished second to Chicago in 1963 and tied the surprising Vikings for runner-up status in 1964. The Packers finished with a winning record in 1969, meaning their only losing campaign was 1968 when they finished 6-7-1. Victories in the first two Super Bowls highlighted Green Bay's efforts. Meanwhile, the Vikings compiled a 52-67-7 record for a .440 winning percentage, which ranked 17th out of 26 professional teams during the decade.

Their first winning season was 1964, when the Vikings fashioned an 8-5-1 mark. Minnesota won its first division title in 1968 and went to Super Bowl IV after the 1969 season, winning its second straight Central Division crown on the way. The Vikings lost 23-7 to the Kansas City Chiefs at Tulane Stadium in New Orleans.

Mick Tingelhoff was there for that game and the Vikings' three other futile attempts to bring the Vince Lombardi Trophy home during the 1970s. Regardless of how much they dominated the series, the University of Nebraska product and his teammates knew that one of their annual chores was getting past the Packers.

"I remember my first game as a rookie, lining up across from [Ray] Nitschke," Tingelhoff said of the 34-7 defeat in the 1962 season opener at Green Bay. "That was a thrill because he was such a tough guy and good player. I remember seeing Ray at the Pro Bowl and he said to me with that growlly voice of his, 'Wait until next year, I'm gonna get you.'

"But I played under Coach Lombardi and with guys like Forrest Gregg and Fuzzy Thurston at the Pro Bowl," the seven-time All-Pro said. "They were great players and real gentlemen. Going up against Henry Jordan and Willie Davis was tough, but we would laugh about it later."

Tingelhoff got in his share of good licks, earning Pro Bowl selection six times. He played in 240 consecutive contests for the Vikings, second only to Jim Marshall's 270-game streak.

He has lived in Prior Lake, a south Minneapolis suburb, for 23 years. Tingelhoff has worked in the investment business, owned restaurants with former teammate Paul Krause, and run filling stations among his many career endeavors. One of Tingelhoff's fondest memories was snapping the ball on kicker Fred Cox's game-winning field goal in the Vikings' first victory in the series, a 24-23 triumph at Lambeau Field in 1964.

However, he said it didn't matter who was the better team, the wars they fought on the gridiron stayed there.

"We always looked forward to playing them, and one of our goals every year was to beat the Packers," said Tingelhoff, whose jersey No. 53 was retired by the team during the 2001 season. "We knew we had to play hard and well. It was really a friendly rivalry. If you won, you won, and if you lost you tried again the next time. It never carried over after the games."

That may have been true, but spectators wouldn't know it after the rugged foes tightened their chinstraps. And stalwarts such as Minnesota's Bill Brown didn't earn or keep their nicknames for being nice or having fun. Then again, players called "Boom Boom" relished the thought of contact in the violent world they lived in every weekend.

The Mendota, Illinois, native attended the University of Illinois, where he was a fullback/linebacker between the tenures of Nitschke and future Chicago great Dick Butkus; Brown was a freshman when Nitschke was a senior and was a senior when Butkus was a freshman.

Brown, whose son-in-law, Rich Gannon, played for the Vikings (1987–92) and later became the starting quarterback for the Oakland Raiders, was selected in the second round by the Bears in the 1961 draft. That happened a round after somebody picked Ditka. A year later Brown was traded to the Vikings, also in their second season in the NFL, for a fourth-round draft pick and stayed there until 1974.

"Trading me was the best thing Mr. [George] Halas ever did," Brown said with a raspy laugh. "He did it on the Thursday before the opening game of the season, but I came back to haunt him. He wrote me a letter later that said it was the worst move he ever made."

Brown showed why, as the four-time Pro Bowler rushed for 52 touchdowns and added another 23 receiving. More times than not he portrayed the Vikings' version of the Packers' Paul Hornung, both called upon to find the end zone once their team reached scoring position.

"Fullbacks were asked to do everything," said Brown, who's lived in the Bloomington area for 30 years, settling in the northern suburb of Coon Valley, where he most recently worked in sales.

"I was capable of doing a lot of things, so they used me. I blocked, could catch the ball, and ran decent. And I played on most of the special teams units. Some players felt it was above them, but that never bothered me. It was part of the game."

And so was battling the Packers twice a year.

"It was a damn good rivalry," said Brown, third on Minnesota's all-time rushing yardage list behind Robert Smith and 1970s star Chuck Foreman. "Even when we were neophytes in the league, we were one of their nemeses. We had some real knock-down, drag-out games here and over there."

One person he wishes he hadn't met so often was Green Bay middle linebacker Nitschke, meetings he might have avoided had he signed with the AFL's New York Titans or in Canada, places he said he could have made two or three times more money than the $11,000 deal he inked with Chicago.

"God bless him, but as the fullback I had to hit him many times and we knocked each other down some," said Brown of the late Nitschke. "I got to meet Ray more than I preferred. I thought maybe because we were from the same alma mater that I wouldn't have to take so much abuse from him and Mr. Butkus."

One old warrior who called Nitschke and Brown friend and foe alike was Billy Butler. The Berlin, Wisconsin, native was taken by Green Bay out of Tennessee-Chattanooga in the 19th round in 1959, Lombardi's first draft as coach and general manager. Green Bay lost him to Dallas in the 1960 expansion draft, and then he joined the Vikings from 1962-64 after arriving from Pittsburgh for a sixth-round choice.

Butler handled the most kickoff and punt returns for the two division rivals all four years with the teams, taking back punts for scores from 61 and 60 yards in 1959 and 1963, respectively.

"I averaged about 58 minutes per game in college, and in those days you only had 37-man rosters [in the NFL], so you played both ways," said Butler, who settled in his hometown in 1989 after 20-plus years in the auto business in Milwaukee. "I returned punts and kicks, backed up [Paul] Hornung at halfback, [Boyd] Dowler, who was my roommate, at receiver, and [Emlen] Tunnell at free safety. And I played free safety and backup halfback at Minnesota."

Butler has attended NFL Alumni Association meetings and events several times but said he hadn't really kept track of his former football employers. He remembers the rivalry, though.

"It was kinda intense," he said. "You gotta remember that Minnesota Viking fans prior to them getting a team were Green Bay fans, and then they switched sides. And Green Bay fans were always half nuts. You had packed houses, people all drunk and raisin' hell. It was quite a show."

The action was just as nasty on the field, said Butler, who scored the first interception return for a TD in Minnesota history when he scampered

39 yards against the Rams on October 21, 1962.

"[Norm] Van Brocklin was fiery as hell, and Lombardi was just as bad," Butler said. "It was knock-down, drag-out stuff. It was probably one of the better additions to the NFL getting Minnesota in. It was a pretty damn good rivalry."

Jerry Kramer agreed wholeheartedly with Butler's assessment, and he saw firsthand how the games turned into dogfights because the teams were reflections of their coaches, who were both later inducted into the Hall of Fame.

"Coach Lombardi was so frustrated with us," said Kramer, one of the best of many storytellers to grace this series, recalling a locker room incident in which his boss took center stage. "He couldn't understand why we were letting up or what was going on, but the Vikings were playing their tails off. It was halftime, and he was stormin' around the room raisin' hell. He kicked a wastebasket over and ended up limpin' around the locker room. We got a giggle outta that one."

Kramer, the author of several books about his beloved Packers, garnered All-Pro honors five times and earned Pro Bowl selection three years from his right guard position. He also remembered how the hot-tempered Van Brocklin could erupt.

"We were a pretty straight group of guys on the field, ya know, like 'yes, sir,' and stuff like that," Kramer said. "But one game it was halftime and we were heading to the locker room in different directions, and I get pretty close to Van Brocklin and he hollers, 'Kramer, you c---------.' I almost dropped my teeth. I couldn't think of any particular reason other than that he was very frustrated and a competitive guy, and I happened to be the one who walked by at the time."

Longtime Green Bay trainer, the late Domenic Gentile, recounted an episode involving both temperamental coaches in his 1995 book, *The Packer Tapes*: "Once the Vikings were driving against our defense at the Met. They scored an apparent touchdown on a pass play, but Lombardi ran up and down the sidelines screaming 'Interference, interference!' One of the officials saw the offensive penalty and threw a flag. Both teams were on the same sideline and Van Brocklin thought Lombardi had influenced the guy to make a call. He hollered at Vince, 'Nice call, you [bleep] dago.'"

Gentile continued: "Vince, of course, was extremely upset about the slur, but he didn't say anything. However, after the game, which we won, he threw a tantrum in the locker room, calling the Vikings a bunch of crybabies. He became so worked up he almost passed out. Packers Hall of Famer Tony Canadeo, then one of the team's radio broadcasters, had to calm him down and bring him into the training room to sit down."

Tarkenton knew that Van Brocklin, "The Dutchman," always welcomed mixing it up with Lombardi's crew, as these comments from his book *Tarkenton* demonstrate:

"I think he [Van Brocklin] was at his best when we played Green Bay. Maybe the competition with Vince Lombardi and the idea of matching his underdogs against the champions motivated him. His preparation for those games was always excellent. We played some tremendous football, tactically as well as physically, against the Packers."

According to Gentile, Lombardi believed strongly in taking precautions when it came to injuries.

"He had a rule that every player had to have his ankles taped for practices," Gentile wrote in *The Packer Tapes*. "If you were caught without your ankles taped it was a $150 fine. In the 1960s, when most players were making $25,000 or $30,000, that was a lot of money.

"Lee Roy Caffey, one of our starting linebackers, didn't bother getting his ankles taped for a light workout the day before a game against the Minnesota Vikings. Sure enough, he sprained his ankle.

"Lombardi came over and said, 'Lift up your sweats and pull down your socks, Lee Roy.' He saw that there was no tape. 'OK, Lee Roy, that'll be $150.'

"The next morning we were at the stadium getting ready for the game. Lee Roy was sitting on the training table, his ankle swollen and an ugly shade of purple. There was no way he was going to play that day. Lombardi walked in, took the ice bag off Caffey's ankle and studied it for a few seconds. 'Well, Lee Roy, I'll tell you what. If you play today, the fine will be rescinded,' he said. "Caffey didn't hesitate. He looked straight at me and said, 'Tape up.' He went out and played the entire game."

That tough-as-nails mentality was no more evident than with Minnesota quarterback Joe Kapp, whose will to win rivaled his bruising approach to the game.

The Salinas, California, native led the University of California to the Rose Bowl and the British Columbia Lions to the Grey Cup in Canada before quarterbacking Grant's Vikings to their first Central Division title (1968) and first appearance in the Super Bowl after the 1969 season.

Kapp's personality fit perfectly into the kind of rough-and-tumble play that dominated the NFL's toughest division.

"It was a challenge playing head-to-head in the Black and Blue Division, a lot of tight ball games," said Kapp, who coached his college alma mater from 1982–86. "It was a privilege and honor to play against guys like Bart Starr, Jerry Kramer, Nitschke, Adderley and Willie Wood.

"They were champions and always had the great linebackers," Kapp added. "Shit, you had better be tough. There were lots of great linebackers in our division and in the league, like Nitschke, Butkus, [Mike] Lucci, and [Tommy] Nobis. That was the way football ought to be played."

Kapp, although he struggled mightily against Green Bay, led the Vikings to five wins in six games against the Packers during his three years at the helm.

"None of us on the offense was too famous," Kapp said. "We were the ugly ducklings. Our defense, the Purple People Eaters, had our stars. We played a lot of close games because that's how our offense was designed. I didn't necessarily have a lot of love for Coach Grant, but I sure had a lot of respect for him."

Dale Hackbart made the Packers roster in 1960–61 and then joined the Vikings for five seasons starting with the 1966 campaign, which happened to be Van Brocklin's last in Minnesota. He also witnessed the wrath of Lombardi and Van Brocklin and got to play for Grant, so he knew exactly how much winning meant to them and the players in this series.

Hackbart was always an aggressive player, accruing more than 100 yards in penalties in 1967. He said it was a thrill to square off against the team he grew up cheering for.

"Playing against Green Bay was a big event for me," said Hackbart, a versatile University of Wisconsin alumnus and Madison native who also played with the Washington Redskins, St. Louis Cardinals, and Denver Broncos. "They were the team of the 1960s. The games were always close, and it was a bitter rivalry, but I have a lot of good friends from those Packer teams."

He led the Vikings in interceptions with five in his first year with the club, including a 41-yard touchdown return. Usually a free safety, Hackbart played strong and weak side linebacker in Jimmy Carr's scheme that became known as "The Hack" defense.

Hackbart has lived in Colorado the past 30 years, working in the mining division for Bridgestone/Firestone the last 18. Most of his family resides in Wisconsin and Illinois, and some of the greatest moments during his professional career revolved around the Minnesota–Green Bay series.

"I'll always remember the game at the University of Minnesota [October 5, 1969]," said Hackbart, who played quarterback at Wisconsin and was a fan of Packer greats Tobin Rote and Tony Canadeo. "Bobby Bryant intercepted a pass and I blindsided Forrest Gregg. I hit him in the ribs real good, but it was a clean block. And he didn't know who it was, but he also got hit from the other side by Lonnie Warwick.

"But Forrest gets up and cold-cocks me with his forearm," Hackbart said. "Well, the official sees that and throws him outta the game. The interesting thing that didn't get printed in the newspaper was that when I was leaving, Forrest was outside near the Green Bay bus. I told him to look at the film tomorrow, but I could see the fire in his eyes. He started chasing me around the bus, but he wasn't nimble enough to catch me."

The Boulder resident and avid skier said his career may have been much different if not for a fateful day against the Detroit Lions.

"It was my second year with the Packers and Willie Wood returned a punt like 70 yards for a touchdown," Hackbart said. "I threw a couple of blocks and got into a skirmish with a guy who thought I had clipped him. It happened right in front of the Green Bay bench. Well, Phil Bengtson starts chewing my butt off, that I could have cost us the game. I told him I didn't clip and ended up by telling him where he could go.

"Well, Fuzzy Thurston is standing right next to us and tells me I shouldn't have said that," continued Hackbart. "So, I told Fuzzy where he could go, too. The next day during the film session, Phil watches the play and sees that my block is what sprung Willie, and he apologized to me. Then after practice, Lombardi points his big finger at me and tells me that I'd been traded to Washington.

"It was devastating at the time, but making the Packers roster my first year was a career highlight for me. I can't help but think if I would have kept my mouth shut that day that maybe I would have spent my whole career there, but we'll never know."

However, several Green Bay receivers got to know Hackbart and his Minnesota secondary mates up close and personal. One of them was long-striding flanker Boyd Dowler.

The University of Colorado graduate never reached the 60-catch plateau, but he was a consistent producer and threat for Bart Starr and others during his 11 years (1959–69) wearing No. 86: He grabbed between 29 and 54 passes every year. He finished with more than 6,900 yards receiving and contributed nineteen 100-yard days. Dowler led or tied for the team lead in catches seven times, including four straight from 1962 to 1965.

Many of those highlights came against his rivals to the west. He caught touchdown passes in six of the foes' first 10 meetings, including a 70-yarder in the 1961 series opener. Dowler downplayed those efforts.

"The truth is, when they first came into the league they weren't very good, so when we threw the ball we did pretty well," said Dowler from his home in the Tampa, Florida, area. "They played a whole bunch of zone defenses, and Bart was good at reading where to go and what to do, so we were effective and productive against them.

"But then they came up with guys like Alan Page and Carl Eller to put pressure on the quarterback, and we started going downhill after our championships, and we couldn't do much with them. They won all four games in 1968 and 1969.

"I remember guys like Karl Kassulke, Bobby Bryant, Ed Sharockman, and Dale Hackbart, all pretty tough guys and hitters, and then they had Paul Krause sitting back in the middle to go get the ball," added Dowler, who has coached for five teams and scouted for two, most recently with the Atlanta Falcons. "Their personality was, bend but don't break, and if you couldn't run on them it was tough."

Sharockman said the Packers offense never made it easy for the Vikings. The Pennsylvania native was a quarterback and free safety at the University of Pittsburgh, but he played almost strictly at cornerback for the Vikings. Sharockman, who now sells residential real estate for RE/MAX in the Twin Cities area, said the Packers weren't fancy. But getting the upper hand against them was another story.

"Green Bay was always the team to beat, and it seemed like we did that at least once most years," he said. "Everybody likes to play their best against the best. Vince [Lombardi] was pretty basic. They ran the sweep and play action off of it, but they did it so much better than anybody else. We had good days and bad days against them. It was a friendly rivalry, nothing wild, just good smash-mouth ball.

"They had a good line to protect Bart, so when they ran that play-action stuff it was tough," Sharockman added. "Max McGee gave me a tough time. He had quick feet and ran good patterns."

Ron Kramer was another weapon the Vikings had to contend with. The tight end from the University of Michigan was a bruiser either blocking or catching passes for seven seasons in Green Bay (1957, 1959–64).

"The one game up there [October 13, 1963] we were kicking the shit out of them at halftime [24-7] and scoring touchdowns like nothing," Kramer said, "but the next thing you know it's the last two minutes, it's 30-28 and they're lining up to kick the winning field goal. Thank God we blocked it and ran it back for a score.

"This division had great rivalries, and that's the way the league was set up," he added. "This has always been a good rivalry because they're right across the state border. A lot of people forget that there was football before the Super Bowl."

Jerry Kramer definitely would second that notion. The Idaho native and resident said there was just something about these showdowns that usually brought out the best in the players.

"There's a mishmash of memories from those times, but one thing I know is that the Vikings always gave us fits," the former No. 64 said. "No matter if they were the worst team in the division; they gave us a hell of a ball game. Bill Brown, Francis, Carl Eller, Jim Marshall, and the boys.

"I don't remember a game where we said we could relax because we got in a cat fight no matter what," Kramer added. "They didn't care if we were world champs. That one game (37-28 win in 1963), we about had it won and we had to fight for our lives. We knew we'd get a tremendous ass-chewing if we lost, but Herb saved the day for us."

Jerry Kramer said knocking heads with the Purple People Eaters was a microcosm for life in the NFL of the 1960s.

"Alan Page was sensational and the most difficult challenge for me, and their linebackers were always pretty good players. I thank heaven that Page didn't have more experience to go with that talent his first couple of years. And Dale Hackbart, we tried to greet him like we would any of our friends," Kramer said with tongue firmly in cheek.

"I've been at a bunch of golf outings with guys like Bill Brown, Tommy Mason, and Mick Tingelhoff, and we have good relationships with the old Vikings," Kramer said. "But you know what? That didn't dim the intensity one bit, it probably increased it. You want them to think highly of you, so you bring a little extra energy to those confrontations.

"It was part of the violent nature of the game, but it was also ego, or the mano-y-mano," he added. "You didn't want them to think you weren't one of the warriors, so you didn't shirk away from the contact. It was a pride thing. You'd whale the hell out of each other and then go have a beer afterwards. It was a different time with different guys."

Former Packer player and retired broadcaster Max McGee enjoyed many of the same recollections.

"They were noted for their front four, but they had a hell of a defense," McGee said from his Twin Cities office. "And Van Brocklin wanted to beat us bad. They always got up emotionally because we were the world champions, and so we knew we'd have to be up to play them, too."

McGee didn't have trouble doing that, twice catching two touchdown passes in a game (1962 and 1964) in lopsided Packer victories. Both happened to be at Minnesota.

"They were our next-door neighbors, so they were tough games," said McGee, who spends much of his time working with the Juvenile Diabetes Foundation and Children's Hospital of Wisconsin in raising funds for research. "They read our papers, and we read theirs. It was always a struggle."

Ditto that sentiment for Hall of Fame defensive end Willie Davis, who endured hand-to-hand combat against such on-field enemies as Errol Linden, Larry Bowie, and Tingelhoff.

"Oh, I'd love to trade for the money they make today, but not the game itself," said Davis, who made the Pro Bowl and earned All-Pro laurels five times from 1960 to 1969. "I would never trade those experiences. I don't think most players today enjoy the game like we did."

All of that dedication to your sport, love for teammates, and respect for the opposition from people who had to survive Lombardi's hellish training camps. But Davis was one who welcomed the conditioning, at least when it came to the Packers' yearly confrontations with the Vikings. That's because he got paid to chase Minnesota's No. 10 around twice a year from 1961 to 1966.

"There was one guy, a writer up there, who called us things like 'Green Bush' and picked on me a lot," Davis said from his Los Angeles workplace. "He rode me pretty good after [I was] running around after Fran so much. I guess I chased him as much as anybody. I remember thinking that maybe if I just stopped, invariably he'd come back to me. I loved those games because you knew you'd have to be ready to play and that it would be a long day. Today I think if we were ever at the same function, maybe I would have a chance to actually meet him.

"Seriously, I certainly had some good games against him and the Vikings, but you never knew what he'd do," Davis added about Tarkenton. "You usually tried to do something a little different, and one time the whole idea was to surround him, keep him pinched inside the pocket. But he hurt us badly anyways, so that went on for about a half. Then Vince says, 'The hell with that, get after him.'"

Another blocker he had to contend with later in his career was Doug Davis, the Vikings' fifth-round draft pick from Kentucky in 1966. The younger Davis remembers a small victory in their showdowns, one that didn't last too long.

"Willie was not that big, but he was very quick," said Doug Davis, who now works for U.S. Filter near Tampa, Fla. "I remember the first time in my rookie year, I had a real good game against him. I heard he had made the comment about being embarrassed by a rookie. He definitely changed that in a hurry the next time.

"I felt that I invented the 'look-out block,'" he added with a laugh. "Fran Tarkenton spoke at one of our annual meetings out in Anaheim a few years ago. He had me stand up and told that story and got quite a chuckle from the audience. But our games against the Packers were always close, so you never knew who was going to win."

Willie Davis, who serves on corporate boards across the country, including the Green Bay Packers, returns to Wisconsin once or twice a month because he owns several radio stations in Milwaukee among his many broadcasting holdings. He said the Vikings have built an excellent organization from such meager beginnings.

"I remember the first time we played up there and we got more cheers and excitement than they did, but seven or eight years later they had transformed and built their own identity," said Davis, the defensive end. "During my tenure we played against them with Norm Van Brocklin and Bud Grant, and one thing that was always interesting to me was how unassuming Grant acted on the sidelines. Even when one team was kicking the other's butts, it was almost impossible to read him."

Carroll Dale got to read Grant, albeit for only one season. This speedy wide receiver from Virginia Tech spent five years with the lowly Los Angeles Rams before being traded to the Packers, where he spent eight seasons

(1965–72). Dale ended his career with the Vikings in 1973. Despite starting most of the year he caught only 14 passes. However, the Vikings won the NFC Championship before losing to Miami in Super Bowl VIII.

Upon retiring, Dale worked in the coal business in Virginia for 17 years. The last 12 years he's been the athletic director at Clinch Valley College in his hometown of Wise, Virginia. He said he is thankful for the time he spent in the Central Division.

Dale missed action because of a pulled leg muscle his first year but started most of his seasons with the Packers, where he recalled the annual grudge matches against the men from the Twin Cities.

"Even while we were winning three straight championships, we always had trouble with Minnesota," Dale said. "And in 2000, the Vikings won the division but lost both games to the Packers. The Bears rivalry has always been there, but the Vikings-Packers series has moved up the ladder since both have been contenders.

"The key for us was always whether our line could block Eller, Page, Gary Larsen, and Jim Marshall, the Purple People Eaters," he added. "If we could keep them away from Bart, then we usually had success."

Dale caught touchdown passes in three straight postseasons (1965–67) and led the team in receptions three consecutive years (1969–71). He also caught passes in eight playoff games in a row, a mark topped only by Robert Brooks, Dorsey Levens, and Antonio Freeman.

He finished his Green Bay career with 275 catches for 5,422 yards, which is an all-time Packers' record average of 19.7 yards per reception. His highest output was 205 yards in a September 1968 home loss against Detroit (six catches). One play in particular stands out against Minnesota: October 15, 1967, at Milwaukee.

"In those days, you could go back to the huddle and tell the quarterback or tell Vince what the defense was doing," Dale said. "Well, I told Zeke [Bratkowski] they were overplaying the short routes and that I could beat [Ed] Sharockman on a fly. Vince says to Zeke, 'Throw it or I'm gonna take you outta the game.' He did, and it was an 86-yard touchdown."

However, the Vikings rallied for a 10-7 victory that day. Such was life in this highly contested series. And with so many close decisions, special teams and the kicking game proved paramount time and again. Nobody knew that better than Fred Cox.

Cox booted field goals and extra points for Minnesota from 1963 to

1977 after starring at the University of Pittsburgh. He was drafted by the Cleveland Browns but was traded to Minnesota with three other players in 1962 for a sixth-round pick in the 1963 draft.

"I was drafted as a running back and a kicker, but they had someone named Jim Brown and a guy named Lou Groza," Cox said with a chuckle about the two future Hall of Famers.

But he found his home with the Vikings, leading the team in scoring 12 of his 15 seasons, including his first 11. He surpassed 100 points four times and is by far the Vikings' all-time leading scorer with 1,365 points.

He has lived in the Twin Cities area since 1969, settling in Monticello, which is about 40 miles west. Cox retired two years ago from his long career as a chiropractor.

"The highlights and memories are too numerous to mention, but a couple of things stick out," said Cox, who booted a career-long 53-yard field goal during a 24-19 loss at Green Bay in 1965.

"I remember having a field goal that could have won the game blocked by Herb Adderley, and they ran it back for a touchdown. But the next time [October 4, 1964] I made one [from 27 yards] to beat them in Green Bay.

"I never felt that the weather was really a factor for us or the Packers," said Cox, "but when it was bitter cold we knew it would be a struggle, that it would be low-scoring and that a field goal could win or lose it. There was no question it was a good rivalry, and I had some of my best games against Green Bay."

Somebody who saw that more times than most was Bratkowski, who played as a backup to Starr from 1963 to 1968 and in 1971, and later as an assistant coach with Green Bay.

The University of Georgia product was drafted by the Rams and came to Green Bay in a midseason trade in 1963 after Starr had broken his hand.

"I arrived there the week before their second game against the Vikings and got to play later in the game because we were way ahead," Bratkowski said of Green Bay's 28-7 win at Lambeau in which John Roach had started and thrown three scoring strikes to overcome a 7-0 deficit. "My first pass as a Packer went for a touchdown to Tom Moore. We were trying to run the clock out, but the down and distance dictated throwing, and he scored on it."

Bratkowski's final aerial in a Packers' jersey also went for a score as he hit tight end Rich McGeorge in a loss to New Orleans at Milwaukee in 1971.

Besides being on the Chicago and Green Bay staffs, Bratkowski also coached with the New York Jets (twice), Cleveland, Indianapolis, and Philadelphia.

He's retired now and living in the panhandle of Florida, but Bratkowski recalled that preparing to play against Minnesota was a challenge as a player and a coach.

"Being an expansion team, their roster was filled with a lot of veterans who were in their last years of playing, but through the draft and acquiring players, they slowly became a real powerhouse," Bratkowski said. "Jim Finks orchestrated much of that and did a great job, and then they brought in Bud Grant, an excellent coach. They had a good defense, and they had Fran Tarkenton and Joe Kapp at quarterback.

"There was a parallel," Bratkowski said, between being a quarterback and then a coach. "You based things on their defensive tendencies and quality of their personnel. Early on we did everything by hand and used film. Then we had computers and video tapes. So nowadays the preparation doesn't take near as long because of computers. You can cut stuff up by formation, down, and distance, so your information is more accurate and time-saving."

Still, it came down to getting it done on the field against a formidable defensive unit, one of the best in NFL history.

"Alan Page was a major factor, Jim Marshall was outstanding, and Carl Eller was great," Bratkowski said. "Their defense was very solid and team-oriented. They didn't make many mistakes, so you had to work hard for what you got. They weren't complicated in their approach, but they were very good athletes. The linebackers complemented their line, and the secondary worked well because of their great pass rush.

"We had some great battles, and that's because nobody talked a lot," he said. "Everybody played hard and fair and did their jobs. We had our success and they had theirs."

Bob Jeter agreed. The University of Iowa player was a backup wide receiver before working his way into a starting role in Green Bay's secondary, finishing his Packer career with 23 interceptions.

"The most important thing I recall is that we knew we had to beat them twice, Detroit twice, and Chicago at least once to win the division," said Jeter, who was drafted in the second round in 1960 but played in Canada until joining the Packers in 1963. "Fran Tarkenton used to give our defensive linemen hell. I know Willie Davis hated playing them because Tarkenton was so elusive."

Jeter, who now works for Unilever Best Foods, was traded to Chicago in 1971 and has lived in the Windy City since 1972. He had several ties to the Vikings over the years.

"When I was at Iowa, Jerry Burns was our offensive coordinator, and then he was with us in Green Bay during our two Super Bowl seasons. And I played against Bud Grant's teams up in the CFL."

Minnesota fashioned a 15-7 record against Green Bay during Dave Osborn's 11 seasons with the Vikings (1965–75). The rugged running back said matching wits and brute force against the Packers represented what football meant to him.

"I always figured you were supposed to get muddy, wet, and bloody, and it didn't feel right if you didn't," said the Lakeville, Minnesota, resident, who has worked in the car, office equipment, and landscaping businesses since his playing days ended. "It was a challenge out in the elements, the snow, rain, and wind. I remember playing in 25-below wind chills. The team that adapted best to the conditions usually won."

The Kandu, North Dakota, native was drafted in the 13th round out of the University of North Dakota and became a key cog in the Vikings' diversified offensive attack along with Brown and later with Clint Jones and Chuck Foreman.

Osborn led Minnesota in rushing three times, including a career-high 972 yards in 1967, while also hauling in a team-high 34 catches that fall. Osborn said life in the Black and Blue Division was often brutal because great defenses ruled and field goals often decided 6-3 and 9-6 games.

"One of the years they won the Super Bowl [1967] we played over here on a cold day and I gained 155 yards against them, and after the game Vince Lombardi said, 'Where in the hell did they get that Osborn guy from?'

"But whenever we played the Packers, the guy I looked for was Nitschke. No matter if we went left or right, he was there. When I think of the Green Bay Packers defense, he's the one."

Fuzzy Thurston didn't have to worry about Nitschke, except for during practices. But he said it didn't matter who lined up for the Vikings, it was going to be a long afternoon.

"I don't think I played anybody tougher than Alan Page," Thurston said during one of his visits to his Green Bay bar, Fuzzy's. "We had a very difficult time with that defensive line. With Fran Tarkenton and a great defense, they got very good very quickly. We never had many easy ones up there."

The Altoona, Wisconsin, native and Valparaiso University graduate has been one of the state's most visible reminders of the Lombardi era, having been in the bar business for 40 years. Although he spends much of his time in Florida these days, Thurston loves to talk about the Glory Days. And naturally, discussing the Vikings gets the former left guard's adrenaline flowing again.

Thurston, who gained All-Pro honors in 1961 and 1962, grew up right next to Eau Claire and almost played for Grant when the latter was coaching in Canada, so he knows all about the early days of the rivalry.

"Throughout the '30s, '40s and '50s it had been the Bears and Packers, and when a new team came to town in 1961 a lot of our fans from around the border and in Minnesota had to make a decision about whether to become Viking fans," he said. "It was a big, big change. At first it was just another game, but that didn't last long. I know many people in Eau Claire and La Crosse feel like this is the number one rivalry for the Packers. And if it isn't, it got to number two real quick."

Thurston said it's taken over the top spot for him. "The series has gotten much more intense over the years, and there are a lot more fisticuffs and talking these days, a lot more 'Let's whip each other's butts' stuff. The fans get very loud and disgusted with each other and there's a lot of yelling. As the years go by, I've hated the Vikings more [than the Bears], especially since they started playing on that stupid turf. I think it's the number one rivalry today."

That would mean skipping a lot of history, so here is a look at highlights and lowlights from the rivalry's first 10 years. It was a time when "America's Team," the Packers, dominated pro football, only to have the upstart franchise 270 miles to the west start building a dynasty of its own.

1961

OCT. 22 AT MINNESOTA: Green Bay romped to a 33-7 win at Metropolitan Stadium in the teams' first meeting.

The Vikings charged $40 for season tickets in their first year, and all 40,809 seats were sold out two days before this game, so the Vikings put the $3 standing-room-only tickets up for grabs as the Packers opened as 17-point favorites.

Norm Van Brocklin jokingly said that he was going to call for a two-week delay in playing the game so Green Bay stars Paul Hornung and Ray Nitschke would miss it because of military commitments. That didn't happen.

Hornung scored 15 points on four field goals and three extra points as the Packers turned a 13-7 halftime lead into a laugher.

The Packers gained 467 total yards, highlighted by backup halfback Tom Moore's 159 yards rushing. Bart Starr hit Boyd Dowler for a 70-yard score on their first snap from scrimmage, a play in which Dowler got behind Vikings' defensive back Rich Mostardi by more than 30 yards.

Starr then led Green Bay on methodical 68-, 67-, and 57-yard drives to set up Hornung field goals before directing an 82-yard march that was keyed by Moore's 69-yard jaunt. Moore, who was knocked out of bounds on his long run by former Packer cornerback Dick Pesonen, also completed an option pass to cap his day.

Dowler booted a 75-yard punt, and although it allowed 328 yards, the Packer defense intercepted four passes and recovered three fumbles.

Hugh McElhenny rambled for a 41-yard gain in Minnesota's only scoring drive, an 80-yard march.

OCT. 29 AT MILWAUKEE: Green Bay whipped the Vikings again, 28-10, one week later in a scheduling quirk. The hosts jumped out to a 14-0 lead after two possessions and were never really threatened after that despite losing the Kramers, Ron and Jerry, to ankle injuries.

Paul Hornung rushed for 70 yards and one touchdown and threw for another. Max McGee caught six aerials for 102 yards, while Bart Starr finished with 301 yards on 18 of 24 passing.

The Packers traveled 67, 70, and 69 yards, while holding the Vikings to one first down until the last two minutes in taking a 21-7 halftime lead. Green Bay finished with a 478-280 margin in yards gained but lost three fumbles and faced a third-and-53 situation on one drive in the second quarter.

Hornung passed the 100-point plateau again (102) as Green Bay won its fifth straight game, its longest streak since the 1944 championship season.

Van Brocklin called it the worst officiated game he'd seen in his 13 years in the league, the first 12 as a player. It seemed appropriate that the contest ended in a driving rain.

1962

SEPT. 16 AT GREEN BAY: The Packers won 34-7 in the season opener.

The teams' first tussle in Green Bay had been sold out since the spring.

Paul Hornung was golden again, providing enough scoring to manhandle the Vikings: three rushing touchdowns, two field goals, and four PATs for 28 points, the fourth-highest total in team history. He also completed a 41-yard halfback option pass, and his day included a 44-yard run. He scored the Packers' first 20 points despite missing a 36-yard field-goal attempt.

Jim Taylor and Hornung combined for 132 yards on 27 tries as Green Bay outgained Minnesota 334-229. The Packers, again 17-point favorites, registered five interceptions, including two apiece from Willie Wood and Herb Adderley. Wood set up one Packers' score with a 65-yard punt return.

Minnesota's lone score came at 13:15 of the fourth quarter when Fran Tarkenton tossed a 17-yard pass to wide receiver Jerry Reichow.

OCT. 14 AT MINNESOTA: Green Bay continued its domination with a 48-21 victory at Metropolitan Stadium as the Vikings slipped to 0-5 and the Packers stayed unbeaten.

Bart Starr threw three touchdown passes, two to Max McGee, as the Packers rolled again. Fullback Jim Taylor rushed for 164 yards on 17 carries, the fifth-highest game total in team history, while McGee hauled in 10 catches for 159 yards as the visitors registered 29 first downs.

Green Bay's defense had surrendered only two touchdowns in its first four games, but that changed as the Minnesota offense equaled its four-game total for points. Tarkenton threw two TD passes, one a 41-yarder to Steve Stonebreaker, and finished with 260 yards. But two of the hosts' scores came in the final quarter, much too late to make a difference.

Meanwhile, the Packers rolled up 522 yards, their highest total since 1942. Starr connected on his first 10 pass attempts, finishing 20 of 28 for 297 yards and three scores. Besides McGee, Boyd Dowler accumulated 121 yards on seven receptions. Jerry Kramer booted two field goals and finished with 11 points. Green Bay outrushed their rivals 225-46.

Green Bay had a 16-play, 90-yard drive to make it 34-7 in the third quarter. However, several Packers were banged up in the typically rugged encounter, including Paul Hornung, who injured his right knee.

When asked who'll beat the Pack, Lombardi responded in the *Press-Gazette*, "We'll beat ourselves before we finish."

The paper also quoted Norm Van Brocklin: "They'll get beat, and they'll lose more than one. They're not invincible. No team is invincible."

He was partially correct. Green Bay went on to outscore its opponents 415-148 in completing a 13-1 regular season and then claimed a 16-7 win over the New York Giants in the NFL championship game.

1963

OCT. 13 AT MINNESOTA: Green Bay won a thriller, 37-28, in its first road game after going 3-1 at home to start the campaign.

Minnesota scored two defensive touchdowns, one on a 47-yard interception return by Ed Sharockman and the other a 26-yard fumble return by linebacker Roy Winston.

Green Bay had outscored the Vikings 143-45 in their first four meetings, but it needed Hank Gremminger's 80-yard TD return of Herb Adderley's blocked field goal to secure the triumph in a game that saw the Vikings rally from 24-7 halftime and 27-7 third-quarter deficits.

Starr passed for 253 yards, including TDs to Ron Kramer and Elijah Pitts, but the Packers fumbled seven times and threw two interceptions. Three of Green Bay's scores were set up by Minnesota turnovers in their own territory.

The clubs combined for 773 yards of offense, 522 of them through the air. But the game wasn't decided until Adderley's maneuver in which he switched from the left to the right side of the formation.

As for Gremminger, it proved to be his only NFL touchdown in 10 years with Green Bay (1956–65).

(More on this game in chapter 6.)

NOV. 10 AT GREEN BAY: The Packers didn't give the Vikings any room during a 28-7 victory in the rematch.

Minnesota went ahead 7-0 in the first quarter on an 18-yard Fran Tarkenton to Paul Flatley scoring play. The two had connected for a 62-yard gain to highlight the drive. It was the first time the Vikings had held a lead in the series. The Vikings outgained Green Bay 209-60 by halftime but could gain only a 7-7 tie.

Fred Cox missed three field goals and the visitors dropped two potential touchdown passes, enabling the Packers to rally behind backup signal caller John Roach. He tossed three TD passes, and Tom Moore scored twice to lead the Packers back.

Green Bay gained 334 yards in the second half, including 200 passing, to overcome a combined three fumbles by Jim Taylor and Moore. The Vikings keyed on Taylor, stuffing him for 37 yards on 18 carries. But Moore gained 82 yards on 15 tries, broke the game open with a 45-yard TD catch, and closed out the scoring on a pass reception from the recently acquired Zeke Bratkowski.

Boyd Dowler caught eight passes for 134 yards, while Tommy Mason topped Minnesota's ground game with 10 carries for 76 yards.

1964

OCT. 4 AT GREEN BAY: Minnesota won its first game against the Packers, 24-23, in exciting fashion. A missed extra point was the difference as Bill Brown scored twice from a yard out for the Vikings.

Fran Tarkenton connected with tight end Gordy Smith for a first down on a 4th-and-22 play from his 35-yard line. The 44-yard gain set up Fred Cox's 27-yard field goal with 18 seconds left.

(More on this game in chapter 6.)

NOV. 1 AT MINNESOTA: Green Bay rebounded with a 42-13 shellacking at rainy Metropolitan Stadium, outscoring the Vikings 21-3 in the second quarter and 14-0 in the fourth.

The Vikings managed only 95 yards passing, topped by a Fran Tarkenton to Tommy Mason 63-yard play, and gained just 72 yards rushing while earning eight first downs. Green Bay's offense was another story.

Jim Taylor scored three times, including on two of his three pass receptions for 57 yards, and rushed for 108 more on 17 carries. Max McGee scored twice, highlighted by a 45-yard score on a third-and-1 play in the final quarter. Bart Starr became the third Green Bay quarterback to register four touchdown passes, which trailed Cecil Isbell's then record of five. He finished 12 of 18 for 186 yards, directing drives of 55, 77, and 82 yards.

A Met record 44,278 fans, which broke the mark set the year before against the Packers, watched Green Bay take advantage of two Minnesota fumbles in the second quarter and Elijah Pitts' 57-yard punt return to set up the visitors' final score.

Tom Moore rumbled in from 26 yards out as the Packers dominated the trenches with 186 yards rushing behind a makeshift offensive line. Fuzzy Thurston was out with an injury, so right guard Dan Grimm moved to left guard, Forrest Gregg from right tackle to right guard, Bob Skoronski from center to left tackle, Norm Masters from left to right tackle, and rookie Ken Bowman started his first game at center.

"I really had shakes out there at the start," said Bowman, an eighth-round pick from Wisconsin, in the *Press-Gazette.* "When you're on the platoons, you can go all out on one play and then get a rest. But when you go all out on every play, it starts catching up to you about the third quarter."

One guy who appreciated the effort was Taylor. "We just overpowered 'em," Taylor said in a *Press-Gazette* story. "From the opening whistle we owned 'em. I've always had some rough luck against the Vikings. Maybe they didn't key on me as much as they did in the past."

The visitors took control during a 53-second span of the second quarter. Henry Jordan jarred the ball loose from Tarkenton, with Willie Davis pouncing on it at the Vikings' 23. Two plays later it was 21-7. On Minnesota's next play from scrimmage, Ray Nitschke recovered Bill Brown's fumble at the Vikings' 26 and Moore went the distance for a 28-7 cushion.

From the Vikings' viewpoint, it was dismal all the way around.

"They kicked the hell out of us," Norm Van Brocklin told the Green Bay publication. "They came to play."

1965

NOV. 21 AT MINNESOTA: Green Bay saved its best for last during a 38-13 win at the Met as Norm Van Brocklin ended his short-lived "retirement" after a disappointing 41-21 home setback to Baltimore the week before.

Bart Starr threw three touchdown passes, and the visitors blasted the Vikings 28-0 in the fourth quarter.

Minnesota went ahead 13-10 on Fran Tarkenton's 27-yard pass to Paul Flatley, but Starr scrambled 38 yards to set up the Packers' first score of the final quarter, a 17-yard pass to Boyd Dowler.

Jim Taylor rushed for 111 yards on 25 attempts, his first 100-yard outing of the season. Starr finished with 44 yards rushing as Green Bay gained 339 yards and didn't allow a sack.

Tarkenton rushed for 54 yards on eight carries and had identical passing numbers as Starr, completing 9 of 19 attempts, as the Vikings gained 364 yards. However, Green Bay intercepted Tarkenton twice and recovered four fumbles, including three in the fourth quarter, highlighted by Doug Hart's TD return to cap the scoring.

Hart had an end zone interception called off in the first quarter because the Packers were offsides. However, the Packers finished off the key goal-line stand despite giving the Vikings five plays.

DEC. 5 AT GREEN BAY: The hosts rallied and held on for a 24-19 win and the season sweep. Fred Cox kicked four field goals for the Vikings, including a 53-yarder (tied for second-longest in team history), but it wasn't enough.

Elijah Pitts and Bill Anderson scored TDs, and the Packers overcame a 16-14 halftime deficit.

Bart Starr and Boyd Dowler collaborated on a 27-yard score 51 seconds into the game for a 7-0 Green Bay advantage, but it needed Willie Wood's 73-yard return of Cox's missed 59-yard field goal with a 20 mph wind at his back to climb to within two points at the break. Wood grabbed the errant kick at his 6 and raced to the Minnesota 21.

Backup quarterback Zeke Bratkowski hit Bill Anderson for a 21-19 lead, and then Pitts connected with wide receiver Carroll Dale on a 51-yard halfback option to set up Don Chandler's field goal for a 24-19 cushion after Chandler had missed a 27-yarder earlier in the fourth quarter that could have helped seal the victory. Bratkowski threw three interceptions, including one at the Vikings' 3.

Tarkenton wound up only 11 of 30 passing, but Minnesota did the brunt of its damage on the ground, churning out a 251-113 margin. Mason led the way with 21 carries for 101 yards, and Brown chipped in 13 tries for 85 yards.

Starr was replaced in the third series because he couldn't continue after jamming fingers on his throwing hand during pregame warm-ups.

Minnesota, which held a 21-16 advantage in first downs, including a 15-7 difference on the ground, almost pulled the game out twice in the waning seconds.

But Tom Hall was called for offensive pass interference on one catch in the end zone, and Jim "Red" Phillips was ruled out of bounds on the last-ditch effort to end the game.

"I was just going for the ball," Hall said in a *Press-Gazette* interview. "I can't say I was at fault or vice versa."

As for Phillips' effort, there were obvious differences of opinion.

"It looked like he trapped the ball," Herb Adderley said in the newspaper article. "He was lying across the flag and half out of bounds. I don't know why they raised so much Cain."

"It was no trap at all," Phillips argued in the story. "The official called me out. I don't have the money to say I wasn't [out], if you know what I mean."

1966

NOV. 6 AT GREEN BAY: Minnesota used two time-consuming drives in the second half to secure a 20-17 comeback victory, its second win in a three-year span at Lambeau.

Minnesota trailed 17-10 but controlled the fourth quarter, scoring 10 points for the win while handing the Packers their only home loss of the season.

Green Bay took 15 plays to march 86 yards, using 7:35, to take the seven-point cushion on Elijah Pitts' 2-yard run. But the Vikings chewed up the rest of the third quarter, getting Fred Cox's field goal to close to within 17-13 on the second play of the final quarter. Minnesota then scored the game-winner after a 10-play, 73-yard drive that ended with Bill Brown's second short plunge with 6:53 left.

Fran Tarkenton completed seven third-down passes for 119 yards, the biggest being a 38-yard hookup with wide receiver Jim Phillips on a third-and-three situation from the Minnesota 34 in the final scoring drive.

Tarkenton explained the broken pattern that proved crucial in *Press-Gazette* coverage: "It was originally supposed to be a square out to the left, but [Bob] Jeter did a good job of covering Phillips. So I waved him down field. When he sees me fake a throw and hit the palm of my left hand with the ball, he knows the pattern isn't there and hit him down the middle."

Both teams scored their first touchdowns after 80-yard journeys and then took advantage of good field position to tack on field goals for a 10-10 halftime deadlock. Donny Anderson's 61-yard kickoff return put the Packers at the Minnesota 40, while the Vikings started at the Green Bay 48 after Pitts fumbled.

Jim Taylor and Pitts rumbled for 157 yards and two scores in the defeat, with Pitts churning for 89 yards. They also grabbed Bart Starr's first nine completions (out of 11 total) as the Vikings took away the Packers' deeper routes.

The Packers held onto first place despite falling to 7-2 in front of 50,861 fans, while the Vikings improved to 3-4-1.

NOV. 27 AT MINNESOTA: Green Bay didn't let down three weeks later as it won a 28-16 decision in the frigid Twin Cities.

The Packers raced to a 21-3 halftime lead as part of a five-game, season-ending winning streak that led to the playoffs and Super Bowl I.

Green Bay's margin was cut to 21-16, and Minnesota was 52 yards from victory with two minutes left. However, cornerback Herb Adderley intercepted a pass, and Jim Grabowski then scooted 36 yards to secure the triumph with 52 seconds left. It was the Packers' longest run from scrimmage so far that season.

Punter Don Chandler pulled down a high snap from center and scampered 33 yards to the Minnesota 17 to set up Green Bay's first TD. Willie Davis' sack and Ray Nitschke's fumble recovery put the Packers at the Minnesota 37 en route to their second score. And then Adderley partially blocked Bobby Walden's punt, which traveled only four yards, giving the visitors a first down at the Minnesota 11. Bart Starr then connected with tight end Marv Fleming from 10 yards out for the 21-3 margin.

But the Vikings bounced back. Tarkenton hit Jim Phillips on a 61-yard play and hooked up with Dave Osborn from 38 yards to bring them within five points in the fourth quarter before Adderley stepped in front of a flea-flicker pass for the interception.

Fran Tarkenton passed for 229 yards, but 99 of them came on the long fourth-quarter drive, and Tom Brown's 38-yard interception return for a Green Bay score was nullified by a penalty. Starr produced a 20-for-31 effort for 149 yards and two scores after overcoming a hamstring injury. The Packers also sacked Tarkenton four times after getting to him only once in the previous meeting.

1967

OCT. 15 AT MILWAUKEE: Minnesota again enjoyed success on the road, claiming a 10-7 verdict for its third triumph in four seasons on Wisconsin soil. A County Stadium record crowd of 49,601 watched the defensive battle in a cold drizzle.

Minnesota scored all of its points in the fourth quarter. Ed Sharockman returned a Zeke Bratkowski interception 37 yards to the Green Bay 37 to set up Bill Brown's one-yard TD run to tie the contest after the visitors escaped disaster by recovering their own fumble near the goal line just before scoring. Then Earsell Mackbee pilfered another Bratkowski pass with 2:04 left to set up Cox's 12-yard game-winning kick that knocked the Packers from the unbeaten ranks (3-1-1) and gave the Vikings their first victory of the year (1-4).

However, Bud Grant's strategy and one of quarterback Joe Kapp's team-record low two completions proved crucial. The Vikings played conservatively on offense and kept the heat on the Packers defensively.

In Bill McGrane's 1986 book, *Bud: The Other Side of the Glacier*, Grant discussed the strategy.

"Whenever there was a timeout, Joe would come to the bench scowling and say, 'When are we gonna open up?' I told him we weren't going to open up. That was a great football team we were playing, we couldn't afford to take a chance and risk turning the ball over. I told Joe to be patient. I said we'd get an opportunity if we kept on sawing wood."

On the deciding drive, Grant sent Brown into the line five straight times, and with Green Bay packing the middle against another thrust, he finally gave Kapp the "open it up" call.

The former CFL signal caller faked to Brown again and tossed a completion to Dave Osborn to set up Cox.

"Joe told me after the game that he never would have believed he could feel like a contributor on a day when he completed just two passes," Grant continued in his account. "But he did . . . he was happier than anybody."

Meanwhile, Bratkowski, who was picked off three times, hooked up with Dale on an 86-yard TD in the second quarter, the longest scoring play in either player's career.

However, defense still dominated most of the afternoon as each team managed just 10 first downs. It was the first game against the Packers for both Grant and Kapp as part of the Vikings' organization.

Bratkowski, who had his eight-game winning streak in relief of Starr broken, completed 15 of 25 attempts for 240 yards. But the Packers were stymied on the ground, gaining only 42 yards on 26 carries. The Vikings gained 158 yards rushing, led by Bill Brown's 14-for-72 day, but finished with only 183 total net yards.

Both teams had other scoring chances. Don Chandler missed a 34-yard field goal in the second quarter, and the Packers committed key penalties in the third quarter, while Bob Jeter picked off a Kapp pass at the Green Bay 10 in the first.

Minnesota had allowed 27 or more points in three of its four outings, surrendering 179 yards per game and 4.4 yards per carry before handcuffing the Packers' running attack.

The Vikings' victory snapped the Packers' 17-game unbeaten streak of 16 wins and one tie (regular and preseason). Minnesota was also the last team to have defeated the Packers before that streak, beating them at Green Bay the year before.

Grant said the victory was vital regardless of who it was against or how it happened.

"It was important that we win today," he said after the game in the *Press-Gazette*. "It didn't make any difference if it was the Packers or the Little Sisters from the Poor. It was the timing. We're not that bad. Certainly we're not the best team, but we're not the worst. Now we should start moving a little."

They moved a little, finishing 3-8-3 for the Central cellar.

On the other bench, things didn't smell so rosy, either.

"Neither one of us had an offense worth a damn," Lombardi said in the *Press-Gazette* article.

But his Packers recovered to win six of their next seven games to finish 9-4-1 and win the division crown.

DEC. 3 AT MINNESOTA: Green Bay came away with a 30-27 triumph, having clinched the division title a week earlier against runner-up Chicago on its way to Super Bowl II.

The Packers' 24-14 advantage in the second and third quarters proved to be the difference during a contest that featured three ties and three lead changes. Dave Osborn rushed for what was then a team-record 155 yards on 21 carries for the Vikings.

However, Green Bay won it after safety Tom Brown's fumble recovery at the Minnesota 28 with less than two minutes left set up Don Chandler's 19-yard field goal with eight ticks left on the clock.

Donny Anderson's 11-yard punt gave the Vikings the ball at the Green Bay 43, which Osborn covered in one carry to give Minnesota a 10-3 lead. But Bart Starr connected with Boyd Dowler, who finished with three catches for 100 yards, from 57 yards out that tied it again. Then backup running back Chuck Mercein recovered the loose ball at the Vikings' 22 on the kickoff to set up Chandler's 34-yard three-pointer and a 13-10 margin at the break.

Ed Sharockman's interception on a tipped pass meant the Vikings needed to go only 4 yards to grab the lead again when Joe Kapp hit tight end John Beasley. But Starr and Carroll Dale responded with a 34-yard pass play, and Ray Nitschke's interception led to another TD as the visitors surged ahead 27-17 in the third quarter.

Kapp collaborated with Jim Phillips for a score after Clint Jones raced 44 yards with a kickoff return. Then Ben Wilson's fumble put the Vikings at the Green Bay 30, which they took advantage of with another Fred Cox field goal to tie it in the fourth quarter.

Anderson, who had 11- and 28-yard boots to his credit, uncorked a 59-yard punt that pinned the Vikings at their 7 late in the game.

Both teams gained 276 total yards. Green Bay's balanced attack finished with 133 yards rushing, 143 passing. Minnesota struggled passing, earning 219 yards on the ground.

1968

SEPT. 22 AT MILWAUKEE: Minnesota doubled up the Packers for a 26-13 victory in a contest that marked the first time in the series that Vince Lombardi wasn't patrolling Green Bay's sidelines.

Bill Brown again hurt the Packers, scoring on two runs. The Vikings added the first safety of defensive end Jim Marshall's career. He sacked Bart Starr in the end zone to grab a 16-0 lead.

After the second-half kickoff, however, Starr surprised the visitors with a 10-yard TD run to end a 10-play, 66-yard drive to shave the Packers' deficit to 16-6 and gain the momentum. Then Green Bay thought it had stuffed Joe Kapp on a quarterback sneak on a controversial fourth-and-inches call from the Vikings' 26. Officials gave Minnesota the first down, however, and the visitors drove down for a TD to push their margin to 23-6.

Green Bay could have made another run but was stopped on consecutive third and fourth-and-1 plays from the Vikings' 25.

The teams combined for 242 yards, but the Packers hindered their chances with eight penalties for 90 yards.

As for the almost disastrous strategy of going for it from his own 26, Bud Grant told a *Press-Gazette* reporter, "Of course I made the decision. That's what I'm getting paid for."

NOV. 10 AT MINNESOTA: The Vikings followed that up with a 14-10 decision at home for its first season sweep of the Packers en route to an 8-6 finish, which gave them their initial Central crown in a season in which nobody seemed to want to win it.

Jim Grabowski gained 89 yards rushing for Green Bay as the two-time defending Super Bowl champions slipped to 3-5-1.

Bill Brown did his usual damage, scoring twice to cap 69- and 89-yard scoring drives as the Vikings took a 14-3 margin into the locker room at frosty Metropolitan Stadium.

Green Bay, which fumbled three times and was called for two major penalties in the game, dominated the second half. The Packers failed to capitalize on a 16-2 advantage in first downs after the intermission. Anderson's one-yard burst pulled the visitors to within 14-10 midway through the third quarter to finish off a seven-play, 66-yard march. Anderson's 28-yard jaunt highlighted the drive.

However, a clipping penalty from the Minnesota 5-yard line forced Green Bay to try a field goal. Carl Eller blocked former Viking Mike Mercer's attempt with 10 minutes left.

"I was extremely lucky," Eller said in the *Press-Gazette*. "I just happened to get through and stick my hand up. The ball hit it. I didn't even get in that far. I just sort of got through sideways and put my hand up. It was a big break for us."

Minnesota got several more breaks to hang on, holding the Packers to only one score despite allowing them into their territory five times in the second half.

Another Green Bay march was thwarted when Lonnie Warwick's hit caused Donny Anderson to fumble, with Paul Krause recovering at the Vikings' 18 with 2:54 left. And a fumble by Claudis James at the Viking 45 with 51 seconds left sealed the outcome. Earl Mackbee also intercepted a pass as the Vikings claimed their first home triumph against the Packers in the series.

The Packers outgained the Vikings 263-226, including a slim 172-160 difference on the ground. Backup running back Jim Lindsey carried 10 times for 48 yards for the Vikings. Green Bay's defense held Joe Kapp to 8 of 16 passing for only 80 yards.

1969

OCT. 5 AT MINNESOTA: The Vikings dominated again for a 19-7 victory in a game played at Memorial Stadium on the University of Minnesota campus in front of 60,740.

Green Bay avoided its first shutout loss since 1958 (56-0 to Baltimore) when Bart Starr tossed a pass to running back Dave Hampton with 5 seconds left, the only thing the Hall of Fame quarterback could do against the vaunted Purple People Eaters front four, who sacked Starr eight times for 63 yards in losses.

Green Bay's two early fumbles and an interception helped give the Vikings a 13-0 cushion at halftime. Fred Cox kicked his first two field goals in a 4-for-4 effort.

The fumbles set the Vikings up at the Green Bay 48 and 24 en route to the field goals, and Bobby Bryant's interception and the first career personal foul against Packers' All-Pro tackle Forrest Gregg, who was ejected despite denying any wrongdoing, gave Minnesota first-and-goal at the 6 to set up Dave Osborn's 3-yard touchdown.

Gregg got into a confrontation with former Badger star Dale Hackbart.

"Somebody hit me after the play was over, at least I felt it was, and we kind of squared off," Gregg said in the *Press-Gazette*. "We were standing up face to face and I thought he was going to hit me. He made a move as though he was going to, so I hit him first. The referee caught me and put me out."

Green Bay reached the Minnesota 13, but back-to-back sacks forced it into a 4th-and-31 situation from the 34. A 42-yard pass interference call helped set up Cox's third field goal, and his final boot capped a 55-yard drive.

Minnesota limited the Packers to 173 yards but gained only 217. Joe Kapp struggled again, connecting on 6 of 16 attempts for a paltry 60 yards but completing key passes when needed. Kapp was coming off a team-record seven TD tosses against Baltimore (a 52-14 win) the week before.

Green Bay linebacker Lee Roy Caffey, who came away with a shiner on his right eye and a gash on his nose, summed up the Packers' problems in the *Press-Gazette*: "The hardest lick all day, and I got it from my own man. Nitschke and I were going after the same guy and he stuck a finger in my eye. I guess it was a short-yardage situation."

Members of the Green Bay offense took their share of blows.

"We got in a hole and they knew we had to pass, and they just blew in there," said guard Bill Lueck in the Green Bay paper. "They weren't worrying about the run, just rushing the passer. It puts a lot of pressure on you."

"The defense deserved a better fate," Bart Starr added in a *Press-Gazette* story. "They played very well. We didn't do anything offensively to help them."

NOV. 16 AT MILWAUKEE: Minnesota pulled out a 9-7 win for its second straight season sweep en route to qualifying for its first Super Bowl.

Green Bay's Doug Hart scored on an 85-yard interception return in the second quarter. But Bobby Bryant intercepted Bart Starr's pass intended for Dave Hampton on first down at the Minnesota 8 with 1:47 remaining to seal the visitors' triumph, one of what was then a team-record eight thefts for the season for Bryant.

Starr finished 12 of 21 for 151 yards and was sacked only once, but suspect kicking and a Vikings' offense that held a 39-19 advantage in plays from scrimmage in the second half helped secure the win.

Joe Kapp, who entered the contest as the league's top-rated passer, was sacked twice and benched in the first half after a 4-for-11 performance and only 41 yards. Gary Cuozzo then completed 11 of 16 aerials for 105 yards in relief.

Minnesota punter Bob Lee pinned the Packers at their one-yard line, and then Anderson's 27-yard punt gave the Vikings the ball at the Green Bay 31 to set up Fred Cox's first field goal from 10 yards out. Then Mike Mercer's 42-yard field-goal attempt in the second quarter was blocked by Karl Kassulke. And Bart Starr's 48-yard pass to Carroll Dale to the Minnesota 17 was wasted when Mercer missed a 22-yard try that could have won the game in the third quarter.

"It was a bad kick," Mercer told the *Press-Gazette* about his errant try. "I just hit it wrong. I rushed it. Everything was good but me. The center, the hold, the block, all were good. It's the first time in my nine years in pro football that I've blown a crucial kick."

Cox gave the Vikings the points they needed with field goals after 49- and 68-yard drives, including the clincher from 20 yards out with 5:03 left. It was set up when the Packers had to give the ball up with 7:51 remaining after Hampton slipped on a third-and-inches carry from his 35 and lost a yard.

It was Minnesota's eighth straight victory of the year during a 12-game winning streak that it sandwiched between defeats on the first and last weekends of the season.

As for Green Bay, it was another low in a season of peaks and valleys that saw it finish 8-6.

"I've never seen a squad that wanted to win a ballgame more than this one," said Starr in the *Press-Gazette*. "It's hard to take."

CHAPTER TWO

THE 1970s
THE RISE AND FALL

Linebacker Don Hansen (58) and linemen Clarence Williams (83) and
Dave Pureifory (75) helped stuff Viking star ball carrier Chuck Foreman (44)
in this 1976 contest. Minnesota swept Green Bay that season.

GREEN BAY WON THE FIRST and last games against Minnesota during the 1970s, but the Packers would just as soon forget the rest of the decade after going 2-15-1 vs. the Vikings in the other 18 contests.

Defensive back Steve Luke, a hard-hitting player who Green Bay selected from Ohio State in the fifth round in 1975, summed up many of the organization's frustrations.

"You could take a pick of almost any of the games, and they were great battles, but they seemed to have a knack of finding ways to win in the end," said Luke, who manned the strong safety spot for the Packers for six seasons. "The game in 1978 at Lambeau (10-10, the only tie in series history) was key, that if we would have won, it could have helped us get into the playoffs. But Ahmad [Rashad] scored in the last minute. And another time he burned us [a 27-21 overtime loss in 1979]. Those stick out because they broke our backs."

Still stuck in the omnipresent shadow of Lombardi and Green Bay's championship machine of the 1960s, Phil Bengtson, Dan Devine, and Bart Starr failed to rekindle that magic, instead stumbling and struggling to only two winning seasons combined.

Retirement, injuries, and age had robbed the franchise of most of its Super Bowl players. Devine cleaned out most of those who remained, and his inexcusable trade for quarterback John Hadl left Starr's drafting cupboard starving for ammunition when he took over.

The moribund team compiled the 10th-best percentage (.413) of the 14 teams in the National Football Conference, finishing above .500 in only 1972 and 1978. They won the Central Division in 1972 with a 10-4 mark but lost a tiebreaker to the Vikings in 1978 after a promising 6-1 start dwindled to an 8-7-1 record. Former Vikings running back Dave Osborn didn't recognize many of the faces in the locker room when he ended his playing career with a final season in northeastern Wisconsin in 1976 after 11 good years in the Twin Cities.

He got to see firsthand just how drastically fortunes had fallen in Titletown.

"I had been released by the Vikings in the preseason, and then Bart called me up and asked if I would come over," he said. "I told him I wanted some kind of guarantee that I'd play. Barty Smith was starting because [John] Brockington had gotten hurt, and they needed some insurance. So I played the last six or seven games.

"It was a different feeling seeing the Purple and Gold lining up on the other side of the field," he said of his two encounters with his former friends during the final month of the season. "With the Vikings there was constant pressure because we were always winning. But when I got to Green Bay they had a poor record, and I sensed that many guys felt beaten before they went out there, and you can't play like that."

However, Osborn said his experience wasn't all negative.

"I was very impressed with the Green Bay fans and organization," Osborn said. "They all cared about the team. It was like one big family, and I had a lot of respect for them. They live and die with the Packers."

While Green Bay usually battled to stay out of the division's graveyard, the unflappable Bud Grant captained one of the most consistently excellent ships to double-digit victories six times in 10 years, tying the Los Angeles Rams for the second-best winning percentage (.694) in the NFC behind the Dallas Cowboys. Minnesota finished 99-43-2 in the decade to claim the divisional crown every year except 1972 and 1979. It tied the Bears in 1977 and Green Bay in 1978 but won tiebreakers to earn the titles and automatic playoff berths that go along with that distinction.

The Vikings did it with their famed Purple People Eaters defense, led by a ferocious front four. Defensive tackle Alan Page earned league Most Valuable Player laurels in 1971.

Minnesota added to its veteran core, which included the return of the mad scrambler, Sir Francis Tarkenton, such young stars as halfback Chuck Foreman and wide receiver Sammy White to keep a stranglehold atop the Central.

However, all of that success never materialized into a championship as the Vikings lost Super Bowls VIII, IX, and XI.

That didn't seem to matter when these guys got together, said Luke, whose teams were 0-8-1 against Minnesota until the Packers finally tasted victory with a 19-7 triumph in 1979 and swept their rivals in 1980.

He remembers the games being tough mentally and physically regardless of the outcome.

"It was always intense, and we knew we'd be in a battle," said Luke, who became a sports agent after retiring and is now involved with former Packer Bob Long and a company that works with various charities. "They had the great defenses, but offensively they had quite an arsenal with Tarkenton, Rickey Young, Chuck Foreman, Sammy White, and Ahmad."

An opposing player Luke failed to mention was former Wisconsin Badger standout Stu Voigt, one of the Vikings' many unsung heroes who did the grunt work necessary to make a good team great.

Voigt (1970–80) was a 10th-round draft choice who caught 20 to 34 passes each season from 1973–77 after being the last Big Ten athlete to participate in three sports: football, baseball, and track.

The Madison native starred at West High School and became a key target for Tarkenton, catching five TDs in 1974 and four in 1975. He lives three miles south of where Metropolitan Stadium used to stand in the suburb of Apple Valley. Voigt has worked in broadcasting since his retirement and does color commentary with Dan Rowe on the Vikings radio network flagship station, WCCO. He still has business interests in the Madison area and is on the "W" Club board for the Badgers, so he knows all about the tradition surrounding the Packers and their series against Minnesota.

"I was a total Green Bay fan and followed the Milwaukee Braves, so growing up in Wisconsin in those days was great," said Voigt, who was nicknamed "Chainsaw." "My early years in the NFL were a thrill and a dream come true because I played against the Packers. It was kinda surreal facing guys like Ray Nitschke and Kenny Bowman, having grown up while knowing so much about them. Bumping heads with Dave Robinson and Willie Wood. It was a lot of fun.

"The scores and statistics don't stand out, but I know my parents came up for most games at Lambeau early in my career, so I always wanted to play well," added Voigt, who works in banking and real estate development when not enjoying his weekend job. "I caught a number of touchdowns against the Packers, and even though playing in Milwaukee wasn't the same as being in Lambeau, all 11 years were special."

They weren't that way for Green Bay's defensive backs, including cornerbacks Ken Ellis (1970–75) and Willie Buchanon (1972–78).

While they had no problems keeping up to the slow-footed Voigt, staying close to Minnesota receivers while Tarkenton bided his time with his nimble feet proved to be another story indeed.

Ken Ellis led the Packers in interceptions in 1971 with six and tied for team honors the next two years, earning Pro Bowl recognition twice and All-Pro three times in his career. He also topped Green Bay in punt returns twice, accumulating a 15.4 average to lead the NFL in 1972, an effort that included an 80-yard touchdown against Detroit that helped the Packers turn a 17-0 deficit into a key 24-23 victory en route to the division title.

The Georgia native was drafted in the fourth round out of Southern University in Baton Rouge, Louisiana, where he met his wife. He is currently an associate pastor with Bethany World Prayer Center.

Ellis was the honorary captain for Green Bay's 13-7 victory over Tampa Bay during its 1996 Super Bowl run and was named to the Packers Hall of Fame in 1998.

He was a collegiate running back and flanker but was switched to cornerback as a rookie under Bengtson, replacing Herb Adderley.

"There are a number of things I remember about the rivalry, but one in particular was during my rookie year in the game at County Stadium," said Ellis, whose career ended after the 1979 season with the Los Angeles Rams. He was in coverage against Gene Washington, the wide receiver from Michigan State, not the flanker from Stanford who's with the NFL office today.

"He ran an out pattern for the corner of the end zone and I went for the interception," Ellis said. "I tipped it, but he caught it for a touchdown, the only one I gave up that year."

Ellis said he keeps in touch with several former teammates, including John Brockington, MacArthur Lane, Al Matthews, Mike McCoy (the defensive tackle), Scott Hunter, and Buchanon.

"I recall that when we played at Minnesota, both teams were on the same sideline and Bud Grant didn't let them have heaters," said Ellis, who was involved in the trade with the Houston Oilers that brought Lynn Dickey to Green Bay.

"That included the 1972 game that we won 23-7 to win the division. I remember Alan Page getting called for several penalties and getting kicked out of the game. He was so irate. But that was a miraculous season for us."

It couldn't have turned out better for Buchanon: first year, a division championship and postseason berth. However, the victories were few and far between after that.

The former San Diego State star was named an All-Pro in his final season with the Packers, which was also his third Pro Bowl selection. He earned Defensive Rookie of the Year honors after being Green Bay's first of two first-round draft picks.

"I remember the game up there my rookie year, the one we clinched the (division) title in," said Buchanon, who finished his career with the San Diego Chargers, qualifying for the AFC playoffs each of his seasons there from 1979 to 1982. "It was like 29-below wind chill for that game. The week before I had convinced Coach Devine to let us wear gloves, which up to that point only quarterbacks were allowed to do. I gave him this spiel about being a poor California boy who had never played in this kind of stuff, and he reluctantly gave in. I had two interceptions against Tarkenton that day. After that, more and more guys started wearing gloves."

Buchanon, who works in real estate and advertising in the San Diego area, laughs about another game against the Vikings and one of his good buddies, former wide receiver and current broadcaster Rashad.

"He always called me 'Willie B.,'" Buchanon said. "Normally when a guy would catch the ball near the sidelines I'd tap him out of bounds. But one time he ran an out pattern and I just leveled him. He says, 'What the heck you doing?' I tell him, 'We're right in front of my bench. I can't let you get away with that.'"

Buchanon, who missed most of the 1973 and 1975 seasons because of broken legs, also recalled a time when Mr. Tarkenton showed his mettle.

"Dave Pureifory, who was my roommate, knocked some of Tarkenton's teeth out in the second quarter. I think he threw for over 200 yards in the second half.

"But they had a bunch of tough guys. . . . Alan Page, Jim Marshall. That's when defense was defense. I know wide receiver John Gilliam always gave me fits, and their offensive line was excellent. And then when they drafted [halfback] Chuck Foreman, he added a whole new dimension. You could break your ankle trying to stop him, and that shake-and-bake of his."

However, more times than not there wasn't anything fancy about either team's strategy and Minnesota linebacker Wally Hilgenberg (1968–79) will attest to that.

The University of Iowa graduate, who was a captain with future Viking teammate Paul Krause, played for four years with Detroit before being traded to Pittsburgh and subsequently picked up off waivers. He then became a mainstay on the right side for the next decade in Minnesota.

Hilgenberg was one of the league's real tough guys on and off the field, having wrestled a 550-pound bear during one off-season. But he knew that Sundays against Green Bay were going to be rugged affairs.

"Lombardi loved the power running game, so he had big offensive lines and a bunch of running backs, such as Donny Anderson and Jim Grabowski, and they added MacArthur Lane and John Brockington later," Hilgenberg said. "They weren't great, but they were all big, physical running backs. And, of course, when I was with the Lions, they had Paul Hornung and Jim Taylor.

"We weren't a lot different," Hilgenberg continued. "We relied on defense. Bud's attitude was not to give up points and try to win games in the fourth quarter, which made it tough on linebackers because one mistake could be the difference, unlike today when teams are scoring 30 to 40 points."

Hilgenberg said it was like two locomotives colliding.

"It was the old Black and Blue Division at its best, it was that mentality," he said. "You knew it was going to be physical and that you'd have to tolerate the cold. As far as that goes, the Packers were a little wimpier than us because they had heaters.

"I thought that kind of weather was easier for both of us because you're cold regardless," Hilgenberg said. "We practiced in subzero temperatures, so I thought it was harder for us to go down South because the heat and humidity affected us more in the third and fourth quarters."

Hilgenberg said it was always hot in the Minnesota–Green Bay series, but he welcomed those games as much or more than any others.

"The first game I ever started, when I was with Detroit, was at Lambeau Field," he recalled. "The aura. I was excited about playing against guys like Bart Starr and everybody. Looking at the stadium and seeing all of the tailgaters, knowing that you'd be playing on grass. To hit and be hit. It was like going to war.

"I really enjoyed playing against those guys because it was like a cat and mouse game," Hilgenberg added. "They had their tendencies and we had ours. We knew Bart liked to go to a running back on an option out of the backfield on short yardage. So we would bait him. One time I faked like I would cover him and stayed tight and Paul Krause snuck up and intercepted it. We had practiced it and it worked like a picture. It was fun and competitive. We played against them so many times and laughed about it later. It was a great, great series.

Another old-school player who enjoyed himself on and off the field was defensive lineman Bob Lurtsema, better known as "Benchwarmer" Bob.

The Grand Rapids, Michigan, native attended Western Michigan University and was drafted by the Baltimore Colts in 1966. He was traded to the New York Giants for a fifth-round draft pick and spent five years in the Big Apple. He then played with the Vikings before being shipped to Seattle in the trade for Rashad in 1976.

He's published the *Viking Update* newsletter for almost 20 years, and even though Minnesota dominated the series during his time in the Twin Cities, he said there were few gimmes.

"I remember the first game I played for the Vikings was when we kicked their butts, 3-0 (in 1971). It was just a great defensive game. Somebody from Green Bay fumbled going into the end zone, and we went on to win it. And in 1972 they came up here and beat us to win the division title."

Lurtsema, who picks on Cheeseheads every chance he gets, said he learned a few lessons the hard way while competing against Green Bay's veteran offensive linemen.

"Playing against Gale Gillingham, their guard, I get in the ballgame, and we had noticed on film that depending on where he put his right foot meant the difference between a running or passing play," Lurtsema said. "So I jump in there and I look over, and Jesus, I can't remember which was which. I drew a blank. I tried a pullover move and he caught me. It was like I was on roller skates. He got me good and knocked me outta there.

"One other time, I was a rookie, and I'm lined up across from Fuzzy [Thurston]. It was a short-yardage play and I stuffed it. And Fuzzy says, 'Good play, Bob.' I was so amazed that he even knew my name. I'm thinking, 'This is great.' He says I'm the toughest rookie he's ever played against. The next play we're in the same defense and he blasts me. I look up and he's got a big smirk on his face. He suckered me with all of that talk."

Lurtsema wasn't the only foe who fell victim to Gillingham's talent and tenacity. The Wisconsin native starred from 1966 to 1974 and in 1976, replacing two legends in Packer history, Thurston and Jerry Kramer. He made a reputation for himself, earning All-Pro honors four times, including three straight from 1969 to 1971. He also was selected to five Pro Bowls, and he accomplished that while playing against the Purple People Eaters just as his famous predecessors had.

"I played both sides when I started, but then I replaced Fuzzy on the left side for a couple of years and then moved to the right side in '69 after Jerry retired and [Bill] Lueck took over at left guard," said Gillingham, a Madison native who also lived in Stoughton and Tomah before moving to Minnesota as a junior in high school. "Alan Page was a good player, and Gary Larsen. They had a great defense, with linebackers like Roy Winston, [Lonnie] Warwick, Jeff Siemon, and Matt Blair."

Gillingham played offensive and defensive tackle at the University of Minnesota and was drafted No. 13 in the first round by the Packers. Green Bay had taken fullback Jim Grabowski four picks earlier with a choice they had obtained from Detroit for Ron Kramer.

"With few exceptions, the games against the Vikings came down to the end or a key play or two," said Gillingham, who sells real estate in Little Falls, Minn. "We always moved the ball, especially when we still had Boyd Dowler, Carroll Dale, and Marv Fleming, and Bart was still in one piece. But after they left we never replaced them and couldn't throw the ball. Then we got [John] Brockington and we ran our way through the Central Division in 1972.

"Minnesota threw the ball well with Fran, but the games were always extremely intense because of tough defenses. They were slugfests where you would pound, pound, and pound until you got something done."

One game against Minnesota stands out for Gillingham because of what happened during the game and shortly thereafter.

"Dave Hampton returned a kickoff for a touchdown to clinch it," Gillingham said of Green Bay's 13-10 win at Milwaukee on October 4, 1970. "And then he collapsed in the locker room after the game with an appendicitis or something. He damn near died."

Nothing that traumatic happened to Gillingham or one of his linemates, center Larry McCarren, but the man nicknamed "The Rock" absorbed and dished out his share of punishment while tangling with the Norsemen.

McCarren (1973–84) played in 162 consecutive games, tied for second highest in team annals. The Illinois native and former member of the Fighting Illini was drafted in the 12th round and became a fixture at center for the Packers.

McCarren said the Packers had tough sledding when it came to their showdowns with the Vikings throughout the 1970s.

"When I came into the league they had Eller, Page, Gary Larsen and Jim Marshall," he said. "Facing that crew for the first time was kinda special because I had heard about them while growing up in football, from high school to college and then the pros. The reputation they had. Page, when he started with the Vikings, was a good 250 and quick as a cat. He was a Hall of Famer and you had to account for him. He gave us most of the headaches."

McCarren was chosen to play in the Pro Bowl in 1982 and '83, retiring before the 1985 campaign because of a neck injury. He has worked at WFRV-TV in Green Bay, where he's been sports director since 1988. In 1995, he joined Jim Irwin and Max McGee in the WTMJ radio booth, where he has provided color commentary for play-by-play man Wayne Larrivee after the famous duo hung up their microphones.

McCarren said most of the contests run together, but one stands out in his mind, even though it ended in a 32-17 victory for Minnesota.

"The first time I started a regular-season game was the opener against the Vikings in 1974, so that was a significant event for me."

Another force in the trenches, except on the opposite side of the ball, was defensive tackle Mike P. McCoy (1970–76), who was the No. 2 pick in the NFL draft. Green Bay obtained the selection in a trade with the Chicago Bears that involved Elijah Pitts, Bob Hyland, and Lee Roy Caffey.

McCoy led or tied for the team lead in sacks twice, including a career high 8 1/2 in his final season with the Packers. The Notre Dame product finished his career playing two years with the Oakland Raiders and then two more with the New York Giants.

He said defense often won out in these border wars, even though Minnesota held a commanding 11-3 advantage in McCoy's seven campaigns in Green Bay.

"It was always a defensive battle, 10-3, 13-10, or something like that. They were good, hard, clean games, not like when we played the Bears. It was hard-nosed and let's strap it up."

McCoy got involved in the Fellowship of Christian Athletes and Athletes in Action while still playing and has continued in the ministry ever since. The last 12 years he's been in Lawrenceville, Georgia, and is affiliated with Bill Glass Ministries, founded by the former Cleveland Browns star and based in Dallas.

"The Vikings had guys like Mick Tingelhoff, Ed White, Wes Hamilton, and Ron Yary, all really good offensive linemen," McCoy said. "Their quarterbacks were Fran Tarkenton and Gary Cuozzo, and running backs Bill Brown, Ed Marinaro, and Dave Osborn, the mudder. None of them had a lot of speed, but they were good all-around backs.

"Their defense had more big names, with the Purple People Eaters, Jeff Siemon and Paul Krause," McCoy added. "I think the Vikings respected us, and we respected them."

Ron Yary would agree on both counts, missing only two games while anchoring the Minnesota offensive line from 1970 to 1981 after serving in a reserve role as a rookie and splitting time his second year at right tackle.

The USC grad earned All-Pro selections from 1971–76 and made the Pro Bowl team those years plus after the 1977 season. The first-round draft pick is a member of the 2001 NFL Hall of Fame class because he won most of his individual battles, including those against the Packers.

He said he learned what to expect from the rigors of playing pro ball just before his rookie campaign.

"I played against Willie Davis in the college all-star game in 1968," Yary said. "It was a real good introduction to the NFL. He was a lot stronger than anybody I'd gone up against, and much quicker and faster. He must have been 32 or 33 and near the end of his career."

However, Davis's successors didn't necessarily make Yary's job any easier.

"The Packers always had big tough ends," Yary said from his Los Angeles-area home. "Clarence Williams was big and strong, and Mike Butler was big and tough. And one game Bob Brown popped my eardrum. He wound up and faked with his right and then head-slapped me with his left."

Yary said that surviving those types of conflicts was the key to victory and gave Minnesota a chance at the postseason.

"Bud Grant always told us that if we wanted to get into the playoffs, you had to beat the teams in your conference and those in your division twice, and that usually gave you at least 10 wins. That's why we took each of those Central Division games so seriously."

Matt Blair was his teammate, starting in 1974, and remained a major cog in Minnesota's defense through the 1985 season. He knows exactly what Yary was talking about.

The Twin Cities resident promotes golf tournaments and does sports marketing for groups around the country for major events that have included the Masters, the Super Bowl, and the NCAA basketball Final Four.

But as a player, he spoke much more loudly on the field.

"Over the years, you can look at all of the games and scores to see who won, and there weren't many blowouts," said Blair, who finished his career behind only Scott Studwell in total tackles.

He blocked a team-record 20 kicks, equaling Page's season mark of five during 1979. That year he blocked two kicks in a game twice, the second time during a 19-7 loss to the Packers at Milwaukee.

"It was always special to play in the Central Division," Blair said. "However you want to say it, you didn't have to get motivated to play the Packers."

Greenwood, Wisconsin, native Larry Krause got a taste of the rivalry for four years, ending his career the same year that Blair began his. Krause (1970–71, '73–74) starred at St. Norbert College in De Pere, the Packers' training camp headquarters. He was the Packers' 17th and final pick in the 1970 draft, excelling on special teams.

"I played fullback and halfback," said Krause, who has moved from Madison to Wausau and then to Waunakee, where he has been since 1989, working in commercial real estate for M&I Bank. "We carried five running backs, so I was the swing guy. I mostly played special teams and returned kickoffs."

He scored only once in his career, but it was highlight material, racing 100 yards with a kickoff return in his rookie season. He finished that year with 18 returns for 513 yards (28.5 average), which placed him third in the NFC and seventh in the NFL.

Krause and the Packers won only twice in eight meetings against the Vikings during his four active seasons, but he said playing against them was special because they were a top-flight organization.

"They ran a pretty classy operation," Krause said. "The Packers-Bears rivalry was different. The Bears weren't very good at the time and were thuggish, and things escalated from there. But Minnesota had Bud Grant, one of the most respected coaches in the league. Every year they were the class of the division and the team to beat."

Mike Butler learned that the hard way, especially during his matchups against Ron Yary.

"He was tough," said Butler, now an assistant director of operations for the Tampa Bay Housing Authority. "I remember chasing Fran Tarkenton around all day. Him and those Hail Mary passes and Ahmad Rashad coming down with those catches. I remember one time covering Chuck Foreman out of the backfield. Luckily they didn't throw him the pass."

Butler is a Washington, D.C., native who starred at the University of Kansas. He was the No. 9 pick in the 1977 draft, 19 picks before defensive end running mate Ezra Johnson in the first round. Butler played with Green Bay through the 1982 season, spent two years in the USFL and then returned to the Packers for a couple of games in 1985 before injuring his neck.

One moment stands out in his mind about the Minnesota series.

"It was the game in Milwaukee in 1979," Butler said. "Ezra caused a fumble, I recovered it and ran it 70 yards for a touchdown, which was a Packer record at the time."

That mark stood until Scott Stephen rumbled 76 yards (no TD) against the Bears in 1989 and was bested again when Keith McKenzie scooted 88 yards for a score against Pittsburgh in 1998.

Butler's score helped the Packers down the Vikings, 19-7, in that November 11 showdown.

Willard Harrell was a third-round pick, No. 58, a selection the Packers got in the Bob Brown trade. He played his third and final season with the Packers during Butler's rookie campaign, and the St. Louis–area insurance salesman said returning kicks and carrying the pigskin wasn't a picnic against the Purple Gang.

"They didn't call it the Black and Blue Division for nothing," said Harrell, a northern California native who attended the University of the Pacific. "That was when football was football, so there are a lot of fond memories, even though you came out of those games all battered and bruised.

"The Vikings were such a big rivalry, so it was something special," added Harrell, who played his final seven seasons with the St. Louis Cardinals. "Going against those famous Purple People Eaters, it was awesome."

Here are highlights and scores from those encounters and the remainder of the decade's contests.

1970

OCT. 4 AT MILWAUKEE: Green Bay's 13-10 win broke its four-game losing streak in the series. Dave Hampton provided a spark with a 101-yard kickoff return for the deciding score.

Dale Livingston's 28- and 33-yard field goals held up until the exciting fourth quarter. His Vikings' counterpart, Fred Cox, cut their deficit in half, but Hampton found room behind his wedge and scored the clincher on the ensuing kickoff.

Minnesota gained 216 yards behind Gary Cuozzo's 19-for-38 effort passing, but the Vikings mustered only 57 yards rushing. Meanwhile, the Packers gained 143 yards on the ground.

However, Green Bay got outstanding play from its defense. Bob Brown, who joined Hampton in receiving a game ball, registered three sacks, Lionel Aldridge added two, and Kevin Hardy chipped in a sack and a key deflected pass in the fourth quarter.

"One of the greatest thrills I've had has been playing in two Super Bowls," Bob Brown said in the *Press-Gazette*. "And beating the Vikings after losing to 'em two years in a row is just as big a thrill. It was a great team victory."

In the secondary, Doug Hart's interception set up Livingston's first field goal, and safety Willie Wood's pick at the Green Bay 10 with 1:42 left before halftime proved crucial.

Linebacker Dave Robinson recovered a Minnesota fumble at the Packers 20 after Donny Anderson's fumble had given the Vikings a first down at the Green Bay 33.

Anderson chipped in offensively and on special teams. He gained 59 yards on 11 carries and averaged 43 yards on eight punts, including a 60-yarder. Cuozzo connected with Gene Washington on a 12-yard score with 1:51 left to shave Green Bay's margin to three. But Bart Starr, who had been intercepted by Paul Krause at the goal line early in the second quarter, completed a 9-yard pass to Carroll Dale on a third-and-3 play with 48 seconds left to help the Packers run out the clock.

"You have to give credit to the kid [Hampton]," Minnesota's Grant said in the *Press-Gazette*. "He hung in there and broke it. He came up with the big one."

Hampton almost didn't make it afterward. He had been hospitalized two weeks earlier for cramps, then after this game, suffered what was thought to be appendicitis. He underwent abdominal surgery for an abscess.

NOV. 22 AT MINNESOTA: The Vikings got revenge with a hard-fought 10-3 triumph at wind-swept Metropolitan Stadium despite Packer halfback Donny Anderson's 19-carry, 93-yard outing.

Green Bay outgained the Vikings 282-202 but lost a fumble and an interception, and northwest winds that reached 35 mph played havoc with Dale Livingston. He missed 25- and 31-yard tries in a first half that ended 3-3 and then bounced a 13-yard attempt off the upright with six minutes left in the game.

Anderson also fought Mother Nature from his end zone, when the Vikings took over after one of his punts at the Green Bay 41. A 37-yard pass to wide receiver Gene Washington set up Clint Jones' plunge for the game's only TD in the third quarter.

Despite the conditions, Bart Starr completed 12 of 23 passes for 131 yards, but he had to leave the game with a knee injury. Backup Don Horn led the Packers down the field before Livingston's shortest miss and then moved Green Bay to within a tying touchdown. But rookie running back Larry Krause fumbled and Minnesota's Jim Marshall recovered at the Vikings' 18 with two minutes left, eliminating the Packers from Central Division contention.

1971

OCT. 17 AT GREEN BAY: Minnesota controlled the contest at Lambeau Field, winning 24-13 for its fifth victory in the last six years on Packer turf in Dan Devine's coaching debut against the Vikings.

A spokesperson from the Packers ticket office said during the week that, "We could have filled another half a stadium with all of the requests we've had."

Those in attendance saw an entertaining contest until Green Bay's miscues mounted in the second half against a superior Minnesota squad, which entered the game having allowed only three touchdowns in four games and had registered back-to-back shutouts against Buffalo and Philadelphia.

Jim Marshall's recovery of rookie standout John Brockington's fumble gave the Vikings possession at the Green Bay 32. Gary Cuozzo then passed to Dave Osborn for the TD. Green Bay tied it up at the half on quarterback Scott Hunter's run, and the home team grabbed the lead when Hunter and Carroll Dale hooked up on a 56-yard score to cap a four-play, 80-yard journey. But Vikings' defensive tackle Alan Page, who later won Defensive Player of the Year and Most Valuable Player honors, worked his magic, blocking the extra point to keep the score 13-7.

Donny Anderson's fumble at the Green Bay 8-yard line gave Minnesota the life and momentum it needed. Cuozzo hit tight end Stu Voigt on the first play as the Vikings grabbed the lead for good after the extra point.

Bobby Bryant's interception put the visitors 38 yards away, and Cuozzo and wideout Bob Grim connected for a 24-yard pass play to push Minnesota's cushion to eight. Then Fred Cox clinched the win with a 22-yard field goal after Green Bay lost the ball on downs at its 47.

Dale finished with eight catches for 151 yards, while Grim topped Minnesota with seven receptions for 101 yards. Hunter was 12 of 24 for 230 yards.

NOV. 14 AT MINNESOTA: The Vikings won 3-0 in the lowest-scoring game of the series.

The Vikings set futility marks on offense, registering team records for fewest first downs (5) and yards gained (87) but still won.

Fullback John Brockington churned out 149 and Donny Anderson added 68 of the Packers' 245 yards rushing, but they still failed to score. Turnovers in the red zone killed Green Bay, which finished with 301 total yards.

Kicker Lou Michaels missed a 23-yard field goal in the first quarter after defensive end Clarence Williams recovered a Vikings fumble at the Minnesota 22. Then the Packers 82-yard march ended in disappointment when they were stopped twice from the 1-yard line, including Anderson's dive on fourth down. Green Bay held and drove again, but Paul Krause intercepted his 50th career pass at the 3-yard line.

The visitors' ineptness continued when Krause recovered Anderson's fumble 10 yards from the end zone in the third quarter. Then Scott Hunter was intercepted by Charlie West on a second-and-8 play from the Vikings 10 with 8 minutes remaining. West returned it to midfield, where the Vikings drove to Fred Cox's 25-yard difference maker.

Of the West interception, the rookie quarterback, Hunter, told the *Press-Gazette*: "I got greedy. I wanted 7 instead of 3. Rich McGeorge ran a good route and was open by five steps, but I threw it a little late. I saw West but I thought I had it over his head."

Brockington summed up the Packers' plight by saying in the *Press-Gazette*: "This is the most frustrating day of all, and we've had quite a few. To play as hard as we did and come out with nothing. God must not dig somebody on this team."

Minnesota coach Bud Grant still tipped his cap to the Packers.

"The Packers played as sound a football game against us as anybody has in the last three years," he said in the Green Bay paper.

Dan Devine saw things more like Brockington.

"I've been through a lot of frustrating experiences in my 23 years of coaching, but this has to rival the most frustrating ones," he said in the *Press-Gazette*.

1972

OCT. 29 AT GREEN BAY: Minnesota whipped the eventual division champions, 27-13, at Lambeau to hand the Packers their second straight loss and drop them to 4-3.

The Vikings intercepted Scott Hunter four times, returning two of them for scores, including Paul Krause's 32-yard jaunt that broke a 13-all tie and linebacker Wally Hilgenberg's 14-yard scamper as the visitors tallied 17 points in the fourth quarter.

Safety Jeff Wright, in his first starting assignment, grabbed Hunter's other two errant aerials. Hunter had been intercepted only once through the first six weeks.

"I thought the ball was thrown well," Dan Devine said in a *Press-Gazette* article, "but it was a big play by Krause. We didn't get the big plays from the defense like they got."

DEC. 10 AT MINNESOTA: Green Bay returned the favor with a 23-7 victory to clinch its first Central title in five years, while snapping the Vikings' four-year reign atop the division. The Packers won the next week to finish 10-4, while Detroit slipped to 8-5-1 and the Vikings faltered to 7-7.

MacArthur Lane's 37-yard run ignited Green Bay's offense, and the defense forced four second-half turnovers. John Brockington surpassed 1,000 yards to become the first NFL running back to do so in his first two years.

(More on this game in chapter 6.)

1973

SEPT. 30 AT MINNESOTA: The Vikings earned an 11-3 win in another slugfest. The Vikings flopped on John Brockington in the end zone after the latter had fallen on MacArthur Lane's fumble for the hosts' first score. It was set up when Mike Eischied's punt was downed on the Green Bay 8-yard line.

A short Ron Widby punt and Ed Marinaro's 27-yard return set up Fred Cox's 23-yard field goal after the safety for a 5-3 Minnesota lead. Cox added a 13-yarder in the third quarter when the Vikings recovered another Lane fumble, this one at the Green Bay 7.

Minnesota took over at its 20 after one of rookie kicker Chester Marcol's two field-goal misses (37 and 34 yards), putting the game out of reach with 5:51 left on a 14-yard Cox kick. The key play in the drive was Chuck Foreman's 37-yard run on third-and-2.

Foreman gained 89 yards on 16 attempts, and the Vikings completed 12 of 16 pass attempts in totaling 315 yards. Meanwhile, the Vikings limited Green Bay to 160 net yards, including only 7 of 20 passing. Left-handed signal caller Jim Del Gaizo was 4 of 14 for 36 yards and Scott Hunter was 3 of 6 for 44 in relief. Marcol booted a 42-yard field goal to give the Packers a 3-0 lead in the second quarter.

Minnesota, despite losing three fumbles, finished with a 206-90 advantage in rushing as Ed Marinaro chipped in 83 yards on 20 carries. Brockington led Green Bay with 14 attempts for 58 yards.

"You couldn't call it very artistic, but it was emotional," Minnesota head man Bud Grant told a *Press-Gazette* reporter. "Neither team really played very well."

"I didn't throw well and I have no excuses," Del Gaizo said in the *Press-Gazette.* "I think I had ample time to throw. It was my fault."

Even though those statements were much more accurate than the lefty signal caller was, his coach spread the blame for another demoralizing set-back to the Vikings.

"The things that won or lost the game had nothing to do with the quarterbacking," Dan Devine said in the Green Bay paper. "We had several crucial penalties, like the one that wiped out a 16-yard gain by John Brockington shortly before half. In a game of field position, those things are very important."

DEC. 8 AT GREEN BAY: Minnesota whipped the Packers, 31-7, to complete the season sweep and finish 6-0 in the division.

The Vikings dominated this Saturday contest, scoring two touchdowns in the first and second quarters en route to a 31-0 cushion after three. All four scores went for 20 or more yards, including Chuck Foreman's 50-yard run and Bobby Bryant's 46-yard interception return.

Green Bay outgained the Vikings rushing and passing but threw four interceptions, including three by Jerry Tagge. John Brockington surpassed 1,000 yards rushing for the third consecutive season, the first player to do so in his first three years in the league.

Bryant corralled three interceptions, becoming the first Viking defender to accomplish that feat twice; he had done it in 1969 against Cleveland.

Stu Voigt hauled in a 21-yard reception for the game's first score. Bryant and Foreman followed suit before wide receiver John Gilliam made it 28-0 with his 20-yard catch.

Foreman equaled his scoring play in his other 18 carries to finish with an even 100 yards, but Brockington hammered for 124 on 27 tries as the Packers won the running battle 152-138.

Green Bay also claimed a 148-83 margin passing despite a lousy 14-of-32 effort, including a 10-for-25 showing from local product Tagge. Minnesota was 10 of 19 passing.

The Packers slipped to 4-7-2 one season after being the class of the division, and two Vikings offered their viewpoints as to why.

"When you lose a couple, things start going badly," said former Packer Carroll Dale in the *Press-Gazette*. "It's hard to put your finger on."

"A couple of injuries, some bad breaks and, of course, their unsettled quarterback situation," Bryant said in the story.

Dale made his first and last appearance at Lambeau as a member of the opposition.

"It was odd coming into town and riding to the Port Plaza Inn with the Vikings," Dale told the *Press-Gazette*. "But it's been 13 weeks and I didn't feel that odd out there on the field in a Viking uniform."

1974

SEPT. 15 AT GREEN BAY: Minnesota triumphed, 32-17, on opening day to kick off a season that ended in the Vikings' second trip to the Super Bowl. It was the Vikings' 11th victory in their last 13 games against the Packers, giving them a 14-13 series lead.

Minnesota rushed for 165 yards as halfback Chuck Foreman scored three touchdowns. However, the contest was deadlocked at 10 at halftime. Then cornerback Nate Wright intercepted a Jerry Tagge pass on Green Bay's first possession of the third quarter to turn the game in the Vikings' favor, one of his two thefts for the afternoon.

The Packers rushed 17 times for only 50 yards on first down, and that included an 18-yard reverse by Steve Odom. Green Bay ran 33 times and passed 20 while playing without starting offensive tackles Bill Hayhoe and Dick Himes. Center Larry McCarren and guard Lee Nystrom made their first regular-season starts. Guard Bill Lueck, coming back from a three-week absence due to injury, tried to fight off Alan Page, and recently acquired tackle Harry Schuh filled in at one end of the line.

Minnesota's Amos Martin keyed the defensive charge with a 15-yard score on a fumble recovery, and fellow linebacker Fred McNeill, a rookie, forced a fumble on a punt return.

Nate Wright's key play proved controversial, as the Packers contended and TV cameras seemed to confirm that Tagge tackled and forced the Viking cornerback to fumble before he was knocked out of bounds.

However, the Green Bay quarterback shouldered the blame for his miscue that was intended for wide receiver Barry Smith.

"I hung the ball out there too high," Tagge said in a *Press-Gazette* article. "Nate Wright made a great play. He looked at my eyes the whole way. He took a chance and came out the winner."

NOV. 17 AT MINNESOTA: Green Bay upset the Vikings, 19-7, to earn a split of the season series.

Chester Marcol booted four field goals for the Packers, the fifth time in his career he had accomplished that feat. In the process, he tied a mark that he had shared with Paul Hornung with six field-goal attempts.

John Brockington gained 137 yards on 32 carries for the victors, who also got a key 68-yard pass play from veteran quarterback John Hadl to fullback MacArthur Lane for the game's clinching and final score.

Green Bay also blocked a 29-yard Fred Cox field-goal attempt that cornerback Ken Ellis returned 68 yards to the Minnesota 13 to set up Marcol's short field goal. Another Packer drive ended when Brockington fumbled into the Minnesota end zone. Green Bay outgained the Vikings 393-282, including 202-74 rushing. The Packers ran 40 plays to Minnesota's 19, while holding the ball for 18:18 in the first half.

Minnesota's lone score came on a Fran Tarkenton pass to Chuck Foreman from 25 yards out with 5:08 left in the game.

It was only the Vikings' sixth loss in their last 36 division contests despite two more interceptions from Nate Wright.

Green Bay linebacker Jim Carter told the *Press-Gazette*, "There's been a lot of pressure on the coaching staff and the ballplayers. There are rumors circulating all the time about some new coaches. Two victories in a row, I hope will help some. I sure hope so."

The Packers went on to win their third in a row the next week over San Diego (34-0), but they lost the final three games, all on the road, to finish 6-8 and out of the playoffs. That proved to be the end for Dan Devine.

1975

NOV. 2 AT GREEN BAY: Minnesota again found success at Lambeau, claiming a 28-17 win in Bart Starr's first game as a coach in the series.

Fran Tarkenton, who completed 24 of 30 passes, hit John Gilliam and Chuck Foreman with fourth-quarter touchdowns to rally the Vikings from a 17-14 deficit. Minnesota outgained Green Bay 266-113 through the air.

Green Bay overcame a 14-10 halftime deficit with the help of a stout running game without John Brockington, who was injured on the first play from scrimmage and missed the rest of the day. Barty Smith, who entered the game with only 14 carries for 44 yards on the season, led the way with 88 yards on 16 attempts as the Packers outgained the Vikings 132-101 on the ground. But Green Bay couldn't make up for John Hadl's three interceptions, two by Paul Krause.

Minnesota won its seventh straight en route to going 10-0 to start a 12-2 campaign.

Green Bay didn't have any turnovers until the fourth quarter, relying on its ground attack on all eight plays during its first scoring drive, a 57-yard march, and 9 of 12 plays during a 68-yard trek in the third quarter for a 17-14 lead.

Tarkenton finished 6 of 6 on the Vikings' 13-play, 83-yard drive to open the game, including a TD toss to Stu Voigt. The Vikings converted 11 of 16 third-down opportunities.

DEC. 7 AT MINNESOTA: The hosts cruised to a sweep with a 24-3 victory. John Gilliam hauled in two more TD aerials from Fran Tarkenton, and Chuck Foreman added a third as the Vikings' 24-3 halftime lead provided all of the scoring. Gilliam's first TD grab helped give the Vikings a 14-3 lead after the first quarter, and his 37-yard play gave the hosts a 21-3 cushion in the second quarter. All three plays came against man-to-man coverage.

Green Bay was limited to six first downs and 122 total yards, 51 rushing and 71 passing. The Packers' miserable aerial display produced only 11 completions in 30 attempts and three more interceptions. John Brockington was limited to 13 yards on 10 carries.

Meanwhile, Tarkenton was an efficient 20 of 30 for 211 yards on his way to the NFL's Most Valuable Player award.

1976

NOV. 21 AT MILWAUKEE: Minnesota won, 17-10, to clinch its fourth straight division crown in a game in which ex-Viking star Dave Osborn was honorary captain for the Packers.

Green Bay outrushed the Vikings 146-100 but lost, the only time in the Packers' 14 games that the team that gained more yards on the ground failed to win. Safety Johnnie Gray returned seven punts for the hosts (for 30 yards), tying for second most returns in team history.

John Brockington tied the contest at 10 with a 1-yard plunge as the Packers traveled 74 yards with the second-half kickoff, but the Vikings got the game-winner when Ahmad Rashad hauled in an 11-yard TD with 14:16 left to finish off an 88-yard march.

Before that, the Packers, who had three sacks, handcuffed Rashad and fellow wideout Sammy White for most of the game. The two combined for four receptions, including only one for 7 yards by White, who entered the game with 38 catches and a 19.5 average.

The home faithful watched the Vikings outgain their foes 151-82 passing as the Packers threw four interceptions, including three by Carlos Brown, later known as actor Alan Autry (*"Heat of the Night"* and *"Grace Under Fire"*).

Second-year running back Robert Miller hauled in nine passes for the Vikings, who finished 23 of 43 through the air, including 16 catches by their running backs. A critical one occurred when Fran Tarkenton found Chuck Foreman for a 25-yard gain on a fourth-and-21 play from the Green Bay 33 to help the visitors grab a 10-3 halftime lead with 11 seconds left. Bart Starr could only admire the talents of his former quarterbacking foe in a *Press-Gazette* interview.

"It was typical of how he can eat at you," Starr said. "You can never seem to take it all away from him. If you stymie something, he'll beat you with something else."

Foreman carried 19 times for 84 yards, while John Brockington churned for 51 on 13 tries and Willard Harrell, who was intercepted on an option pass, gained 42 yards on eight attempts for Green Bay.

Linebacker Fred Carr blocked his fifth and sixth kicks of the season, 47- and 33-yard Fred Cox field-goal attempts, but Green Bay's problems again centered on its bumbling offensive unit.

Brown was sacked four times and two of his interceptions came on passes that deflected off of his receivers' hands. Green Bay's troubles were best illustrated in its final shot at tying the game.

A fake punt and one completion gave the Packers a first down at the Minnesota 37 with 2:14 left. Four plays later they had lost 24 yards to their own 39.

DEC. 5 AT MINNESOTA: The Vikings survived in the snow for a 20-9 win as they geared up for a fourth trip to the Super Bowl.

Green Bay grabbed a 6-0 lead but Bobby Bryant blocked Chester Marcol's extra point, an omen of things to come. Green Bay won the turnover battle 3-0 but never took advantage of the opportunities, being outgained 218-59 rushing and 195-85 passing. The Packers completed just 8 of 26.

Chuck Foreman reached pay dirt on two one-yard bursts en route to 22 touchdowns for the season. And Robert Miller added five more catches, giving him 14 of his season total 23 against Green Bay, and rushed for 95 yards to lead the ground attack. Foreman's scores completed 72- and 73-yard drives, while Fred Cox booted three-pointers after 44- and 56-yard journeys.

Cox's two boots knotted things up before Foreman's first dive gave the Vikings the lead for good early in the fourth quarter.

Tight end Rich McGeorge dropped a potential TD pass, forcing the Packers to kick a field goal for a 13-9 deficit with 7:24 left. Foreman then put the game out of reach with his second tally with 2:11 showing.

Minnesota dominated by a 29-8 margin in first downs, including a 16-2 rushing advantage, but Fran Tarkenton had his streak of 155 consecutive passes without an interception broken when cornerback Perry Smith made a theft in the third quarter. Ahmad Rashad led Viking receivers with six catches for 61 yards, but Green Bay's anemic arsenal averaged the same (2.8) per pass as it did per rush.

Physical play was typical again, and according to some, it went beyond that.

"Some of the Packers did play it a little dirty," said Viking running back Brent McClanahan in the *Press-Gazette*. "No. 52 [Gary Weaver] was one. He was pretty cocky and pulled a couple of cheap shots."

1977

OCT. 2 AT MINNESOTA: The Vikings survived a shaky start in claiming a 19-7 triumph.

Lynn Dickey connected with wide receiver Steve Odom on a 95-yard pass on the third play from scrimmage to open the scoring, the third-longest in team annals and the longest ever against the Vikings.

But Minnesota controlled the rest of the game despite two errant extra-point conversions.

The Packers stumbled to 8 yards on the other 17 plays besides the Odom score in the first half, as Minnesota ran 45 plays, held a time of possession advantage of 21:21 to 8:39, earned 15 first downs to Green Bay's one, and gained 207 yards.

All of that, and the Vikings managed only a 13-7 lead.

Green Bay finished with 81 yards rushing against a shuffled Minnesota defense. Injuries to two linebackers forced the Vikings to move Jeff Siemon outside and insert rookie Scott Studwell into the middle.

Manfred Moore returned seven punts for the Vikings as they finished with a 24-8 margin in first downs and 194 yards rushing. Sammy Johnson accounted for 65 yards on 12 tries and Chuck Foreman added 53 yards on 19 attempts.

Trailing 13-7, the Packers drove from their 6 to the Minnesota 36, trying and missing a 53-yard field goal. The Vikings drove 64 yards to the clinching TD, which gave Bud Grant his 100th career NFL victory against 39 losses and four ties, and a 17-4 mark against Green Bay.

One of the most colorful characters to grace this series was defensive lineman Dave Roller, who, like many Packers before him, spent the afternoon trying to catch Fran Tarkenton.

"We were just exchanging vows," Roller said of their verbal gamesmanship in a *Press-Gazette* story. "He was trying to intimidate me, and I was trying to intimidate him. I can't repeat what he said. But I told him, 'Hold onto that ball and let me sack you.' And he said, 'You think I'm crazy.' And I said, 'Yeah, you're a Georgian,'" said Roller, a native of Kentucky.

"Everyone else sticks in the pocket. I don't think he knows what a pocket is."

NOV. 27 AT GREEN BAY: Minnesota again held the Packers to single digits in earning a 13-6 victory at snowy Lambeau Field.

A temperature of 26 degrees and winds of 16 mph created sometimes blizzard-like conditions with five inches of snow.

Green Bay again jumped out first as quarterback David Whitehurst ran in from 3 yards out, completing a 21-yard drive set up by a fumble recovery. But Chester Marcol's extra point attempt hit the upright.

Backup quarterback Bob Lee, subbing for Fran Tarkenton, who had broken his leg two weeks earlier in a win against Cincinnati, connected with Sammy White on a 40-yard pass, his only catch of the game, for a 7-6 lead. Fred Cox's first field goal came after Willard Harrell fumbled at the Green Bay 43, and he added another three-pointer after a 13-play, 46-yard drive for a 13-6 halftime score.

Green Bay had excellent scoring opportunities turned away in the second half. The Packers drove from their 17 to the Minnesota 5 after White-hurst hit tight end Bert Askson with a 34-yard pass. However, Paul Krause recorded his 78th career interception.

With just more than four minutes remaining in the game, fullback Barty Smith coughed up a fumble at the Minnesota 8. It was his first of the season and came after the Packers had recovered Chuck Foreman's fumble at the Viking 21. Bryant's end zone interception on the last play preserved the triumph.

The slugfest saw the Vikings win the first down battle only 12-9 and finish with a 158-108 rushing advantage. Green Bay held a 61-60 margin in the air as Minnesota attempted only eight passes.

Green Bay's passing was again anemic, as Whitehurst completed 6 of 23 tries with two interceptions. Foreman led Minnesota's ground attack with 26 carries for 101 yards in a game in which each team lost two fumbles.

The victory helped Minnesota win three of its final four games to finish 9-5 and gain a tiebreaker edge over Chicago for the division championship.

1978

OCT. 22 AT MINNESOTA: The Vikings continued their dominance with a 21-7 decision to break the Packers' four-game season winning streak.

Green Bay entered with a 6-1 record and control of the division race and limited the 3-4 Vikings to 60 yards rushing on 32 carries, but still lost the game.

Fran Tarkenton completed 26 of 43 passes for 262 yards, spreading the pigskin around as usual: Running backs Chuck Foreman and Rickey Young hauled in seven catches apiece and wide receivers Ahmad Rashad and Sammy White grabbed six and five, respectively. Rookie tackle Frank Myers negated the pass rushing prowess of Ezra Johnson, and two pass interference penalties and two personal fouls kept Minnesota drives going.

One of the crucial calls also got Packer defensive tackle Dave Roller booted out of the game because of a late hit on Tarkenton on the Minnesota sideline.

"Roller had definite intent to injure Tarkenton," Grant said in a *Press-Gazette* article. "He hit him 2 or 3 yards out of bounds. Those are the kinds of people who give this game a bad name."

Roller defended his actions in the story.

"I didn't do it deliberately. I swear it was nothing flagrant. I hope the films prove it. Our momentum carried us into the sideline. I didn't try to elbow or kick him. We were laying there and Bud Grant said, 'Kick him out.' Then everybody said, 'Kick him out.' To me everybody acted too quick. I can't believe the referee did that."

Tarkenton told the newspaper that he didn't want to stir up anymore controversy about the play involving his former teammate when both were with the New York Giants.

"I do like Rollerball," Tarkenton said of Roller, who later played two years with the Vikings. "He's an interesting character. He hit me in the back, and that's all I know."

In the real game, the Vikings sacked David Whitehurst five times and limited him to an 8 for 30 day and 120 yards in a game in which Green Bay ran the ball seven less times than it passed despite averaging 5.2 yards per carry.

One promising scoring opportunity came with the Packers trailing 14-7. The visitors faced a third-and-2 at the Minnesota 38, but guard Darrel Gofourth jumped offside.

Tarkenton said in the *Press-Gazette* that the Vikings still had to concentrate on the bigger picture.

"When you're 4-4 you don't enjoy this. When I'm 10-4 I'll be smiling. This is only today's game. This win doesn't mean a damn thing. It means we're 4-4."

NOV. 26 AT GREEN BAY: The teams tied, 10-10, in the first overtime game between them.

Halfback Terdell Middleton set a Packers' record with 39 rushing attempts (for 110 yards), becoming the first Green Bay back since John Brockington in 1973 to reach 1,000 yards.

However, it wasn't enough to ignite the hosts' offense, as David Beverly punted 10 times for a paltry 29.9 average. Minnesota's Greg Coleman averaged 44 yards on his six boots.

Fran Tarkenton, in his final game against the Packers, threw four interceptions and had only 35 yards passing through three quarters as Green Bay defensive ends Mike Butler and Ezra Johnson applied constant pressure and cornerbacks Willie Buchanon and Mike C. McCoy blanked wide receivers Ahmad Rashad and Sammy White for no catches until their game-tying drive to force the extra quarter.

But the future Hall of Famer hooked up with Rashad on a 5-yard pass play to tie the score at 10, finishing 20 for 37 for 199 yards.

Green Bay's Chester Marcol missed a 40-yard field goal, and Minnesota's Rich Danmeier shanked one from 21 yards in overtime as both teams walked off the field with a frustrating outcome, although it proved to be more beneficial to the Vikings.

Minnesota's 42 rushes averaged only 2.6 yards, so it used Tarkenton's arm to move within range in overtime, as he passed for 56 of the 85 yards as the visitors marched to the Green Bay 4, where Danmeier's errant effort came up wide.

The Packers traveled 70 yards in 12 plays to take a 7-3 lead, but not much else worked, even though David Whitehurst didn't throw any interceptions.

Middleton's fumble at the Green Bay 9 set up Danmeier's lone field goal, and on the first play of the fourth quarter, the halfback from Memphis State lost a yard on a third-and-one play from the Minnesota one, forcing Marcol's chip-shot field goal and a 10-3 advantage instead of 13-3 or 14-3. Barty Smith also was stuffed on a third-and-1 situation at midfield in OT, and the Packers punted.

The teams each went 1-2 the rest of the way, with Minnesota winning the division title and earning the playoff berth even though both finished 8-7-1 overall and 5-2-1 in Central games because of the Vikings' 21-7 win October 22.

1979

SEPT. 23 AT MINNESOTA: The Vikings came out on top 27-21 in a second consecutive overtime battle between the foes.

Wide receiver James Lofton and Bart Starr had a run-in after the Packers conservatively used three running plays during the final 1:41 of regulation and then didn't get the ball back in overtime.

Green Bay took a 14-7 halftime lead and maintained that margin at 21-14 in the final quarter, but the Vikings rallied with a Rickey Young TD run to force overtime. Then Ahmad Rashad pulled in a 50-yard pass from Tommy Kramer to win it.

Rickey Young (19-71) and Ted Brown (15-77) led Minnesota to a 161-141 rushing advantage, and Kramer, despite two interceptions, finished 19 of 26 for 245 yards. Rashad was his favorite target with nine catches for 136 yards.

Green Bay finished 10 of 15 passing with no interceptions, but gained only 108 yards. Terdell Middleton led the ground arsenal with 90 yards on 20 carries.

NOV. 11 AT MILWAUKEE: Green Bay claimed a 19-7 decision to earn its first win over Minnesota in nine games, handing the Vikings their third straight setback en route to a 7-9 final mark and first losing season since 1967.

Packers' defensive end Mike Butler returned a fumble recovery 70 yards for a TD, while Terdell Middleton recorded his last 100-yard game (27 carries for 135 yards) as a pro to give County Stadium fans their first win over the Vikings since 1974.

Despite all of that, Tommy Kramer completed a club record 16 consecutive attempts as Minnesota finished with a 230-115 edge in passing yards. However, the Vikings had two interceptions and fumbled three times, two of which were recovered by Green Bay safety Johnnie Gray.

The Packers gave away three interceptions, had two of Tom Birney's extra points blocked, and committed eight penalties for 59 yards. But they surged to a 178-117 rushing margin.

CHAPTER THREE

THE 1980s
MIRED IN MEDIOCRITY

Green Bay's Brent Fullwood, left, and Minnesota's Keith Millard chat after the Packers held on for a 20-19 victory in November 1989, one of the hosts' record four one-point victories that year.

M ike Ditka's Chicago Bears awoke from 20 years of slumber to dominate the Central Division from 1984 through 1988, regularly steamrolling past their closest rivals behind a suffocating defense that fit the term Monsters of the Midway just as, or more, profoundly than the teams of the 1960s.

Meanwhile, the Vikings and Packers seldom emerged from hibernation, instead hovering around the .500 mark much of the decade.

The Vikings tied for the seventh-best record in the NFC at 77-75-0 (.507), winning tiebreakers with Detroit in 1980 (9-7) and Green Bay (10-6) in 1989 to claim their only division titles. Minnesota finished within one game either side of the break-even mark seven times in eight seasons from 1980-87 but also earned playoff berths in 1982, '87, and '88.

Green Bay's only postseason appearance came in 1982's Super Bowl tournament/strike season when it posted a 5-3-1 record. Otherwise, the Packers suffered through another mostly dismal stretch with a 65-84-3 mark (.438), which placed them 10th among the 14 NFC franchises.

The Packers took parity to a new level, fashioning 8-8 seasons four times, including three in a row (1983–85).

Both teams displayed awesome offensive firepower much of the time but gave up as many big plays on defense, thus middle-of-the-road finishes were all that could be expected.

The decade saw Minnesota coach Bud Grant retire, come back after Les Steckel got booted following a 3-13 record in 1984 and then retire again one season later, closing out his illustrious career. That issued in the Jerry Burns era as one of Grant's and Vince Lombardi's former assistants got a shot at the top position with the Vikings.

In Green Bay, Bart Starr's nine-year run closed after another disheartening loss to end the 1983 campaign, when a win over the Bears would have sewed up a playoff spot. His former teammate and fellow member of the Hall of Fame, Forrest Gregg, never rose above Starr's mediocrity. And like Dan Devine before them, a major house cleaning failed to pan out after four years.

That brought Lindy Infante on board for four years. But besides the heart-stomping 1989 season in which the Don Majkowski–led Packers pulled out a league-record four one-point victories, Infante couldn't turn things around either.

Despite that lack of overall success, Green Bay had little trouble figuring out the Vikings, winning 14 of 19 games.

However, players said these were some of the most hard-fought contests they faced.

Greg Koch manned the right tackle spot for Green Bay from 1977-85. A partner in a law firm in his hometown of Houston, this second-round draft pick from Arkansas said he survived 11 years in pro football's battle zone (10 as a tackle and one as a guard) "relatively injury-free."

However, Koch said those Sunday afternoons were more bearable because his Packers often got the upper hand on their rival Vikings, with whom he finished his career in 1987 after a year with the Miami Dolphins.

"It was weird because no matter what our record was, we went to the playoffs in 1982 and then were 8-8 the next three years, but we almost always beat the Vikings," said Koch, who relaxes these days by playing the piano. "They may have been the better team, but we always had the mindset that we could beat them. We didn't have much of a defense, but we were always pretty good on offense."

Still, Koch said the Vikings never backed down.

"Scott Studwell, who was drafted the same year I was (in the ninth round), was a great linebacker," Koch said. "And when I was a freshman at Arkansas, we played against a guy at Iowa State who was about 6-foot-5 and 220 who played safety (Matt Blair). He knocked one of our running backs unconscious. I said to myself if defensive backs look like that in the NFL, I don't want to play.

"And I always thought (defensive end) Doug Martin was much underrated. I remember the last game I played against the Vikings was in 1985 and Doug got hurt on the second or third play, and I don't recall his name, but I just destroyed his replacement," Koch said of the 27-17 victory that completed Green Bay's season sweep.

Koch doesn't bask in the limelight of being a former NFL player, but he said he holds those memories dear.

"My career transcended two eras," said Koch, whose best friend from his playing days is former Green Bay center and current Packers' broadcaster Larry McCarren. "I played against guys like Carl Eller and Jim Marshall, the Purple People Eaters, my first couple of years, guys I grew up watching. I got to see greatness, and it was a thrill to go up against them and Bud Grant.

"Being from the South, I still knew about the legendary Black and Blue Division, and once I got up there I certainly learned about the big rivalry with the Bears because it was the oldest," Koch said. "But I hated the Vikings just as much, maybe because they had had more success. There definitely was no love lost there. Minnesota was the coldest place in the world to play, but that was old-time football."

Paul Coffman enjoyed his best seasons with the Packers (1978–85), and like Koch, he ended his playing days with a final fall in the Twin Cities.

The Kansas State alumnus became the most productive pass receiving tight end in Green Bay history after coming aboard as a rookie free agent.

Coffman finished with 322 receptions in Green Bay, surpassing the 50-catch mark three times, including a team-high 56 in 1979. He caught passes in 50 straight games from 1979 to 1982, scored 11 TDs in 1983, and made three Pro Bowl appearances before spending two years with Kansas City and one with Minnesota.

The Peculiar, Missouri, resident grew up a Vikings fan in his native Kansas.

"Throughout high school and college I followed the Purple People Eaters, Joe Kapp, Chuck Foreman, and Matt Blair," Coffman said. "As a senior at K-State, my best friend, Gary Spani, and I went over to a preseason game between the Vikings and the Chiefs at Arrowhead. I watched Stu Voigt all night, and I'm telling myself that if this guy can play, I can make it in the NFL. And I've told Stu that story since. It was nothing against him, but he wasn't big, fast, or a great athlete, but he just kept plugging away. And that's the way I was."

Coffman said it didn't take him long to learn what life in the NFC Central was like in general and what the rivalry against Minnesota was all about in particular.

"My rookie year I played in short-yardage situations, and we're down around the goal line," Coffman said. "I come up to the line of scrimmage and Jim Marshall is lined up across from me. I look over at him and I'm thinking, 'Golly, he's like 41 years old,' and I see his gray beard and everything. Well, he knocked me on my butt. That was my introduction to the Vikings and Metropolitan Stadium. They beat us that day, we both ended up 8-7-1, but they went to the playoffs."

Even though the 1980s weren't especially kind to either team, Coffman said the competition was still fierce.

"We went through some lean years, and they suffered through the Les Steckel thing," he said, "but I had to go against guys like Matt Blair. Then they got players like Joey Browner and Chris Doleman. Doleman came into the league as a 260-pound linebacker and I'm at 225, 228. He was the John Randle of his day, always talking trash, so it was a battle.

"I got to know Joe Senser, one of their tight ends, who was a super guy," Coffman added. "We would meet before the games. It was a heated rivalry, so you always got up for those. It was a lot of fun and brought out the best in you. We developed respect and friendships from those games."

Most players agreed, but despite all of their division championships and playoff and Super Bowl appearances, the Vikings used a younger-brother attitude as motivation against the Packers.

"Bud and Burnsie [Jerry Burns] approached it like we didn't have as long of a history, that we were an afterthought," said former Minnesota wide receiver Leo Lewis (1981–91). "There were a lot of Packers fans in Minnesota originally, and many people had long family histories of following the team. So when we came along many fans figured they dare not switch [allegiances]."

He and his teammates were sometimes confused after looking up into the Metrodome stands when facing Green Bay.

"I was always surprised to see all of the green and gold, and not just in one section, but spread out all over," Lewis said. "I'm wondering, how did they get all of those tickets? And to this day, despite their records, the Packers have a loyal following, whereas our fans are more trendy. So, all of that gives this series the feel of playing your cross-town rival and a bragging-rights mentality."

Lewis was used to that underdog approach, toiling for 11 seasons as a 5-foot-8-inch, 170-pounder. He played valuable roles as a pass catcher and punt returner for Minnesota after being drafted by the St. Louis Cardinals and signing with Calgary of the CFL.

Lewis was a backup most of his career, but he caught a career-high 47 passes for 830 yards (17.7 average) to lead Steckel's squad in 1984. He took over the number-one punt return duties in 1987 and led the team in that category for five years, including 58 for 550 yards in 1988.

"I was very fortunate to have played 11 years here," Lewis said from the Vikings' offices in Eden Prairie, where he is director of player programs. "I got the label as being a kick returner, but I didn't return punts (with the Vikings) until I was 30. My first six years I was a receiver."

Karl Swanke (1980–86) also used his versatility to his advantage in earning playing time in many ways for Green Bay. The sixth-round pick from Boston College lined up at tackle, guard, center, short-yardage tight end, and H-back positions during his seven seasons.

Swanke, a project manager with IBM in Vermont, and the Packers won nine of 11 outings against the Vikings until being swept in his final season. However, not everything was peaches and cream for him.

"I remember in my second year. We had played out in L.A. and then they came to Milwaukee the next week," Swanke said of the 30-13 defeat the Vikings hung on Green Bay in 1981. "We were returning a kickoff and one of their linebackers dove down and hit me and I tore out my knee, so I missed the rest of that season. And in '83 when we won that 'Monday Night Football' game over Washington, they beat us the next game and that was one of the reasons, unfortunately, that we couldn't turn the tide that year.

"And then there was the game in my rookie year toward the end of the season over at the Met," Swanke said. "I was the short-yardage tight end and also at the end of the line for extra points and field goals. So in case of a fake field goal they'd holler 'fire' or something and I'd go out for a pass. Well, we mishandled the snap and it never got thrown to me."

However, Swanke said the Packers' success in the series overshadowed those setbacks.

"Minnesota was like a second home for us 'cause we won there most of the time, and it seemed like we had as many fans there as they did," he said. "Somehow we were able to beat them. In my first year, when Eddie Lee Ivery and Gerry Ellis both gained more than 100 yards, the line got game balls. And Bart [Starr] let us have a day off, so I got to stay with my brother who was living in Minnesota at the time.

"Even though Alan Page was in Chicago by then and I didn't get to play against their great defensive line, it was an intense rivalry," Swanke said. "Forrest Gregg had played against them and told us how he hated to be head-slapped by Carl Eller and those guys. We knew the history, so we were cognizant of the fact that it was an important game to win, home or away."

And Swanke and his fellow trench dwellers had a secret weapon for many of their contests against the Vikings.

"My wife, Maggie, and I decided to have a party for the offensive linemen the week before one of the Viking games," he said. "We fed them lasagna or pasta and just enjoyed each other's company. It became a tradition, and I believe we had an undefeated record in those games."

Ex-Viking Carl Lee (1983–93) didn't know anything about that stuff, but he said when it was Minnesota and Green Bay it was always heated.

The defensive back played some safety but spent the bulk of his 11-year career at cornerback, where he earned All-NFC honors in 1988 and 1990 and made three straight trips to the Pro Bowl. He was drafted in the seventh round out of Marshall and is the head coach at West Virginia State University in Institute, West Virginia.

Lee led the Vikings with eight interceptions in 1988, including thefts in four straight games. He is sixth in team annals with 29 picks, including two he returned for touchdowns.

He said Green Bay's success was simply because it had good players.

"They had guys like James Lofton, Phillip Epps, some bona fide players, so you did your best to hold your own," Lee said. "When they drafted Sterling Sharpe, that's when the rivalry certainly intensified, at least for me. We became friends from playing against each other and going to the Pro Bowl, so chasing guys like him around was a big challenge.

"It meant that I always looked for those games when the schedule came out, so it was fierce competition," Lee said. "It was one of those deals where we needed to beat Green Bay or I'd hear about it all off-season."

He didn't get to team up with Sharpe, but Lynn Dickey (1976–77, '79–85) led some of the most prolific offensive arsenals in Green Bay history. The Kansas State alumnus passed for more than 21,000 yards for the Packers, including a team record 4,458 in leading the most potent Packer unit ever in 1983 (6,172 total yards).

And Dickey, who spent five seasons with the Houston Oilers before coming to the Packers in a trade, enjoyed some of his best days against Minnesota.

Highlights included 383 yards in a 20-17 setback at Green Bay on October 23, 1983; four touchdown passes in a 45-17 triumph in Milwaukee on November 11, 1984; and his 95-yard TD collaboration with Steve Odom during a 19-7 defeat at Bloomington on October 2, 1977.

"After Fran [Tarkenton] left, we had a lot of success against them," Dickey said. "I don't know why, but we matched up pretty well against them. We beat them three years in a row up at the Metrodome. I looked forward to it because of the style of defense they played. It was pretty vanilla, a standard 4-3 without much blitzing. They lined up and said, 'Here we are, come and beat us.'"

And the Packers obliged, winning 10 of 12 from the second game in 1979 through 1985. However, one player on Minnesota's defense always worried Dickey.

"The guy who stood out to me was Joey Browner," Dickey said of the ball hawking, hitting machine who played safety. "He could play cornerback, strong safety, and free safety. He was a remarkable athlete, big, strong. Thank God they only had one of him back there."

Dickey, a Kansas City area resident, is in the auto service contract business and makes regular visits to Wisconsin. He usually plays in the Lombardi golf tourney in Milwaukee and attends the alumni weekend in Green Bay every year. He also has participated in the fantasy camps three or four times.

He said two memories against the Vikings come to mind.

"All of my life, high school, college, and with Houston, even-numbered plays were to the right and odd-numbered to the left. But the Packers switched that around under [Vince] Lombardi, and Bart [Starr] kept it that way. So I always had trouble getting that straight. Well, one game up at the old Met [November 23, 1980], Gerry Ellis and Eddie Lee Ivery gained over 100 yards. I can count on one hand the number of times we'd had guys do that in my career. But anyway, I call an audible at the line thinking the play would go in the six hole (to his right). Gerry goes the other way, so I turn and see he's not there and I just pitch it to him and he gains about 20 yards on a third-and-8 play.

"Another game, John Jefferson takes a wicked shot going across the middle and gets separated from his helmet," Dickey said. "I thought they killed him. He sits out one play and comes running back to the huddle and tells me to throw the fly. So I throw it up in the end zone and J.J. makes a circus catch and keeps both feet in bounds for the touchdown."

When Dickey and the Packers needed a big play, they often sought out No. 80, wide receiver James Lofton.

The Stanford graduate was Green Bay's first of two first-round picks in the 1978 draft and became one of the franchise's most electrifying offensive performers. In nine seasons (1978–86), Lofton amassed 9,656 yards receiving, still tops in team record books, and his 530 catches are second only to Sharpe.

Lofton scored 50 touchdowns, reached the 1,000-yard plateau five times, and led the Packers in receptions eight times before finishing his career with the Los Angeles Raiders and Buffalo Bills.

"As a kid I remember riding in the car with my dad and hearing them talking about the Purple People Eaters, and then to play against them was a tremendous experience," said Lofton, who was tabbed for All-Pro recognition from 1980–85 and was named to seven Pro Bowl teams while becoming one of only five Packers to surpass 200 yards receiving in a game (11 catches for 206 yards against Denver in 1984).

"I was one of the lucky guys who got to play in old Met Stadium," Lofton said, "and against such great players: Ahmad Rashad, Alan Page, Chuck Foreman, Carl Eller, Fran Tarkenton, Bobby Bryant, and Paul Krause. And they had some fantastic linebackers."

Lofton, a Dallas-area resident, worked in broadcasting for Fox Sports Network and CBS Radio, covering college and pro football, until joining the San Diego Chargers as receivers coach in February, 2002.

He said the players and memories never seem to stop.

"The Minnesota series was always tremendous and right up there with the Packers-Bears rivalry," Lofton said. "They had guys like Nate Wright and Joey Browner, who was always a great hitter. Scott Studwell, Joe Senser, Greg Coleman, Sammy White. The names go on and on. I was working the Vikings' game on the Thursday night they held their reunion ceremonies, and it was fun to see a bunch of the guys I competed against. Not only do you form bonds with your own players, but also the ones from other teams."

Gerry Ellis (1980–86) downplayed his contributions, attributing it to working hard and aggressively, especially against their foes in the Central Division.

The Los Angeles Rams drafted this fullback from Missouri in the seventh round but cut him, and Green Bay picked him up. They were glad they did, as he rushed for more than 3,800 yards and became one of the league's best pass-catching weapons out of the backfield. Ellis hauled in 267 balls, including a personal best 65 in 1981 and 52 in 1983.

Ellis also remembers the day the Packers carved up the Vikings on the ground at Metropolitan Stadium during his rookie season.

"That was a special day for us," said Ellis, who's lived in Green Bay since his playing days ended and works in the printing business. "It was just one of those deals. They had a pretty good defense, but we had guys like Lofton and Coffman."

Ellis said the Packers' high-flying offense usually performed pretty well, but there was one guy he watched out for on Minnesota's defense.

"They were hard-hitting games like against Chicago, but there was one person, Joey Browner, the clothesline specialist, you didn't want to get caught by him. He was one of the head hunters like Ronnie Lott [of San Francisco]. But we did pretty well against them."

Browner played with Lee in the Minnesota secondary for nine seasons before finishing his career with Tampa Bay in 1992. The University of Southern California standout made six Pro Bowls and earned All-Pro honors four straight seasons (1987–90) as a strong safety.

He was one of the biggest hitters in the league while playing many roles in the Vikings' defensive scheme. He intercepted 37 passes, the fourth-highest total in Minnesota history.

The Warren, Ohio, native said squaring off against the Packers was a huge deal.

"They had great players like Sterling Sharpe, Lynn Dickey, James Lofton, and Darrell Thompson," Browner said from his home in Little Falls, Minnesota. "It was like playing against your brothers and sisters. If you didn't know what they were doing, then shame on you. The games were so close because we matched up so well.

"You just knew they were tough and we'd have to play tooth and nail," added Browner, who does consulting work, dabbles in sports memorabilia, and makes charity appearances. "They countered everything we threw at them, and whether we played here or there didn't make much of a difference. It seemed like every year somebody different stepped up to make the key plays, some unsung hero, and that's why the games were so big."

Browner said the only difference between the organizations is that the Packers have taken it to the next level to win championships, while the Vikings have come up short. Regardless, he said guys who didn't get up for those contests probably never would understand what tradition and the sport are all about.

"You have to play for the love of the game, the guys who came before you and for the fans," Browner said. "It you can't feel the tradition, if you don't understand the rivalry, you're losing the concept of what you're out there for. The most important is for the fans, and that often tends to be lost."

Nobody gave more to the sport, his teammates, and the fans than Blaise Winter, somebody who would have made All-Pro every year had it been because of effort alone. That's not to say the Syracuse graduate didn't have talent, because he lasted 11 years in the NFL with Indianapolis, Green Bay, and San Diego.

The defensive lineman suited up for the Packers from 1988 to 1990 and has lived in the Appleton area the past five years, his home base for a motivational/personal growth speaking career.

Winter said there were several intangibles at work when Green Bay hooked up with the Bears or Vikings, and to this day it's hard for him to explain why.

"When I was in Green Bay, the Bears had been on top and the Packers and Vikings were fighting to get back there," Winter said. "Minnesota and Green Bay had proud histories and organizations, and the rivalry was heating up to become something special. There seems to have always been a lot of friction between the two clubs whether they were on top or not.

"They were struggling for an identity, but they both had that success in their pasts. They still had a lot of pride on the field, so when you came in you heard about the Fran Tarkentons, Carl Ellers, Alan Pages, and Chuck Foremans, and were acclimated right away. You knew about Bart Starr, Ray Nitschke, and Fuzzy Thurston, so this series was highly fierce and competitive.

"You knew the teams had pride and tradition and that to be wearing those uniforms it meant you were respected in the league," Winter added. "I always respected them and played hard because it was easy to get up for those games."

Winter, who played on the Chargers' 1994 Super Bowl team, said meeting the Vikings meant digging a little deeper.

"You put aside the fact that Minnesota had lost four Super Bowls because what mattered was that they had been there," he said. "You saw that uniform and the symbol on the helmet and you knew they had laid it on the line over and over. And the Packers were the same way, so it was not just about the wins and losses, it was something more. It was fun to be a part of that, a major high for me.

"As a football player you get fired up for every game, and there are lots of ways to get fired up," Winter said. "You see that to start every game. But in my mind, it was about the heart. I don't know if this makes any sense, but when it came to the Bears or Vikings, it wasn't about the score. It wasn't about the first, second, or third quarters, it was about the fourth quarter."

Ezra Johnson concurred. He finished his Green Bay career (1977–87) with 41 1/2 quarterback sacks, including a whopping 20 1/2 in 1978, which earned him a trip to the Pro Bowl. The second of two first-round picks behind fellow defensive end Mike Butler, a selection picked up in the Ted Hendricks trade with Oakland, Johnson was enshrined in the Green Bay Hall of Fame in 1997.

Since 1992, Johnson has lived in the Atlanta area, where he also attended college at Morris Brown. Now he tackles his four children instead of enemy ball carriers.

"I mostly faced Steve Riley, and he was a good player," Johnson said of the veteran Minnesota lineman. "I really had to work to get to the quarterback against him. I know I never had four or five sacks against them, but anytime we won it was a good game."

Johnson played two seasons each with the Indianapolis Colts and the Houston Oilers after leaving the Packers, but he remembers that the confrontations with the Vikings were among the hardest fought.

"It was a challenge because they had guys like Chuck Foreman and Sammy White," he said. "It was very intense, pretty much like it was with the Bears. I remember it was always awfully cold late in the year.

"And Fran Tarkenton was there," Johnson added. "Man, that was a nightmare. As much as he ran around, chasing him for one or two plays was like playing a full quarter."

Robert Brown didn't have the talent or win the accolades that Johnson and most of his defensive line counterparts did, but the Virginia Tech player was a good run stuffer and turned in many workmanlike performances during 11 seasons in Green Bay (1982–92).

And he said there were no bigger games than the ones against Minnesota.

"It was a huge rivalry," Brown said. "When we looked at the schedule every year, the Vikings were right at the top. They had very talented players, so it was just as big as the old Packer-Bear games, at least to me.

"The Bears pretty much dominated during most of my career, but the Vikings were right behind, and we beat Minnesota most of the time. Even when we finished 4-12 in 1988, we beat them both times. But they were tough games."

The North Carolina native has lived in Virginia for the past 20 years, including the last six in which he has owned and operated Pro Speed Inc., a speed and conditioning program that helps athletes perform better, from kids through professionals.

Brown said facing Minnesota was a tough task, and he proceeded to ramble off the reasons why: running backs Alfred Anderson, Ted Brown, and Darrin Nelson; quarterbacks Tommy Kramer, Wade Wilson, Rich Gannon, and Sean Salisbury; and receivers Anthony Carter and Steve Jordan.

"When we went to Minnesota, sometimes it was almost like a home game, especially when we got on top," said Brown, who battled offensive linemen Riley, Tim Irwin, Gary Zimmerman, and Randall McDaniel in his day. "But it was a nightmare to get behind, with their fans and that big Viking horn. One time it went off during a play, a long pass to Anthony Carter. It sounded before he even caught the ball."

Brown said two games stick out in his memory, the first being the 1989 contest at Milwaukee in which cornerback Dave Brown's two interceptions helped save the Packers' 20-19 victory. The second was the 1991 season finale at the Metrodome in which the visitors gave Lindy Infante a 27-7 triumph in what proved to be his final game as Green Bay's coach.

"I got kicked out of that game," Brown said of the 1991 season-ender. "It was late in the game, I think the last two minutes, and Gary Zimmerman clipped me from behind. I got up swinging at him and they booted me out. I got fined $500."

Money spent on a worthy cause, something Matt Blair probably would have had no problems with.

He said that getting ready for the Packers was exciting, even when he wasn't playing, such as the 1983 showdown at Lambeau.

"I had injured my shoulder against the Bears and Revie Sorey," said Blair, one of the Vikings' captains. "I studied the game plan and prepared like I was going to play, but I couldn't go. It was right before halftime and the Packers were on the move inside our 20-yard line. There was a time-out and I'm standing there in my street clothes. Bud and the defensive coaches asked me what I thought. I told them to watch for a reverse or trick play, and by George, they ran a reverse. We stopped them and held on to win the game. That was something big because even though I didn't participate, I had been mentally into the game."

Irwin patrolled the right offensive tackle spot for all but his rookie season of 1981, giving Minnesota a solid anchor after the Ron Yary era for another dozen years.

The former Tennessee Volunteer said Green Bay had many tough customers on its defensive teams, rambling off such names as Reggie White, Ezra Johnson, Bryce Paup, Mike Butler, John Dorsey, and Mark Murphy.

"Both teams won games that they shouldn't have," said Irwin, a lawyer in Knoxville, Tenn. "It was always a very tough rivalry. I remember they had a guy [tight end Gary Lewis] who always jumped over the top of the pile on extra points and field goals to try and block them. One time I stepped inside and put him down really hard and the official threw a flag at me. After it was all over, I still didn't know what I did wrong."

That wasn't a problem for fellow Viking offensive lineman Dennis Swilley, a Texas A&M standout who played two years at guard and eight at center for Minnesota after being the team's number-two pick in the 1977 draft.

Swilley, who designs homes between San Antonio and Austin, said it only took him one play to have his attitude adjusted in the NFL.

"It was my first couple years and I only knew about 10 percent of what was going on, and the rest of the time I was flying around and flapping my mouth off," Swilley said. "Well, Green Bay had a linebacker, Mike Douglass. I guess I got on his nerves, so he jacked me twice with his forearm. I was so surprised, I just stood there. I tried to look him up; I wanted to know where that blankety-blank was after the game. But he taught me a valuable lesson in that you just need to shut up and play the game."

That Swilley did, suiting up during 1977–83 and 1985–87. He said it was fun playing against the Packers because he had several ties to players there.

"I grew up in Arkansas, so I got to know Greg Koch and Leotis Harris, who I played against in high school," Swilley said. "I enjoyed playing against the Bears because they drafted a lot of guys from the Southwest Conference. Detroit, they always talked a lot of crap. But Green Bay, you always got caught up in the hype.

"I remember their defensive lineman, Dave Roller," said Swilley. "We called him Rollerball. He talked a lot of trash and it was always a headache to block him. But he was a good 'ol guy and played for us for a couple of years. He became the team clown."

Swilley said the overnight accommodations in Green Bay brought back a comical memory.

"I think we only stayed there one year, but there was a place right downtown, the old Green Bay Hotel or whatever it was called," Swilley said. "That was a real Taj Majal. I'm not knocking Green Bay, but it was just a really old place. I told my roommate at the time, Charles Goodrum, that this was like something out of 'Petticoat Junction.'"

Good-natured fun has dominated this rivalry, and Swilley said it was great to have been a part of it.

"I always enjoyed playing against them," he said. "I remember, I think it was my rookie year, it was snowing so hard you couldn't see guys on the other sideline. It was like a white blanket. But seeing those [green and gold] jerseys for the first time and saying, 'That's really the Packers.'"

Here are more highlights from those tangos in the teams' third decade of facing each other.

1980

OCT. 26 AT GREEN BAY: The Packers earned a 16-3 victory as Tom Birney's 36-yard field goal broke a scoreless tie in the third quarter.

His effort was matched when Rich Danmeier booted a 47-yarder in the fourth. However, Lynn Dickey combined with his tight ends, backup Bill Larson and starter Paul Coffman, for fourth-quarter touchdown passes. And running backs Eddie Lee Ivery and Gerry Ellis combined for 139 yards rushing as the Packers improved to 3-4-1 while dropping the Vikings to 3-5.

NOV. 23 AT MINNESOTA: Green Bay enjoyed its first sweep since 1965 with a 25-13 win at Metropolitan Stadium.

The visitors grabbed a 16-6 lead in the third quarter behind Gerry Ellis' TD plunge and Lynn Dickey's 35-yard scoring pass to wide receiver Aundra Thompson. But Ted Brown scooted in from 5 yards out to bring the Vikings to within 16-13 after three quarters.

Tom Birney, who missed one extra point and had a second blocked, added a 33-yard field goal, and Eddie Lee Ivery put the game away with a 38-yard touchdown jaunt. Ivery finished with 145 yards on 24 carries, and backfield mate Ellis chipped in 101 yards on only 15 attempts as the Packers used a 246-89 advantage on the ground to control the clock and the game.

1981

SEPT. 27 AT MILWAUKEE: Minnesota whipped the Packers, 30-13.

The Packers sprinted to a 10-0 first-quarter lead before everything fell apart. Minnesota scored the next 27 points, including a 20-0 run in the second quarter that was highlighted by a 45-yard Randy Holloway fumble return for a score.

Linebacker Robin Sendlein blocked a punt to set up the go-ahead field goal.

Minnesota edged the Packers through the air, 253-245, but it dominated on the ground. Ted Brown rushed for 109 yards on 21 carries as the Vikings won that battle, 157-71.

Safety Mark Murphy recovered two of Minnesota's three fumbles, but the Packers coughed it up twice themselves, including Holloway's scamper. Green Bay also wasted the receiving performances of James Lofton (eight catches for 101 yards) and John Jefferson (seven for 121).

NOV. 29 AT MINNESOTA: Green Bay bounced back with a 35-23 victory in the teams' final meeting at Metropolitan Stadium.

Tommy Kramer equaled his team record of 38 pass completions (in 55 attempts), while Minnesota rushed a team record low 11 times. Kramer tossed two first-quarter TD passes, including a 50-yarder to Ahmad Rashad, for a 14-0 lead.

However, the visitors blew the game open as Harlan Huckleby finished with only 25 yards on 14 carries but scored three times for the Packers. John Jefferson and James Lofton added TD catches from Lynn Dickey, and Gerry Ellis rushed for 77 yards on 19 carries as Green Bay won the ground war 115-28.

The Packers lost two fumbles and two interceptions, but Kramer suffered five interceptions to five Green Bay defenders as the Vikings struggled through their second of five consecutive defeats to end the season.

One bright spot for the Vikings was Joe Senser, who grabbed 11 pass receptions, a Minnesota record for tight ends. However, his right knee was severely damaged when he was tackled near the goal line, an injury that affected him for the rest of his career.

1982

NOV. 21 AT MILWAUKEE: Green Bay manhandled the Vikings, 26-7, in the rivals' lone meeting because of the 57-day players strike.

There were more than 11,000 no-shows as the announced attendance of 44,681 was the first time the Packers hadn't sold out a home game since 1960.

Minnesota took a 7-6 lead in the second quarter, but halfback Eddie Lee Ivery corralled a 5-yard pass from Lynn Dickey to give Green Bay the upper hand for good. Ivery chipped in a 62-yard catch, and Paul Coffman hauled in a 28-yard screen pass to help Dickey finish 15 of 22 with no interceptions before leaving in the third quarter with an injured back.

Substitute David Whitehurst engineered a nine-play, 66-yard march for the final score to sew up the victory. John Jefferson finished with five catches for 80 yards.

Special teams played a vital role in the outcome.

Maurice Harvey scored on a 25-yard return after Minnesota's Sam Harrell fumbled the second-half kickoff. And the Vikings had Jarvis Redwine's 92-yard kickoff return called back because of a penalty.

Meanwhile, the Packers limited their foes to 25 yards rushing on 17 tries. Linebacker John Anderson held Vikings tight end Joe Senser to one catch for 11 yards as Minnesota gained 159 passing.

Tommy Kramer, who left with an arm injury on the first series of the second half, and Steve Dils found Ahmad Rashad and Sammy White for a combined eight catches and 107 yards, but none of them occurred at crucial times, forcing Greg Coleman to punt a team record 12 times. And Dils threw four straight incompletions from the Green Bay 9 early in the fourth quarter.

Phillip Epps set a team standard with eight punt returns (for 49 yards) as Green Bay cruised to 223 passing yards and 136 via the ground in improving to 3-0 for the first time since 1966.

Green Bay finished with 135 yards rushing and drove 76 yards for both touchdowns, and kicker Jan Stenerud's two field goals and two PATs moved him into fourth place on the all-time NFL scoring list with 1,366 points, one ahead of former Viking standout Fred Cox.

Minnesota nailed Dickey six times and Whitehurst twice, with Doug Martin registering three sacks and Mark Mullaney 2 1/2.

That didn't prevent Bart Starr's squad from claiming its fifth win in its last six outings against Minnesota after going 0-8-1 to begin his tenure vs. the Vikings.

1983

OCT. 23 AT GREEN BAY: Minnesota pulled out a 20-17 win in overtime.

Lynn Dickey passed for 383 yards on 23 completions, but the Vikings' Ted Brown churned for 179 yards rushing.

The Vikings improved to 6-2, but mounting injuries helped derail the promising start as they finished 8-8.

Talented rookie safety Joey Browner's third-down sack in overtime forced the Packers to punt and led to Minnesota's game-winning drive as kicker Benny Ricardo hoisted a 32-yard field goal through the uprights.

Browner and Ricardo may not have gotten the chance to make their key plays had it not been for linebacker Dennis Johnson, who blocked a field-goal attempt earlier in the game.

And the Vikings received a stellar contest from Doug Martin, who recorded four sacks for 32 yards in losses, finishing with eight tackles and three assists. Minnesota cornerback John Swain also chipped in two interceptions.

"I can't afford to make those turnovers," Dickey told the Green Bay *Press-Gazette* of his three pickoffs that came against a unit that often deployed four linemen and five or six players in the secondary. "Whatever the pressure or the problem is, I can't do that and expect us to win. We're not that strong a football team."

Especially defensively, as Minnesota's 23rd-ranked rushing attack dominated the Packers. Ted Brown carried 29 times after entering the contest with only 239 yards. And Steve Dils improved to 4-1 as a starter in relief of the injured Tommy Kramer, completing 16 of 27 aerials for 205 yards and no INTs. Both teams blew scoring chances as Eddie Lee Ivery fumbled at the Minnesota 2 in the first half and Minnesota's Sammy White dropped a TD pass.

Brown's 43-yard run to the Green Bay 17 set up a 7-0 Viking lead after a 60-yard drive. Ricardo tacked on a 44-yard field goal for a 10-0 cushion. Jan Stenerud responded with a 48-yarder to shave the Packers' deficit to 10-3, but the visitors went 73 yards in 13 plays for what appeared to be an insurmountable two-touchdown margin with 4:42 left in the third quarter.

Green Bay then came to life, going 70 yards in nine plays, including the final 5 on a pass to John Jefferson, who finished with four catches for 64 yards. The Packers then knotted things up with 2 seconds left in regulation as fullback Mike Meade scurried in from 5 yards out on a pass play. Gerry Ellis' 28-yard reception keyed Green Bay's 80-yard march that started with 1:48 remaining. Phillip Epps brought home a 25-yard catch on a third-and-9 call.

Green Bay's Bucky Scribner averaged 31.2 yards for his four punts into 13 mph winds, including a 34-yarder that set the Vikings up at their 42 to start their only possession of the overtime.

NOV. 13 AT MINNESOTA: Green Bay claimed a 29-21 victory in the teams' first meeting at the Metrodome; the 1982 contest in the Twin Cities was cancelled due to the strike.

Darrin Nelson was the last opponent to gain 100 yards both rushing (119) and receiving (137) against the Packers, finishing with a Minnesota record 278 all-purpose yards, including 22 on returns. It was Nelson's first 100-yard rushing game. His pass receiving total was the highest for the Vikings that season.

But Green Bay's 19-0 halftime cushion proved too much for Minnesota to overcome.

Jan Stenerud started things with a 46-yard field goal and Mike Meade's short TD run made it 10-0. Then John Anderson forced a fumble, with Ezra Johnson recovering, leading to Lynn Dickey's 5-yard toss to John Jefferson for a 17-0 margin. Defensive end Greg Boyd then registered a safety on one of Green Bay's four first-half sacks.

That 19-point cushion could have been worse had tight end Gary Lewis not dropped a TD pass on a fourth-and-1 play from the Minnesota 3. However, the 28th-ranked Packers' defense forced seven fumbles, including six in the first 30 minutes, as the visitors had control.

The second half was a different story. Minnesota sandwiched three consecutive scoring drives around Stenerud's 40-yard field goal to trail only 22-21.

Nelson's 68-yard catch and run, one of seven receptions in the game, set up Minnesota's first score, and Rickey Young went in from 2 yards out to cap a 10-play, 70-yard drive that cut the margin to 22-14. Then Tony Galbreath's 4-yard scamper with 11:18 left made it a one-point shoot-out.

Minnesota had the ball again and was in position to complete the astounding comeback when it was whistled for having 12 men in the huddle, which ended the Vikings attempt for a fourth straight TD drive.

Then a regrouped Green Bay offensive unit regained control, taking over at its 31 with 8:28 remaining. Krazy George was beating his drum in the stands, and the Vikings mascot was stirring up the crowd from on the field. However, the Packers demoralized the Viking players and silenced the Minnesota multitudes with two short passes and 10 consecutive running plays before Dickey's 19-yard strike to James Lofton made it 29-21.

The definitive march consumed 6:16 and helped Dickey equal Cecil Isbell's then-record 24th touchdown pass. He finished the season with 32 as the Packers improved to 6-5 and moved into a first-place tie in the division.

"There were no gimmicks on any of those plays, just straight power football," Dickey said in the *Press-Gazette.*

Despite missing Ted Brown, who had a career day in the first meeting of 1983, because of a separated shoulder, Minnesota outgained Green Bay 417-343, including 303-180 in net yards passing. But the Vikings allowed six sacks while not registering any themselves.

Jessie Clark rumbled 42 yards on his first carry and led the Packers with 10 attempts for 79 yards.

"A loss is always bitter to swallow," said Young in the *Press-Gazette.* "A loss against Green Bay is even more bitter."

1984

NOV. 11 AT MILWAUKEE: Green Bay made it two in a row with a 45-17 rout.

The Packers blitzed the Vikings by scoring the final 28 points after the visitors had tied the game at 17 early in the third quarter. Consecutive TD passes from Lynn Dickey to fullback Jessie Clark ignited the surge. Dickey finished with four scoring tosses, including a 63-yarder to James Lofton.

Green Bay earned a 26-14 advantage in first downs, a 208-110 margin rushing, and a 305-162 passing outburst in finishing with 513 yards while running 25 more offensive plays.

Gerry Ellis rushed for 107 yards on only 10 carries, while Clark chipped in six catches for 43 yards and Lofton led the way with four receptions for 119.

DEC. 16 AT MINNESOTA: Green Bay rolled up a 31-0 halftime lead en route to a 38-14 decision in the season finale.

Both teams lost three interceptions and one fumble, but Green Bay cruised on the ground with a 214-70 advantage in earning a 26-16 margin in first downs. Lynn Dickey completed 16 of 20 passes for 198 yards and no INTs; backup Rich Campbell was picked off three times. Still, James Lofton caught five passes for 91 yards.

Green Bay cornerback Mark Lee intercepted a pass and recovered a fumble, while rookie safety Tom Flynn grabbed his NFC-leading ninth theft.

Minnesota's Willie Teal returned an interception 53 yards for one of its two scores. Minnesota tight end Mike Mularkey pulled in seven of his 14 catches for the season in what was his first career start.

It was Green Bay's seventh win in the final eight games of the season, which gave the team and first-year coach Forrest Gregg an 8-8 mark.

Meanwhile, the Vikings' tumultuous and lone season under Les Steckel came to a fitting end with a 3-13 record and fifth-place finish in the division. A bright spot was linebacker Walker Lee Ashley's six solo tackles and forced fumble.

1985

OCT. 13 AT MILWAUKEE: Green Bay pulled out a 20-17 triumph.

Al Del Greco's field goal won it from 22 yards out with seven seconds remaining after former Packer Jan Stenerud had tied it with 1:17 left. The Vikings had settled for the deadlock instead of going for it on a fourth-and-goal situation at the Green Bay 1.

Stenerud, who had played for the Packers during 1980–83 before being shipped to Minnesota for a seventh-round draft pick, hit the uprights with his two previous attempts in the game; by his count, the former Kansas City Chiefs star had done that only one other time in his 19-year career.

Mike Jones, who led the Vikings in receptions in both games against Green Bay during the season, hauled in six passes and a score.

In a seesaw affair, Minnesota answered every time the Packers gained the upper hand.

Jessie Clark started the scoring with a 5-yard run for Green Bay after Mark Murphy's interception gave the Packers possession at the Minnesota 32. But Jones latched onto a 14-yard pass to even things at 7. Scott Studwell stopped a Packers' threat with an end-zone theft, but cornerback Tim Lewis raced in with a fumble recovery for a 14-7 Green Bay lead. Another Vikings' wide receiver, Leo Lewis, caught a 43-yard pass to knot the score at 14.

John Anderson's interception set up Del Greco's first field goal from 45 yards away, but Jones' 23-yard catch was a key play in the third game-tying drive capped by Stenerud's 18-yarder.

Green Bay blew another shot at points when Paul Coffman fumbled at the Minnesota 12; Joey Browner recovered the loose ball.

Viking Coach Bud Grant explained his reasoning for going for three points instead of six in a *Press-Gazette* story.

"We already had three plays down there and we didn't feel we had the play set up that would work there."

His quarterback, Tommy Kramer, didn't question his leader's strategy, but he couldn't help but wonder what if in his comments to the Green Bay paper.

"We probably should have [gone for the TD]," he said. "Maybe we would have won."

The Packers were glad they had time to do something at the end.

Green Bay took over at its 29 with one timeout left and 1:19 showing. Lynn Dickey started with six straight passes to his running backs, most of them in the flat so his receivers could get out of bounds to stop the clock. Then on a third-and-6 play, the less-than-nimble Dickey avoided pressure and found James Lofton open for 26 yards to set up the game-winning kick.

"I don't know if it was scrambling, or floundering," said Dickey in the *Press-Gazette*.

He finished 15 of 31 for 166 yards and two interceptions and drew these comments from Grant in the article.

"The best play in football is the broken play," Grant said. "Dickey had aborted the play, he was out of the pocket and the rhythm of the play was gone. The defense's timing is [off]."

The hosts had rushed for 285 yards in crushing Detroit the week before and tallied a 135-62 advantage this time as both teams had 18 first downs, 66 plays, and three turnovers. Eddie Lee Ivery led Green Bay with 12 rushes for 83 yards, while Kramer fashioned a 20-for-37 effort for 237 passing yards. He had two TD passes but also two interceptions.

NOV. 10 AT MINNESOTA: Green Bay won, 27-17, scoring the final 21 points in the fourth quarter to erase a 17-6 deficit.

The Packers claimed their second straight season sweep, fifth consecutive win in the series, and improved to 3-0 at the Metrodome in offsetting a 146-yard rushing effort by the Vikings' Darrin Nelson, a career high.

Eddie Lee Ivery and Gerry Ellis scored TDs, and Mark Murphy returned a Tommy Kramer interception for another score. Minnesota linebacker Dennis Fowlkes tied a single-game team mark with three forced fumbles in what proved to be Bud Grant's final contest as a coach in the series.

Nelson's 35-yard draw play to the Packers 22 ignited a nine-play, 66-yard drive to give Minnesota a 7-0 lead. Al Del Greco responded with a 46-yard field goal, his longest with Green Bay to that point, and tacked on three more points after Charles Martin recovered a fumble when Kramer lost the pigskin after one of his blockers knocked the ball out of his hands.

Minnesota then drove 57 yards in 11 plays for a 14-6 advantage to start the second half, highlighted by Steve Jordan's 16-yard catch and Leo Lewis' 7-yard gain on a third-and-6 call from the Green Bay 11. Nelson then ripped off a 37-yard run to set up a field goal and a 17-6 cushion.

That's when the momentum shifted. The Vikings settled for three points on that drive after enjoying a first-and-goal at the Green Bay 5.

Lynn Dickey connected with Phillip Epps for 18 yards and James Lofton for 24 more during an 11-play, 76-yard trek to make it 17-13. Then Packers' cornerback Mark Lee deflected a long pass to Anthony Carter that could have pushed Minnesota's margin to 11 points again, forcing a punt.

Epps beat Carl Lee for a 63-yard gain to the Vikings 5, and Dickey tossed a 1-yard pass to Ivery for what proved to be the game-winner with 5:29 left.

However, the outcome wasn't decided until Murphy pilfered Kramer's pass and scampered 50 yards for his only NFL touchdown. Tim Lewis then grabbed an interception in the end zone to turn out the lights. It was his first of the year after combining for nine the previous two campaigns.

Murphy's steal came despite bruised ribs and a kidney injury he sustained two weeks earlier against Indianapolis.

Kramer reacted to the boo birds he heard after Murphy's crucial play on a pass in which middle linebacker Brian Noble blitzed right in Kramer's face. "You don't call it a [bleep] bad game because you throw the ball in the [bleep] flat and somebody intercepts it like that," Kramer was quoted as saying in the *Press-Gazette*.

Ivery earned his fourth career 100-yard game with 111 yards on 15 carries, including a long of 34, but the Vikings barely won the ground battle 177-175.

Dickey finished 9 of 11 for 135 yards after left-hander Jim Zorn had gone 5 for 13 for 75 yards in his second straight start. Zorn's three-series effort accounted for 6 points after a 23-yard TD toss to Lofton was called back by penalty and Paul Coffman's off-sides penalty at the Minnesota 2 dictated that the Packers kick a field goal just before halftime.

Epps recorded the first 100-yard receiving day of his career on six receptions, while Coffman became the sixth Packer to reach 300 catches. His two receptions gave him 301.

1986

SEPT. 28 AT MINNESOTA: The hosts waltzed to a 42-7 win, the Vikings' largest victory margin in the series and most points they've ever scored in a half (35, in the first).

The Vikings outgained Green Bay 191-1 in grabbing a 28-0 lead after the first quarter. Tommy Kramer tossed six TD passes in the game, second highest behind Joe Kapp's seven, a mark the latter had set in 1969.

Kramer hit Steve Jordan for two of his four first-quarter scoring passes. Hassan Jones also grabbed two of Kramer's end zone connections as Minnesota won the aerial battle 297-138 and finished with a 25-15 edge in first downs.

Jordan (112 yards) and Jones (106) reached the century mark, while Green Bay struggled with only 12 completions in 28 attempts and lost two fumbles. Jordan finished with six catches and his first 100-yard game.

In Forrest Gregg's third year as coach, he equaled Bart Starr's 1975 record as the only Packer teams to start a season 0-4. But Gregg's 1986 version then set the franchise record for futility by also losing its next two contests.

Starting quarterback Randy Wright misfired on his first five pass attempts and exited the game because of illness, leaving the reins to Vince Ferragamo, who finished 12 of 23 for 163 yards and one interception. That total could have been much worse, as Browner dropped one and had two thefts called back on penalties, including an 85-yard touchdown return.

Green Bay's horrendous start to the campaign marked the first time since 1924 that the Packers had scored only two TDs through their first four games.

"I thought the opening game of the season (a 31-3 loss to Houston) was the worst game I'd ever seen a team play," Gregg said in the *Press-Gazette*. "But this one right here will have to live in my mind forever as the worst."

Green Bay's bad play and bad luck started early, as Minnesota's first-quarter explosion overshadowed the fact that the Packers lost one of their best defensive players, linebacker John Anderson, to a broken fibula.

The major talk heading into this showdown was about former Green Bay assistant coach Bob Schnelker, who had taken over as Minnesota's offensive coordinator after holding the same position the previous four seasons under Starr and Gregg.

"I don't want any revenge motives, any talk of animosity," Schnelker told a *Press-Gazette* reporter. "We won another game, and that's it."

However, some of his players weren't afraid to discuss the pot of emotions bubbling under the surface.

"He definitely wanted to get after them," Kramer added in the article. He joined Fran Tarkenton as the only Viking QBs to reach 20,000 career yards passing.

DEC. 7 AT GREEN BAY: Rookie head coach Jerry Burns watched Minnesota whip the Packers, 32-6, giving the Vikings a 74-13 scoring margin in the two games for 1986.

Minnesota won easily despite holding only a 13-6 lead at halftime, finishing with a 20-19 margin in first downs and outrushing the Packers 157-144. Green Bay won the passing battle 233-146 yards but lost three fumbles.

The Packers finished winless at Green Bay for only the second time since the stadium opened in 1957, the other time being the strike year of 1982 when they played only one game at Lambeau.

As they had all year, the hosts self-destructed for their fans as they ended the sorry season having been outscored 125-42 at Lambeau while finishing 1-2 at Milwaukee.

"Intimidating for who?" Forrest Gregg lamented in the *Press-Gazette* about the lack of a home-field advantage. "I think it's intimidating for the Green Bay Packers. Hell, we haven't won here all year. Maybe we'll play all our games away from home."

Green Bay's most glaring trouble came from its punting unit, and they didn't waste much time in showing their ineptitude.

Regular booter Don Bracken was injured in practice on Thursday that week, prompting the Packers to bring in Bill Renner on Friday. Renner's dubious outing started with his first two punts not reaching the line of scrimmage, allowing the Vikings to score 13 points in the first quarter without much sweat.

Cornerback Issiac Holt broke through and blocked Renner' first punt at the 13, with Rufus Bess recovering at the Green Bay 12. Darrin Nelson dashed in for a TD on the next play. On Green Bay's next series, snapper Bill Cherry rifled the ball over Renner's head from the 30. Joey Browner pounced on the ball at the Packer 7. Anthony Carter grabbed a TD pass on the next play.

Middle linebacker Brian Noble summed up Green Bay's plight in a
Press-Gazette story.

"We don't feel that the Vikings are that much better of a football team
than we are," he said. "The thing is we gave them the damn game. We
never fought back."

The Packers fought, but not near hard enough.

Green Bay moved inside the Minnesota 25 on five of their 11 possessions and on three occasions reached the Viking 10 or better, but only
had two field goals to show for it.

"What happened is they were kind of overjoyed with what they did
on Thanksgiving," Gregg said in *Press-Gazette* reports about Green Bay's
thrilling 44-40 win at Detroit 10 days earlier. "I did not have a good feeling going into this game. Every morning by 8:30 when I came to work I'd
see people up here looking at film, but this week, not a soul. I guess they
all learned enough where they didn't have to study anymore. That's sort
of how we played."

1987

OCT. 4 AT MINNESOTA: Green Bay's 23-16 victory was in a replacement strike game.

The Packers had to hang on despite grabbing 13-0 and 20-7 leads
before the intermission. The Vikings closed to within 20-16, but Max Zendejas kicked his third field goal to help clinch the win.

Green Bay didn't turn the ball over and outgained the Vikings 147-
96 rushing. Minnesota earned a 219-153 passing cushion, but 63 of the
yards came on its first scoring play.

Just under 14,000 fans showed up to watch in the Metrodome, by far
the smallest crowd to attend a game in the series.

The outcome wasn't decided until 1:10 remained and the Vikings
poised to send the game into overtime with a first-and-goal situation at
the Green Bay 8.

That's when 37-year-old Viking quarterback Tony Adams, who had not
played football since his 1982 campaign with the Toronto Argonauts, made
the big mistake. Packer safety Jim Bob Morris stepped in front of Adams'
pass at the goal line and raced 73 yards.

"Scabs or whatever, when you play on national TV, it means something," Morris told the *Press-Gazette*. "If it ends tomorrow, it'll still be fun.

I got a game ball out of it."

Green Bay ran out the clock to give Forrest Gregg his first victory of 1987, including the preseason.

"Maybe this doesn't mean much to you, but it means a hell of a lot to me," Gregg said in a *Press-Gazette* story. "As far as we're concerned, we're 1-1-1."

DEC. 13 AT MILWAUKEE: Green Bay earned another win, this time 16-10, in what proved to be Forrest Gregg's last home victory and his final triumph as the Packers' coach.

Anthony Carter scored on a 40-yard pass play from Tommy Kramer to give Minnesota a 7-0 lead in the first quarter. But Kramer left because of a pinched nerve in his neck after completing 7 of 9 passes for 111 yards, giving way to Wade Wilson, who chipped in a 7-for-12, 57-yard effort.

Green Bay finished with four more first downs and outgained the Vikings by only 13 yards, but also benefited from two fumble recoveries.

Halfback Kenneth Davis scored on a 7-yard trap play with 1:09 showing on the clock to upset the playoff-bound Vikings. Tight end Ed West caught three passes for 80 yards for the hosts.

"Maybe we're not a playoff team, maybe we've been fooling ourselves all along," Minnesota head man Jerry Burns told the *Press-Gazette*. "If we can't go out and beat a team like Green Bay, in spite of the fact they played well, then maybe we don't belong in the playoffs."

Well, the Vikings split their final two games to squeeze into the postseason, where they upset New Orleans and San Francisco before falling, 17-10, to the eventual Super Bowl champion Redskins in the NFC Championship contest.

But on this day at County Stadium, another poor Packer team worked its magic against Minnesota, improving to 6-2 vs. its rivals under Gregg's tutelage despite never finishing above .500 in his four seasons.

Randy Wright completed 18 of 31 passes for 192 yards as Green Bay earned its first home win as an underdog since the 48-47 triumph over Washington in 1983.

West's 40-yard catch highlighted Green Bay's 11-play, 73-yard drive that tied the game at 7. Windy conditions didn't help the kickers, including Minnesota's Chuck Nelson, who missed a 35-yarder.

However, his 34-yard boot tied the game at 10 with 9:15 left in the game after Max Zendejas had given the hosts their first lead with a 47-yarder in the third quarter. That score was set up after Viking halfback Darrin Nelson fumbled for the second straight series, the first times he put the ball on the ground after 129 carries.

West, seldom used as a receiving threat, came up big again on the first snap of the crucial march, hauling in a 33-yard pass down the middle to move Green Bay from its 28 to the Minnesota 39. Kenneth Davis then chipped in an 8-yard run and a 12-yard catch before scoring the game-winner, the last of five rushing plays.

Disaster could have occurred as Zendejas shanked what became a 35-yard extra point after John Dorsey was whistled for leg whipping. But Green Bay's defense stopped the Vikings on a fourth-and-1 run from the Minnesota 40 with 44 seconds left.

It was a disappointing end for the Viking regulars, who had averaged 28 points in nine games. And Minnesota's defense couldn't sustain enough of a pass rush, as evidenced by the fact that Green Bay left tackle Ken Ruettgers shut out end Chris Doleman, who had recorded a sack in seven straight games, one short of Carl Eller's team mark.

1988

OCT. 16 AT MINNESOTA: Green Bay won on the road again, 34-14.

Linebacker Tim Harris recorded a safety and scored on a blocked punt, and Max Zendejas kicked four field goals.

The Packers bolted to a 16-0 second-quarter lead before the Vikings rallied to within 24-14 early in the fourth quarter. Green Bay then closed out the scoring on a 10-0 run, capped by Harris' touchdown.

Green Bay won the rushing statistical battle 125-67 but was outgained 257-230 through the air. Tommy Kramer started and was only 3 of 12 for 37 yards before Wade Wilson relieved and finished 17 for 26 for 248 yards.

Walter Stanley caught five passes for 101 yards as Green Bay won the time of possession battle 37:50 to 22:10. The Vikings were penalized 15 times for 129 yards and lost three fumbles.

DEC. 11 AT GREEN BAY: Green Bay turned in another defensive gem during an 18-6 win, snapping a seven-game losing streak for rookie coach Lindy Infante.

The drought had equaled the franchise single-season mark, but this victory helped the Packers avoid their lowest win total since 1958 as they won the next week to finish 4-12.

Tim Harris registered his second safety of the season as Green Bay completed a sweep, limiting the visitors to 44 yards on the ground. It was Green Bay's fourth sweep of the Vikings in five years.

The Packers threw three interceptions and were outgained passing, but they rushed for 97 yards. Perry Kemp caught six passes for 108 yards for the victors, while Steve Jordan led the Vikings with seven catches for 80 yards.

The victory, the Packers' first since the 34-14 triumph at Minneapolis in mid-October, also snapped playoff-bound Minnesota's five-game winning streak in which the Vikings had outscored their foes 167-26.

Temperatures in the teens and a slippery field compelled many of the players to juggle between cleats and turf shoes, and those conditions combined with Green Bay's defense held the Vikings to their lowest point total in 40 games, since a 23-0 loss to Chicago in early October, 1986.

"They have nothing to lose against us," offensive left tackle Gary Zimmerman said in the *Press-Gazette*. "It's their season. They can do some things, experiment. This is their Super Bowl."

Infante didn't go that far, but it was certainly a big victory and a long time in coming.

"Nobody out there, the fans, the media, was giving us a snowball's chance to win this game," he said of his 10 1/2-point underdog squad. "But we knew we had a chance," he told reporters.

The Packers were without running back Brent Fullwood, but quarterbacks Randy Wright and Don Majkowski did enough to keep Green Bay's offense from self-destructing, completing 11 of 20 for 124 yards and 5 of 10 for 85 yards, respectively.

Minnesota's top-ranked defense, playing without Doug Martin, managed only one sack after averaging almost four per game coming in.

A vital juncture of the contest came with Green Bay ahead, 16-6. Majkowski, who was playing because Wright suffered a groin injury, threw an interception that Carl Lee returned for an apparent touchdown. However, All-Pro defensive tackle Keith Millard was penalized for roughing the passer.

"The official? He didn't say anything," Millard said in a *Press-Gazette* story. "I saw the flag. I thought it was for an illegal block on the interception. All of a sudden I see roughing the passer, and I'm looking around to see what the hell is going on."

It was Green Bay's first win at Lambeau—except for one victory by the replacement team against the Eagles during the 1987 players' strike—since the 21-0 whipping of Tampa Bay in the famous Snow Bowl game of

December 1, 1985.

Not including the aforementioned "non-union" triumph over Philadelphia, starting outside linebacker Tim Harris and his Packer teammates had gone 0-13 in Green Bay since he was drafted in the fourth round of 1986. So it was a welcome but strange feeling for the players and the understandably frustrated Packer fans after the Minnesota contest.

"Ever since I started playing at Lambeau, I've been booed walking off that field," said Tim Harris in the *Press-Gazette*. "Today was a great feeling for me because I wasn't booed. They were cheering for us and everything. I've never felt that before, and it was something else."

1989

OCT. 15 AT MINNESOTA: The Vikings turned the tables for a 26-14 victory in Herschel Walker's debut after his arrival in a huge trade from Dallas.

Walker gained 148 of Minnesota's 238 yards on the ground as the hosts tallied 26 unanswered points in the second and third quarters.

The Vikings claimed a triumph as part of Walker's coming-out party with the team, including a 47-yard scamper on his first carry from scrimmage in which he ran right out of one of his cleats.

The former University of Georgia Heisman Trophy winner didn't come close to fulfilling the Viking organization's goal of winning an NFL championship, however. General Manager Mike Lynn gave up three No. 1 picks and three No. 2s in the deal, but for one game, anyway, the Vikings got their money's worth.

Walker carried 18 times and rumbled 51 yards with a kickoff, which was brought back by a penalty. All of that one week after the Packers had stuffed Walker for 44 yards on 12 tries in a 31-13 thrashing of the Cowboys.

Jerry Burns and Bob Schnelker said it didn't take long for Walker's presence to be felt.

"Once I saw him run, I changed my mind," Burns said in the *Press-Gazette*. "I might not be the smartest guy, but I'm not a complete idiot. I said we better leave him out there."

Schnelker concurred in the article: "If you get a great back like Walker, it doesn't take a genius to hand him the football."

Minnesota's defense played as well or better, sacking Majkowski eight times, including four by Keith Millard. And linebacker Ray Berry registered a safety in the third quarter.

Tommy Kramer completed 14 of 24 passes for 172 yards but had one attempt intercepted in the end zone. Fullback Rick Fenney scored on an 8-yard run for a 10-7 lead and added an 8-yard TD catch in the third quarter.

Green Bay, hampered by 11 penalties, was held to 68 yards rushing, including only 14 on seven carries by Brent Fullwood. The shell-shocked Majkowski finished only 9 of 24, including nine consecutive incompletions in the first half.

Sterling Sharpe, limited to two catches for 82 yards, hauled in a 51-yarder to set up the Packers' first score and a 7-0 lead.

However, Green Bay struggled mightily after that, accumulating only two first downs in the second and third quarters combined.

NOV. 26 AT MILWAUKEE: Green Bay bounced back and took home a 20-19 win to split the season series.

Veteran cornerback Dave Brown had two interceptions to help the Packers hang on for their third of an NFL record four one-point victories during the year. Brown's efforts gave him 59 career picks, moving him past Emmitt Thomas into sixth place all-time.

Sterling Sharpe caught 10 passes for 157 yards, the first time Minnesota had allowed a 100-yard game that year. In so doing, he became only the fourth Packer to shatter 1,000 receiving yards in a season. His 10 catches were the most since James Lofton nabbed 11 against Denver in 1984. His performance included a 34-yard touchdown in the second quarter and a 9-yarder to put the hosts ahead for good at 20-16.

Don Majkowski was just as impressive despite having missed practice all week because of bruised ribs. He completed his first 14 attempts and finished 26 of 35 for 276 yards, the first time in 1989 that anyone had gained 200 net yards against the stingy Viking defense.

"The difference today is when they did put pressure on me, I was able to break the pocket and buy some time and throw some key first-down passes," said Majkowski in the *Press-Gazette*. He had been sacked four times after hitting the Metrodome carpet twice as often in October.

Neither team ran the ball well, with the Vikings gaining 76 yards on 27 tries and the Packers trudging for 84 yards on 23 attempts. But the passing attacks went to work, with 301 net for the Vikings and 248 for Green Bay. Minnesota's Wade Wilson passed for 308 yards, completing 23 of 38 tries.

Herman Fontenot chipped in eight catches for 58 yards for the hosts, while Anthony Carter led the Vikings with six receptions for 103 yards.

Minnesota scored only one touchdown in five trips inside the red zone, and that came on a 6-yard Herschel Walker scamper after Packer nemesis Joey Browner had returned an interception 34 yards to the Green Bay 9. It gave the Vikings a 16-10 lead.

After Sharpe's second TD, Tiger Greene and John Anderson stuffed Walker for virtually no gain on a third-and-goal play at the Green Bay 2, as the Vikings settled for a field goal to cut their deficit to one at 20-19. They never got another chance.

The game might have been different, but both teams dropped two interceptions, three of which could have gone for scores. However, nothing mattered to the Packers except the victory.

"It feels pretty good to be tied for first after four years of fighting to stay out of the cellar," Green Bay's Ken Ruettgers said in the *Press-Gazette*.

The Packers joined the Vikings atop the Central standings at 7-5, and both won three of their final four games to finish 10-6. However, the Vikings earned the tiebreaker edge over the Packers by virtue of their 6-2 divisional record compared to Green Bay's 5-3 mark, giving Minnesota its first Central title since 1980.

CHAPTER FOUR
THE 1990s RESURGENCE AND RESURRECTION

Quarterback Warren Moon (1) passes over Green Bay defensive end
Sean Jones, who is being blocked by Minnesota left tackle Todd Steussie.
The Packers won this October 1995 meeting at Lambeau Field, 38-21.

M ark Dusbabek's world almost turned upside down during the 1989 National Football League's annual college draft.

"The Packers had flown me in for a workout and everything and said they might draft me," Dusbabek said. "Yes, it was the NFL, and I wanted to go to a team where I could play. But the fact it could possibly be the Packers . . .

"One of my friends, a big Vikings fan, said he couldn't see me wearing a Packer uniform. It was fortunate how it turned out because I signed as a free agent with the Vikings."

The University of Minnesota graduate and Faribault, Minnesota, native said he's followed the series most of his life.

"It was always special to me because I grew up in Minnesota, and being a huge Viking fan to having the opportunity to play against the Packers meant a lot to me. I remember the old days, when it was Bart Starr and John Brockington, and I didn't like them at all."

Those feelings have become increasingly contentious on both sides of the Mississippi River during the 1990s, as Dusbabek can attest to from playing outside linebacker for the Vikings during 1989-92.

"I was too young when the Packers were very good, but I remember going to the old Met during the '70s when we were very good and the Packers weren't," said Dusbabek, who worked with the Southern California Golf Association. "I never liked the Packers. My dad had season tickets, and coming out of Minnesota, Wisconsin was the big rivalry [in college], which was a carryover from the Packers and Vikings.

"Then in my first year, I got to go up against Darrell Thompson, my former Gopher teammate. Having the chance to hit him a few times was a great thrill. But it was amazing how Packer fans got a hold of so many tickets. Sometimes you couldn't tell if it was a home game or not."

Dusbabek said he has many fond memories despite the brutal meetings against Green Bay.

"I never got to play in Lambeau because they always scheduled us in

Milwaukee, and usually later in the year. We always had the better team, but we could never win there. I played outside linebacker, so I had to go against tight end Ed West all of the time. He was a nice guy and all, but he had as good of a holding technique as anybody in the league, one the referees could never see," said Dusbabek, who suffered ACL and cartilage damage in his left knee.

"We may have lost to Detroit and Chicago, but every year when the schedule came out, one game we wanted to make sure we won was Green Bay. The rivalry, the media, the fans, and the players. The idea that you could throw the records out the window really was the case in this series. And all of that is why you have the border wars."

After four knee operations, he bowed out and hit the golfing scene. However, his career travels haven't prevented him from keeping tabs on what goes on in the upper Midwest every fall.

"It was sad to see what happened with Ray Rhodes, but I actually like the Green Bay team now. I love their tradition and the ambience of it all. Minnesota fans changed a bit when the Vikings moved indoors. The average fan can relate to Green Bay and the close-knit camaraderie the fans have for their team."

Ken Ruettgers was a part of that feel-good relationship during 1985–96. The left tackle from Southern California didn't earn All-Pro or Pro Bowl recognition but was Green Bay's best offensive lineman for 12 years, protecting several Packer quarterbacks' blind sides. He retired during the Green and Gold's 1996 march to the Super Bowl because of chronic knee problems.

Ruettgers entered the Christian publishing business in 1995 but recently joined a Web-based nonprofit venture that he hopes will help athletes make better transitions after retiring from football.

Mention the Minnesota Vikings to Ruettgers and two words come to mind: Chris Doleman. The two squared off 15 or 16 times while the University of Pittsburgh product played in the Twin Cities and again after he moved to Atlanta and San Francisco.

"We really battled," said Ruettgers, who was selected seventh in the 1985 draft, three picks after Doleman. "He got the better of me a few times, but I played pretty well against him. Rich (Moran) and I had some heated competition against him and Keith Millard. But Chris was one of the few guys that came up to me and said I had played a good game. I really appreciated that. There was a great mutual respect."

Ruettgers said the Packers and Bears had a hate-hate relationship and that Green Bay and Minnesota definitely weren't best of friends. But the Sisters, Oregon, resident said visitors had to contend with much more than the Viking players when squaring off in the Metrodome.

"It was the most difficult place to play, even more so than the Silverdome in Pontiac (Michigan), at least in my time with Green Bay," Ruettgers said. "Minnesota was always a contender, so the noise in that place was so loud, and for an offensive lineman, especially a tackle, it was tough. You couldn't hear the quarterback, so we often had to go with the same snap count or cadence, and that put you at a definite disadvantage.

"I remember one time they had wired [John] Randle with some kind of tape recorder or something for the first half so they could listen to our snap count and audibles," Ruettgers added. "So we had to go to some false audibles and stuff, but you couldn't put in a whole new system.

"I remember the game that Brett [Favre] got hurt, then Ty [Detmer] went down and we were down to T.J. [Rubley] and he audibled out of that play," Ruettgers said of the fateful 27-24 heartbreaking loss in 1995. "It's tough under normal conditions, but to be using your third-string quarterback in an atmosphere like that."

Like his teammates, Ruettgers said playing on the artificial turf and indoors proved to be a headache, especially after losing so many times under such unusual circumstances.

"It was a house of horrors and very frustrating for Mike [Holmgren] in those years against Dennis Green," he said. "The games were very competitive, it was a hard place to play and they had a great defensive line. We were on the other side of so many things over there, but that has a way of coming back around. Like when [Antonio] Freeman came up with that catch."

But one thing will forever remind Ruettgers of the rivalry.

"When they blew that big horn, that was the most disheartening thing," he said. "You definitely knew that you were in hostile territory. We pumped in crowd noise at practice and did a very good job of preparing for those games, but you knew you'd really have to gear it up and no matter what, it would be a challenge. But it was a fun challenge."

Not only did the coaches, players, and fans relish these games, but their success and numerous unusual finishes made this one of the marquee matchups of the decade.

Minnesota and Green Bay returned to past prominence, regaining stature as two of the top teams in the league with 95-65 (.594) and 93-67

(.581) records, respectively.

The Vikings won the Central crown in 1992, '94 and '98, also qualifying for the playoffs in 1993, '96, '97, and '99. They made it to the NFC Championship Game in 1998, where they were upset at home by the Atlanta Falcons, 30-27.

The Packers won their first division title since 1972 when they finished a game ahead of the Lions in 1995. The Packers upset San Francisco on the road to reach the conference title contest, but they lost to eventual Super Bowl champion Dallas, 38-27.

However, Green Bay dominated the NFC in 1996 and '97, bringing home its first Vince Lombardi Trophy since 1967 with a 35-21 triumph over New England after the 1996 campaign. They then were heavily favored to repeat but lost, 31-24, to Denver the next year.

Overall, the Packers made the playoffs six straight times under Holmgren, from 1993 to 1998.

Shawn Patterson was around for that first postseason berth, having played along Green Bay's defensive front during 1988–91 and '93. He was a second-round selection, the 34th pick overall, from Arizona State.

Patterson has endured 18 operations because of football, including elbow and shoulder injuries, but it was three ACL surgeries that ended a promising career. However, he still had his chances to enter the fray against the Vikings.

"It was a big challenge facing them twice every year, but our fans made our job a lot easier. I think they were as loud at Lambeau as it is in Minnesota; it's just that it echoes there (in the dome). We got our energy feed off of that.

"We went in with the attitude that we were gonna own the first through the fourth quarters," added Patterson, who returned an interception for a score during Green Bay's 24-10 victory at Milwaukee in 1990. "Nobody expected us to beat the Vikings, but we did it twice in 1988 even though we finished 4-12. We were their Achilles' heel."

Patterson said it was great mixing it up against the Vikings because he often got to renew acquaintances from his days at Arizona State.

"Randall McDaniel was an old college teammate and in my opinion became the best offensive lineman in the league. He was phenomenal. Guys like Tim Irwin and Gary Zimmerman, they had a very good line that contributed to their success. And Todd Kalis, he was my roommate as a freshman. He was intelligent and a good guy, but he was the most analytical person I know. If you broke the wind, he wanted to know every detail. So when we played against him, we might be in an odd formation or shift just so we could make him think about it. I don't know if it worked or not, but it was a lot of fun."

Still, in the heat of the battle, things weren't always pleasant.

"They had good linemen, but sometimes there were cheap shots and stuff. Their center, Kirk Lowdermilk, used to chop block you, where somebody engaged you and another guy tried to blow out your knees. One time we were in a nickel package where I was next to Blaise Winter and we planned to get Lowdermilk back. Well, I hit him up high and Blaise was supposed to go low. I'm looking down and there's Blaise down at our feet. He had shot in and tackled the ball carrier for a loss, and I'm like, "What in the hell are you doing?' I just started laughing. I don't know if Lowdermilk knew what was going on.

"But we became two very capable teams who always slugged it out, which made for interesting warfare. It came down to fundamentals and execution. It was a blast."

One player who lived through as many or more NFL lows than Patterson or anybody else was Don Beebe, who suffered the agony of four Super Bowl losses with the Buffalo Bills. However, he enjoyed the ultimate high, bringing home the Lombardi Trophy as a member of the 1996 champion Packers.

The Sugar Grove, Illinois, native played six years in Buffalo and one in Carolina before joining the Packers for his final two seasons. He said his experience in the league's smallest city made up for any previous career disappointments. The biggest reason for that was because of the Green Bay fans, and it was no more evident than when they faced Minnesota.

"When James Lofton was with the Bills, he told me that if I ever got a chance to go anywhere in free agency, that I should try to sign with the Packers," said Beebe, who attended Western Illinois and Chadron State (Nebraska). "Just walking through Lambeau is eerie or weird. It's a unique atmosphere that would be cool for every player to experience.

"In our rivalry with Minnesota, over in the dome, it was so loud for both teams, and that was just sitting and listening to them announcing the starting lineups," Beebe said. "It you let the home team stay in it, it was very hard to win. But when we went on the road, the Green Bay fans, we had as many there as the other teams. In Lambeau, you might see 100 people from the visiting teams. But in Minnesota, Chicago, Tampa Bay, even when we went to Seattle, there were 20,000 Packer fans. It's kind of unfair for those teams, but it was neat for us."

Beebe returned that support with several blue-chip performances during Green Bay's 1996 run to the title.

On October 6 of that year, he returned a kickoff 90 yards for a score during the Packers' 37-6 victory over the Bears at Soldier Field. The next week, Beebe stole the spotlight in a "Monday Night Football" contest at Lambeau, hauling in 11 passes for 220 yards as Green Bay rallied for a 23-20 overtime win over San Francisco. The 11 catches tied him for fourth-highest in team history, while the yardage total placed him third behind Billy Howton (257 in 1956) and Don Hutson (237 in 1943).

Another highlight many of his former teammates won't let him forget occurred September 22 that year, and it came at the Metrodome. Beebe turned a simple dump-off pass into a long touchdown, but like the team that day during a 30-21 setback, the speedster tripped up at the end.

"Going into that game (both teams were 3-0), Coach Holmgren said we had to win it if we wanted to get where we wanted to go," Beebe said. "The whole week the press had been talking about how we couldn't win in Minnesota. It was a game of big plays. I remember George Koonce returning an interception for a TD.

"On my score, it was just a short hitch route and I reacted. I must have covered 120 yards instead of the 80. When I got to the end zone I looked up at some Packer fans and I stubbed my toe and went down. It was one of the most embarrassing moments, especially the next day when we watched it on film. You can't get away with something like that."

Beebe could run away from most people, having clocked 4.39 seconds or under in the 40-yard dash seven times in his career. Today he operates House of Speed, a company that helps young athletes enhance their sports performances. So he uses that God-given talent to be a role model for youngsters.

However, when it came to Minnesota vs. Green Bay, he was as competitive as the next guy.

"Mike and Denny [Green] worked together in Frisco, so they wanted to win those games more than anybody, they wanted to prove they were the better coach," he said. "And one thing that fueled Mike was that he couldn't seem to win up there. It was a real thorn in his side.

"It's always been the Packers and the Bears, when you think back about George Halas and Vince Lombardi. But really, the rivalry in the '90s has been the Vikings because the Bears have been so bad. The Minnesota game was definitely the one we looked forward to."

Here are highs and lows from the decade's contests, including some of the most unusual finishes in series and league history.

1990

OCT. 28 AT MILWAUKEE: Green Bay won, 24-10, scoring three consecutive touchdowns to break open a 3-3 contest.

Halfback Darrell Thompson and quarterback Don Majkowski registered touchdown runs in the second and fourth quarters, respectively, while defensive end Shawn Patterson scooted 9 yards with an errant Rich Gannon pass in the third quarter.

Rookie cornerback LeRoy Butler snared two of Green Bay's five interceptions against Gannon, who was harassed into a 14-for-41 afternoon for 230 yards, 49 of which came on a late toss to Anthony Carter to close out the scoring.

Carter finished with nine catches for 141 yards, but it wasn't enough to offset six Minnesota turnovers compared to none for the hosts.

DEC. 2 AT MINNESOTA: The Vikings gained a split with a 23-7 victory behind a late flurry.

Green Bay's Tiger Greene blocked and returned a punt 36 yards for a 7-6 lead in the third quarter. But the Vikings dominated the rest of the game, registering 17 straight points.

Rich Gannon's 56-yard scoring strike to Anthony Carter accounted for the Vikings' first touchdown, and defensive end Al Noga recovered a fumble in the end zone for the final tally.

Anthony Dilweg completed 16 of 29 attempts for 172 yards in place of Don Majkowski, but was picked off three times. Green Bay rushed for only 59 yards on 16 tries, while Alfred Anderson topped the Vikings' 137-yard performance with 60.

Gannon finished with 150 yards passing but didn't throw an interception this time.

On the Vikings' side of the ball, Noga earned NFC Defensive Player of the Week recognition with three solo tackles, one sack, and the forced fumble and recovery.

1991

NOV. 17 AT GREEN BAY: Minnesota won, 35-21, behind a huge second half.

Minnesota blitzed the Packers 21-0 in the final two quarters to win going away, including 5-yard TD runs by Rich Gannon and Herschel Walker in the fourth quarter.

The Vikings piled up 32 first downs, which ranked third on the team's all-time list. Wide receiver Cris Carter hauled in seven catches for 94 yards, including TD plays of 29 and 17 yards from Gannon, who finished 19 of 30 for 215 yards and three scores.

Meanwhile, Mike Tomczak hit 50 percent of his 40 attempts for 271 yards and two scores for Green Bay, highlighted by a 75-yard connection to Charles Wilson that gave the hosts a 14-7 advantage after the first quarter. But Tomczak also was picked off twice.

The Packers' anemic ground attack mustered 29 yards on 14 carries, while Minnesota controlled the clock for 39:55 behind 231 yards rushing, which included 95 from Walker, 60 from Terry Allen and 51 from Alfred Anderson. Allen also grabbed a 9-yard TD catch, the Vikings' only such play from a running back that season.

DEC. 21 AT MINNESOTA: Green Bay rebounded for a 27-7 win in the season finale that proved to be Lindy Infante's last game as Packer coach. He registered a 4-12 mark in his fourth year at the helm.

Vince Workman scored twice, one receiving and one on the ground, as the Packers grabbed a 27-0 lead and won easily despite being outgained and getting only 80 yards through the air.

Keith Woodside ran 19 times for 76 yards and provided the final Packer score on a 10-yard run in the fourth quarter as Green Bay controlled the clock for 36:19 despite gaining less than 200 yards of total offense.

Minnesota finished with 47 yards rushing to complete an 8-8 season that also proved to be Burns' final campaign in charge.

1992

SEPT. 6 AT GREEN BAY: Dennis Green and Mike Holmgren had worked on the same San Francisco staff during 1986–88, so NFL schedule makers thought it would be nice to have the rookie head coaches and their teams face off in the regular-season opener at Lambeau.

The Vikings had finished undefeated in the preseason for the first time since 1973, outscoring their opponents 140-6. However, they found much tougher sledding once the games counted, squeaking out a 23-20 victory in overtime, a closely contested slugfest that set the tone for the rest of the decade.

Kicker Fuad Reveiz booted the game-winner from 26 yards away after Terry Allen ripped off a 45-yard run to the Green Bay 11. Allen gained 140 yards (11.7 yards per carry) and set up the Vikings' go-ahead field goal with a 51-yard burst that gave the visitors a 20-17 lead with 4:40 remaining in the fourth quarter.

Green Bay's Chris Jacke was forced to boot a tying field goal with 1:58 left after halfback Vince Workman was thrown for a 3-yard loss on a third-and-1 play from the Minnesota 3.

Workman finished with 89 yards rushing and caught 12 passes, tied for third place in Green Bay history, for 50 yards. Wide receiver Sterling Sharpe chipped in eight catches for 99 yards, including a 12-yarder to open the scoring.

Minnesota's Rich Gannon finished 21 of 44 for 266 yards, like Don Majkowski throwing one interception. Gannon's two touchdown tosses went to Hassan Jones.

Green Bay opened the game with a 17-play, 84-yard scoring drive. Majkowski finished 27 of 38 for 189 yards but completed only 1 of 6 attempts as the Packers lost 7 yards in three possessions in the overtime.

The Vikings lost both of their fumbles, while Green Bay coughed up two of its five in the light rain. Minnesota registered six sacks, including two by defensive end Chris Doleman on successive plays in the third quarter. Doleman finished with seven tackles, three forced fumbles, and one fumble recovery to win NFC Defensive Player of the Week honors en route to Player of the Month laurels.

"We're in this business to win, not to play close games," Holmgren said in *Packer Plus*. "Not to be the underdog and have people tell you it was a nice job. That's not good enough."

DEC. 27 AT MINNESOTA: Dennis Green told *Packer Plus* early in the week leading up to his team's home and season finale against the Packers that he wouldn't rest any of his stars despite having clinched the Central Division title the week before with a 6-3 win at Pittsburgh.

"We have not started thinking about the playoffs at all. This game is important to us because it's against our No. 1 rival. It gives us a chance to finish up our home regular season in a positive vein. All of our focus will be on that."

Minnesota dominated, 27-7, routing the Packers after spotting the visitors a 7-0 lead and dousing Green Bay's wildcard playoff hopes.

Green Bay rushed only 13 times for 29 yards, while the Vikings' Vencie Glenn grabbed three interceptions in front of a crowd of 61,461 at the Metrodome. Glenn's effort garnered him NFC Defensive Player of the Week recognition.

Terry Allen rushed for 100 yards on 20 carries and capped the scoring in the third quarter on a 1-yard run, finishing with 1,201 yards and 13 touchdowns for the season. Minnesota quarterback and current ESPN analyst Sean Salisbury finished 20 of 33 with two TD tosses.

(More on this game in chapter 6.)

1993

SEPT. 26 AT MINNESOTA: The Vikings claimed a 15-13 victory on the turf behind the right leg of Fuad Reveiz on the infamous Terrell Buckley mistake. The brash young cornerback let Eric Guliford get behind him for a 45-yard gain to the Green Bay 5 to set up Reveiz, who attempted six field goals and hit the game-winner with four seconds left.

John Stephens and Edgar Bennett combined for 10 carries and 68 yards in the first quarter, but Green Bay finished with only 106 total yards rushing and converted on just 4 of 12 third-down plays.

Brett Favre completed 20 of 31 passes for only 150 yards and was intercepted twice, while the Vikings' Jim McMahon managed only 17 of 34 for 172 yards before his late-game heroics.

Reveiz nailed five three-pointers, while Green Bay counterpart Chris Jacke nailed two, including a 49-yarder to give the visitors a 10-6 halftime cushion.

"A loss like this can destroy a team. We can't let it destroy us," Packer linebacker Johnny Holland said in *Packer Plus*.

(More on this game in chapter 6.)

DEC. 19 AT MILWAUKEE: Minnesota grabbed a 21-17 win as unheralded fullback Scottie Graham chugged for 139 yards on 30 attempts to give the Vikings their fourth straight win in the series.

The visitors dominated on the ground by a 154-67 margin, giving them a 151-80 average over the Packers during the current four-game streak. Graham, who had just come off the practice squad, was the main culprit as Minnesota's 24th-rated running attack manhandled the Packer defense, which entered with the No. 9 unit against the rush.

"The offensive line did a great job," Graham said in a *Packer Plus* article. "Any back could have done it, the holes we had today."

And Cris Carter put an exclamation point on two of the drives, grabbing TD catches from Jim McMahon in the third and fourth quarters.

Green Bay's goal-line failures and 2-for-10 third-down conversion rate (they also were 0-for-2 on fourth down) sealed its fate.

"I think we had our chances," Mike Holmgren told *Packer Plus*. "It's one of those games we seem to play against Minnesota that's decided by a couple of points or a play here or there."

Special teams star Bobby Abrams, a linebacker, sliced through to nail Green Bay tailback Darrell Thompson for a 5-yard loss on a first-and-goal play from the Vikings' 2. Green Bay failed on the next three plays as Minnesota left town with the sweep.

Vencie Glenn proved to be a thorn in Green Bay's side again, deflecting a pass in the end zone on a fourth-and-1 play and then pilfering another on the Packers final drive in the two combatants' last meeting ever at County Stadium.

1994

SEPT. 4 AT GREEN BAY: The Packers won, 16-10, in the season opener for Mike Holmgren's first win against Dennis Green.

Green Bay's defense, which finished second behind Minnesota's in 1993, limited the Vikings to 194 yards of total offense. Minnesota gained only 48 yards rushing after running through the Packers for 130 per game the year before.

Viking quarterback Warren Moon's numbers suffered from at least six dropped passes in finishing 20 of 37 for 166 yards. But he was sacked three times and intercepted on three other occasions, twice by rookie safety George Teague and once by linebacker George Koonce, whose theft preserved the victory and helped break the Vikings' four-game winning streak in the series.

Minnesota's lone touchdown was defensive end James Harris' 13-yard fumble return that closed what was once a 13-0 deficit to three points in the fourth quarter.

But Brett Favre led the Packers on a 12-play, 48-yard drive that ate up 7:17 to set up Chris Jacke's 49-yard field goal to make the final score 16-10.

Vikings' linebacker Ed McDaniel accumulated 21 tackles, second most in team history.

Edgar Bennett finished with 90 yards in total offense for the Packers, and Favre completed 22 of 36 for 185 yards, including a 14-yard score to Sterling Sharpe, who ended his controversial 11th-hour contract walkout to play a key role.

"We still look up to Sterling, we respect him," safety LeRoy Butler told *Packer Plus*. "We aren't going to let it come between us. We wouldn't be a team. We love him to death. We were overjoyed that he played. And he probably was the difference in the game."

Sharpe led the hosts with seven catches for 53 yards.

"It's not a pretty win, but I've never heard of a bad win," Favre said in a *Packer Plus* article. "A win is a win, and I'll take it any day of the week."

OCT. 20 AT MINNESOTA: Minnesota retaliated with a 13-10 triumph in a Thursday night overtime thriller.

Fuad Reveiz's 27-yard field goal, one of a league-best 34 that helped give him a conference-high 132 points, capped a 14-play, 55-yard march to win it.

Green Bay backup QB Mark Brunell fumbled a snap from center Jamie Dukes early in the fourth quarter as the Packers were driving near the Minnesota 20-yard line with a 10-7 lead.

The Packers, who played without Brett Favre much of the game because of a hip injury, managed only 158 total yards and equaled the Vikings' futility on third downs, going 4 of 16.

Meanwhile, Green Bay's defense didn't allow the Vikings an offensive touchdown for the second consecutive game; the Vikings' lone TD, giving them a 7-0 lead, was Anthony Parker's 23-yard return after teammate James Harris fumbled an interception of Favre.

Warren Moon completed 31 of 50 passes for 271 yards, of which 115 came on his team's final two drives. Minnesota finished with 22 yards rushing on 19 carries.

Brunell led Green Bay to all 10 of its points, including his 6-yard quarterback draw with 50 seconds left before halftime. The southpaw completed 7 of 13 passes in the second quarter, but he finished only 11 of 24 for 79 yards.

"He was a scramblin' little booger," Minnesota defensive tackle John Randle said in *Packer Plus* about trying to chase down Brunell. "He got out from beneath the sacks. He's a tough competitor."

One of Randle's linemates, Harris, batted down three passes, tying him for second-most in Minnesota history.

"We don't take any pride in knocking players out," Dennis Green said in *Packer Plus* of Favre's forced exit. "We'll play whoever is in there. Brunell is a good player, just inexperienced. He kept the ball game close."

Craig Hentrich of the Packers and Mike Saxon of the Vikings each were forced to punt 10 times in this defensive struggle that saw Green Bay slip to 3-4 and Minnesota improve to 5-2.

1995

OCT. 22 AT GREEN BAY: Mike Holmgren entered this game with a 1-5 record against Dennis Green and the Vikings, so the question of why was an obvious topic leading up to this first meeting between the 4-2 Packers and 3-3 Minnesota.

"We don't have a good record against the Vikings since we've been here, and we always wind up talking about this," Holmgren said in a *Packer Plus* story. "We've lost four games, two in overtime and two real close games, of the five. Certainly, we have not done well against them and I'm hoping we can reverse that, get going and have a little streak of our own."

Holmgren's streak lasted one game as Green Bay pulled away for a 38-21 win.

Brett Favre's third of four TD tosses broke a 14-14 tie in the third quarter as Green Bay cruised to a 35-14 lead in staying tied with the Bears atop the division.

The Packer defense equaled its six-game season total of forcing four turnovers and registered three sacks, including the final touchdown in which Sean Jones recovered Warren Moon's fumble in the end zone after Reggie White sacked him and knocked the pigskin loose.

Cornerback Doug Evans turned in an all-star performance, intercepting two passes, knocking down seven others and making nine tackles against the likes of Cris Carter and Jake Reed.

Minnesota entered with the NFC's No. 3 offense but gained only 268 yards, 114 of them coming after Fritz Shurmur's unit had a 35-14 advantage.

Moon finished 16 of 35 for 119 yards before leaving the game midway through the fourth quarter, and Carter grabbed five passes for 58 yards on his way to tying his franchise-record 122 receptions and setting a then team record with 17 TD catches.

Minnesota outgained the hosts 93-69 rushing, but Favre passed for 295 yards and four touchdowns, including five hookups with tight end Mark

Chmura for 101 yards and the game's first TD.

NOV. 5 AT MINNESOTA: After the game two weeks earlier at Lambeau Field, Vikings' head man Dennis Green wasn't conceding anything in the division race or buying the idea that momentum in the series had shifted.

"I think that we've been ahead of the Packers every year for the last three years, so I'm not conceding any damn thing to anybody," he told *Packer Plus*. "I guess at the end of the year we'll see who has the best team."

Minnesota grabbed that distinction in the next showdown, leaving with another close victory at home, winning 27-24 to earn a split.

Minnesota intercepted four passes, including Jeff Brady's theft of third-stringer T.J. Rubley's gaffe to set up the winning field goal.

The Vikings overcame a 16-10 halftime deficit with a 14-0 advantage in the third quarter as Moon connected on two of his three TD passes. The victory was the Vikings' fourth straight in the Metrodome in the Green-Holmgren era.

Brady finished with six tackles, including his first career sack, a forced fumble, and a tackle for loss.

Packers' left tackle Ken Ruettgers said in *Packer Plus*, "It was at all levels, in my 21 years of football, I've never been a part of a weirder swing of events back and forth. Weird, weird. It was just weird."

Green Bay General Manager Ron Wolf echoed his lineman's confusion in a *Packer Plus* story about the Packers' house of horrors: "I'm sick and tired of Fuad Reveiz deciding the outcome of the game. I think we've exhausted ways to lose here."

(More about this game in chapter 6.)

1996

SEPT. 22 AT MINNESOTA: The Vikings handed Green Bay its first loss of the season and improved to 4-0 for the first time since the 1975 squad won its first 10 games with a 30-21 triumph.

Robert Smith's 37-yard scoring run put the Vikings ahead for good in the fourth quarter in a game that featured five scoring plays of 20 or more yards.

Both teams committed four turnovers, but the Vikings controlled the ball for 24:31 of the second half to win going away, their fifth straight victory over Green Bay at home.

Minnesota's smothering pass rush recorded seven sacks and forced Brett Favre to fumble three times, the Vikings recovering two of them, in putting the clamps on the NFL's top-ranked offense. Each of the Vikings' starting defensive linemen registered sacks, with John Randle finishing with a career-high 3 1/2 while forcing two fumbles.

Green Bay gained 60 yards rushing on 15 carries (4.0) and limited the Vikings to 88 yards on 33 tries (2.7), including just 11 in the first half. But Jake Reed's seven catches for 129 yards and big plays in the fourth quarter doomed the visitors.

"They whipped our [expletive], and that's all you can say," said Green Bay center Frank Winters in *Packer Plus*. "I don't know how many times they hit Brett, but every time I looked back, he was laying on the ground. That's not very good for an offensive line."

Dennis Green said that his team's pressure decided the outcome.

"Games like this are won up front," he said in a *Packer Plus* article. "It has to be. Our defensive front kept them off balance and forced sacks and scrambles. We did a great job in our offense in that we were able to believe that we could run the football, so we had balance in the fourth quarter."

DEC. 22 AT GREEN BAY: Jeff Brady, Minnesota's middle linebacker who played for the Packers in 1992 but was cut the next preseason and eventually ended up with the Vikings, made headlines during the week leading up to this donnybrook.

"I'm coming to Lambeau Field ready to headhunt, that's all there is to it," Brady bragged in *Packer Plus*. "You know my feelings about Green Bay. This team right here wants to sweep Green Bay, whether we're in the playoffs or not."

Green Bay safety LeRoy Butler fired a couple of salvos toward Minneapolis, too.

"I remember back in 1992, we needed to win that game, but they kind of rubbed it in our faces and beat us, which is fine," he said in *Packer Plus*. "But payback is a [bleep]. It will be here soon. This time I'm really looking forward to it."

Well, Brady ate his words and a bit of Lambeau sod to the tune of 38-10 in a game that saw the Packers go on a 28-0 second-half outburst to springboard into the postseason and their first Super Bowl win since January 1968.

It was Green Bay's best record (13-3) since going 12-2 in 1966 and gave it home-field advantage throughout the upcoming playoffs.

Brett Favre led the onslaught with three TD passes, while the hosts outgained their foes 233-49 on the ground, recording 18 of their 29 first downs on running plays.

It was made possible by the Green Bay offensive line, embarrassed in the September meeting at the Metrodome. Favre was sacked only twice for -5 yards and shattered his year-old NFC record for touchdown passes with his 39th. Vikings' star Randle wasn't credited with a sack or a tackle in the mud.

Edgar Bennett and Dorsey Levens combined for 29 carries and 182 yards as Green Bay turned in its best ground game since churning out 257 yards in the 1994 Halloween monsoon on "Monday Night Football," in Chicago.

The contest was plenty hot early on, with Frank Winters and Minnesota cornerback Corey Fuller exchanging blows. Winters dove over a pile of defenders who had stopped Levens at the Minnesota 19, hitting Fuller in the ribs after the whistle. Fuller responded in kind by poking Winters in the left eye.

"On the film, he does a lot of hitting after the play, and we knew that," Fuller said in *Packer Plus*. "The play was over with plainly. . . . When someone's out there playing nasty, I'm going to play nasty right with 'em. I'm a clean player, but when you start playing dirty, I'm going to start playing dirty with you."

Winters didn't hold anything back in the article, either.

"I thought he was going to come and talk to me, but when he got close to me he reached in and poked me in the eye for no reason," Winters said.

"That's the kind of player he is. It was kind of cheap. It was blatant because it was after the play. We'll play those guys again. That's the kind of stuff they do. They're a bunch of trash talkers. They've done it all year. And there's nothing you can do about that."

But the league office did something about it, fining Fuller $30,000 and Winters $7,500, even though no flags were thrown on the play. It was the second time during the 1996 season that each player's wallet got a little lighter.

1997

SEPT. 21 AT GREEN BAY: Both teams entered with 2-1 records, and Vikings' quarterback Brad Johnson said before the game that playing the defending Super Bowl champions on the road could be a good remedy after Minnesota was thumped 28-14 at home by Tampa Bay the week before.

"Sometimes the best thing for you is to play the best team in the league in a place where they don't get beat," Johnson told *Packer Plus*. "It's probably the biggest challenge we've faced all year long."

It definitely turned out that way, at least in the first half as Brett Favre threw four touchdown passes to help the Packers bolt to a 31-7 lead.

However, two turnovers gave the Vikings good field position, and Johnson rallied the Vikings to within 38-32 before Green Bay's defense finally stopped Minnesota to clinch its 18th straight home victory.

Favre finished with five TD strikes, tying a team record he shares with three others and passing Bart Starr (156-152) for first in team annals. Favre's effort equaled a mark reached against the Vikings four times but the first since John Elway had done it in 1984.

Robert Smith rushed for 132 of Minnesota's 185 yards on 28 tries, Jake Reed caught nine passes for 119 yards and two scores as the visitors amassed 393 yards, and reserve linebacker Pete Bercich registered a career-high four stops on special teams.

Antonio Freeman latched onto seven of Favre's aerials for 122 yards, and Robert Brooks added five catches for 92 yards and a TD.

DEC. 1 AT MINNESOTA: Green Bay gained its first sweep of the Vikings since 1988 by a 27-11 margin in a "Monday Night Football" contest.

The Packers had exorcised one demon, the Dallas Cowboys (45-17) the week before, and this triumph gave Mike Holmgren his first victory in the Metrodome in six tries.

Minnesota nose tackle Jerry Ball recorded a season-high eight tackles, but Dorsey Levens rushed for 108 yards and scored on two short TD runs as Green Bay took command with 17 straight points to break a 3-3 second-quarter deadlock.

The victory moved the Packers to within one game of clinching their third consecutive Central Division title, which they earned one week later with a 17-6 win at Tampa Bay.

Minnesota's David Palmer established a Vikings' standard with 11 total kick returns for 214 yards, the third-highest in squad history, and a career-high 249 all-purpose yards. But it wasn't near enough as Green Bay out-slugged the Vikings.

Brad Johnson was sacked six times, Robert Smith was held to 54 yards on 16 carries, and Cris Carter managed six catches for 50 yards. Reggie White led Green Bay's defensive charge with 2 1/2 sacks, and LeRoy Butler had nine total tackles.

Meanwhile, Green Bay's offense made enough big plays despite converting only 25 percent of its third-down plays (4 of 16). The Packers were good on both of their fourth-down conversions, Antonio Freeman caught six passes for 85 yards and Favre was an efficient 15 of 29 with no interceptions.

(More on this game in chapter 6.)

1998

OCT. 5 AT GREEN BAY: Minnesota won this matchup of unbeatens, 37-24, in Randy Moss' coming-out party on "MNF."

The Packers entered the contest 4-0, but the rookie wide receiver riddled them for 190 yards on just five catches, including TD receptions of 52 and 44 yards from quarterback Randall Cunningham, who passed for 442 yards, the most ever given up by a Green Bay defense and the fifth-highest passing total for a Minnesota QB. Moss' outburst was the third-highest yardage mark in team record books.

Green Bay's Roell Preston tied a team mark with eight kickoff returns and set a franchise record with 256 yards, including a 101-yard TD scamper.

But the Vikings went on a 27-0 blitz to break a 10-10 tie in the second quarter, limiting Brett Favre to 114 yards passing. Meanwhile, Minnesota exploded for 545 yards of offense.

The Vikings' onslaught snapped Green Bay's 25-game regular-season home winning streak.

(More on this game in chapter 6.)

NOV. 22 AT MINNESOTA: Green Bay linebacker George Koonce assessed his team's frame of mind heading into the rematch at the Metrodome.

"The Packers know all about big games and what we need to do," he said in *Packer Plus*. "We've got to have guys step up and make big plays."

The visitors turned in a few, but not enough to prevent the Vikings from finishing off the sweep with a 28-14 victory that gave 10-1 Minnesota a three-game lead over Green Bay and virtually locked up the division crown.

Minnesota grabbed leads of 13-0 and 20-7 in the first half. Randy Moss again burned the Packers for 153 yards, including a 49-yard TD grab to put the game out of reach in the fourth quarter.

"I just proved that I can play, period," Moss told a *Packer Plus* reporter. "Catching the hitch, the curl, a corner or the deep ball, whatever it may take. I just want to show I can catch the ball if it's thrown in my vicinity. It's all about making plays, man."

Brett Favre did the same in completing 31 of 39 pass attempts for 303 yards, but his only interception was a 58-yard TD return by cornerback Jimmy Hitchcock late in the first quarter to make it 10-0 in Minnesota's favor.

Linebackers Dwayne Rudd and Ed McDaniel each registered 11 tackles for Minnesota's defense, and NFC special teams player of the month, punter Mitch Berger, averaged 54.3 on punts and boomed his kickoffs into the end zone as usual.

Green Bay was successful on 7 of 12 third downs and converted its only fourth-down try but managed 53 yards rushing. Favre hooked up with tight end Tyrone Davis for their second scoring connection to trim the Vikings' cushion to 20-14 in the fourth quarter, but Randall Cunningham and Moss answered on the next drive to decide the outcome.

Bill Schroeder led the Packers with seven catches for 93 yards as Favre completed passes to eight receivers. Favre's passing percentage (79.5) was the second-highest single-game reading of his seven-year Packers career, ranking behind only the 82.1 completion rate he forged with a 23-of-28 effort at Cleveland on November 19, 1995.

However, digging an early hole was too much to overcome.

"The very first play of the game was a fumble," said Favre in *Packer Plus*. "I think it was the loudest (stadium) I've ever played in, anywhere. And I tip my hat to the fans. We just couldn't handle that part of it early. I called the snap count and Frank [Winters] couldn't even hear me. So when I pulled out, he didn't hear me. So we were a little late on it.

"Obviously, that was a concern early, the two fumbles," Favre continued. "We knew coming in that you couldn't turn the ball over against this team. And Hitchcock guessed on a play, made a great play. And that's the kind of plays you've got to make in this type of game. And they made more than we did."

1999

SEPT. 26 AT GREEN BAY: Both teams entered this week three showdown with 1-1 records, so falling to 1-2 would put the loser in an early hole in the division race.

"It's the biggest game, right here," Packers offensive tackle Ross Verba said in *Packer Plus*. "This is the defining point in our season."

Meanwhile, Randy Moss was trying to deflect the media attention from his two marvelous games against Green Bay in 1998 and place it back onto the task at hand.

"I think the memories are always going to be there, but as far as motivating myself to try to go out and do the same things as last year, I don't really want to reminisce too much," Moss said in a *Packer Plus* preview. "That will probably get me away from my game. I'm hopefully not looking at last year. That was a different situation and a different kind of team."

Moss was correct about both squads. Minnesota's juggernaut offense was struggling for consistency, while the Green Bay defense had a new strategy in mind to avoid a repeat of the 37-24 and 28-14 spankings it took in 1998.

"We can't let them have a coming-out party in Lambeau like we did last year," LeRoy Butler said in *Packer Plus*. "Everybody knows what's at stake, and going into the bye week, this game is so important. It's almost as important as a playoff game because we don't want to go 0-2 in our division."

Still, Moss and Minnesota's vaunted offensive arsenal had to be licking its collective chops entering this contest against a revamped Packers cover unit that featured three rookies in some defensive packages.

Linebacker Brian Williams summed up the Packers' chances in *Packer Plus*.

"We say that all the time, it's like a broken record. We have to get rid of those two or three big plays. Everyone keeps saying we did so well with the exception of the big plays. We need to lose 'with the exception' part of the statement."

Despite allowing Jake Reed and Cris Carter to combine for 193 yards, Green Bay handcuffed their nemesis, Moss, for only two catches for 13 yards. One of his receptions was a 10-yard TD that gave the visitors a 20-16 lead late, but it wasn't enough because Brett Favre and the Packer offense saved the day with another last-minute victory, 23-20.

Green Bay's greenhorns, starting cornerback Mike McKenzie and reserves Antuan Edwards and Fred Vinson, earned their stripes, especially Edwards. The No. 1 draft pick pilfered two Cunningham passes, returning one of them for a second-quarter touchdown.

"I know [the media] talks about Randy Moss this and Randy Moss that," Edwards told a *Packer Plus* reporter after the game. "He had a great year last year, but he's not Superman."

(More on this game in chapter 6.)

DEC. 20 AT MINNESOTA: Randy Moss and the Vikings earned a split, rallying for a 24-20 triumph on Leroy Hoard's 1-yard plunge with 8:58

remaining, the third lead change of the second half.

Moss haunted the Packers again, hauling in a 57-yard TD from Jeff George to tie the score at 10 in the second quarter and a 36-yard catch to the Green Bay 1 to set up the final score. He finished with five catches for 131 yards and two touchdowns.

George also helped the Vikings during their scoring drive in the third quarter that gave the hosts a 17-13 lead, scampering for 17 yards on a third-and-9 play. The 60-yard march also benefited from Mike McKenzie's 22-yard pass interference call to the Green Bay 2 on a third-and-11 play.

However, Green Bay, which hadn't faked a kick during Mike Holmgren's seven years in charge, fooled the Vikings with one to grab a 20-17 lead with 12:31 remaining after recovering a Moss fumble on a punt return. Matt Hasselbeck's 9-yard pass went to backup tight end Jeff Thomason after the Packers had set up for a potential 27-yard Ryan Longwell field goal.

Hasselbeck didn't miss the pass, but his celebrating leap at Thomason and others in the end zone missed the mark, with the reserve signal caller hitting the Metrodome turf in front of a national "Monday Night Football" audience.

Green Bay's playoff hopes also took a major hit as it fell to 7-7, while the Vikings enhanced their postseason outlook after improving to 8-6.

"The bottom line is we haven't met some of the expectations that I thought we were capable of meeting," said first-year Green Bay coach Ray Rhodes in *Packer Plus*. "I'm disappointed personally. I was given the opportunity and [we're] not reaching the goals thus far, record-wise."

Ron Wolf fired Rhodes and his staff a few weeks later after just one year as the Packers finished 8-8 and out of the playoffs for the first time since 1992.

CHAPTER FIVE

2000 AND BEYOND

Ex-Wisconsin Badger star Michael Bennett tries to elude Green Bay middle linebacker Bernardo Harris as safety Darren Sharper (42) races in to assist in Green Bay's 24-13 win in the teams' final NFC Central Division matchup Dec. 30, 2001.

THE VIKINGS AND Packers couldn't have started a new decade heading in more opposite directions.

Minnesota opened the 2000 campaign 7-0 and improved to 11-2 with Super Bowl aspirations. Meanwhile, rookie coach Mike Sherman's up-and-down Green Bay squad lost its first two contests and stumbled to a 5-7 mark with slim hopes of reaching the postseason.

However, their respective fortunes have pulled an about-face ever since.

The Vikings tripped over themselves during their final three contests, including a rare slip-up to Green Bay at home (33-28) to throw away their grip on home-field advantage in the NFC. Despite downing New Orleans in their playoff opener, the Vikings were demolished, 41-0, in the championship game by the New York Giants.

In contrast, their rivals turned a season of missed opportunities into a 9-7 mark with four consecutive impressive showings against divisional foes and their first season sweep of the Vikings since 1997—and raised the bar of enthusiasm despite watching the playoffs on TV.

Both teams continued down those paths during the 2001 campaign.

Green Bay roared to a 3-0 start and overcame several subpar outings to clinch a postseason berth for the first time since 1998, Mike Holmgren's last year in Titletown. Sherman added the title of general manager to his resume after Ron Wolf retired, and the Packers battled Chicago for Central Division supremacy all season.

But life was much more difficult in the Twin Cities, where a hodge-podge of issues on and off the field contributed to a dismal showing.

The death of offensive tackle and team leader Korey Stringer to heat-stroke in training camp sent the Vikings into a downward spiral despite an emotional and promising preseason.

Minnesota lost its home and season opener to hapless Carolina in what turned out to be the Panthers' lone victory of the season, and things got worse as the Vikings dropped eight of their final 10 games after evening their record at 3-3 with an impressive win over Green Bay on October 21.

Talk of lawsuits by Stringer's widow, continuing disputes over a new stadium deal, rumors about Coach Dennis Green's job status, and sideline bickering from such stars as Randy Moss and Cris Carter snowballed into a hellish nightmare that resulted in the team's first losing record since 1990.

Green's 10th season at the helm ended abruptly when he and Vikings' owner Red McCombs agreed on a buyout of his contract three days before Minnesota's season finale, a loss at Baltimore that meant the Vikings finished 0-8 on the road. Assistant coach Mike Tice was named to replace Green just a few days later.

Carter's tenure with the team ended when he opted out of his contract and searched for another suitor early in 2002, with some early reports even linking him to Green Bay. However, his career closed with little fanfare when he announced his retirement in May to become a broadcaster with HBO. Linebacker Kailee Wong and veteran safety Robert Griffith departed via free agency, leaving few stars on the Minnesota roster.

Despite much of the uncertainty surrounding the Vikings, these two teams still gave fans something to get excited about, with three of the four contests going down to the final minutes, including the unbelievable first game of the decade.

And that's something that shouldn't change in the years to come.

2000

NOV. 6 AT GREEN BAY: The Packers entered this "Monday Night Football" tussle as a 3 1/2 point underdog, had a 1-7 record against the spread so far during the season, and were coming off an embarrassing 28-20 loss at Miami in which they had blown a 17-0 lead.

The Vikings were one of the NFC's Super Bowl favorites until they packed it in during a 41-13 setback the week before at Tamp Bay.

So, something had to give, and most experts predicted that Minnesota, 7-1, would bounce back against the Packers, who were headed nowhere fast with a 3-5 mark. Well, experts aren't perfect, they're just experts.

Green Bay rekindled hopes for a playoff run with an electrifying 26-20 overtime win on Antonio Freeman's "Miraculous Deflection" play at a windy, soggy Lambeau Field.

Brett Favre finished with two TD passes and 235 yards but completed only 16 of 35 for 192 yards before his 43-yard connection that ended the game. Minnesota quarterback Daunte Culpepper recorded almost identical numbers, going 17 of 34 for two scores. However, the first-year starter's 276 yards, including 45 on one play, were balanced out as he tossed three interceptions.

Freeman caught five passes for 118 yards, and Randy Moss led the Vikings with 130 yards on six catches but didn't reach the end zone. Still, Moss' career numbers against Green Bay improved to 26 receptions for 617 yards (23.7 average) and six touchdowns in five games.

Robert Smith, who completed the 45-yard catch and run from Culpepper, gained 122 yards on 24 carries for Minnesota. Ahman Green slogged away for 68 yards on 23 carries but also hauled in a nifty underhanded toss from Favre for one Packers' score.

Green Bay's Allen Rossum returned a kickoff 90 yards to set up Ahman Green's 2-yard plunge that tied the contest at 20 in the third quarter.

Special teams didn't come through for the Vikings, as holder Mitch Berger bobbled the snap from center in the slippery, rainy conditions with Minnesota trying to kick the game-winning field goal in the final seconds of regulation.

Free safety Darren Sharper had two of his league-leading nine interceptions for Green Bay.

(More on this game in chapter 6)

DEC. 17 AT MINNESOTA: The Vikings had been waiting for revenge, and linebacker Dwayne Rudd summed up his team's mind-set heading into the rematch of the 11-3 Vikings and 7-7 Packers.

"The weather was bad, and we were fighting," Rudd said in the *Minneapolis Star-Tribune* in reference to Green Bay's victory in November. "We were scratching for the victory just as well as they were. They got a great break at the end, a miraculous catch by [Antonio] Freeman. They won the game, but it was a good, old-fashioned Minnesota-Green Bay game. We've got to go out there and redeem ourselves."

Minnesota failed to back up Rudd's words, leaving the Vikings with their second straight setback after being blasted at St. Louis the week before. Green Bay's 33-28 triumph ended Minnesota's 13-game home winning streak and dented the hosts' hopes of securing home-field advantage throughout the NFC playoffs, an honor earned by the New York Giants.

Randy Moss' 78-yard TD to cut Minnesota's deficit to 10-7 was the longest catch of his career up to that point, but it proved to be one of only four plays the Vikings ran from scrimmage in the first quarter.

Robert Smith finished with a season-low 26 yards on 10 carries against a defense led by the inspired play of middle linebacker Bernardo Harris, with 15 of those yards coming on one play. Daunte Culpepper gained 42 yards and a TD on seven tries to lead the way. He also threw for three scores and 335 yards on 23 of 38, but the Minnesota offense never found its customary rhythm.

That wasn't the case with Green Bay, which made mincemeat out of the Vikings defense while scoring on seven of nine drives. The visitors didn't turn the ball over and punted only once.

Tailback Ahman Green rushed for a career-high 161 yards on 25 carries (6.4 average), including a 28-yard sweep around right end on a third-and-9 play to sew up the victory after the Vikings had taken their final timeout with 1:12 remaining.

Green Bay's 159 net yards on the ground (Brett Favre lost 2 yards) was the most it had gained at the Metrodome since 1985. Ahman Green became only the fourth Packer runner to surpass 1,000 yards since 1978.

Favre finished 26 of 38 for 290 yards and three scores. He completed 14 passes to wide receivers Bill Schroeder and Freeman, who each grabbed TDs. But more importantly, Favre avoided the costly interceptions, sacks, and fumbles that had plagued him and the team during a decade of miscues at the Metrodome.

"You might outscore some people, but you're not going to do that very often against a quarterback like Brett Favre," Dennis Green told the *Star-Tribune* of the shoot-out that ended in a Green Bay season sweep.

2001

OCT. 21 AT MINNESOTA: Green Bay had played the role of Jack, climbed the beanstalk, and stolen the hen that laid the golden eggs in dismantling the defending Super Bowl champion Baltimore Ravens the week before, claiming a 31-23 victory that wasn't close until the final minutes.

The Packers entered 4-1, while the Vikings were thankful to be 2-3 after holding on for a 31-26 home triumph against winless Detroit after the Lions scored the game's final 20 points and were deep in Minnesota territory when time expired.

None of that mattered on this day indoors, as the Vikings drubbed the dreadful-looking division leaders, who laid a giant egg on this day by a 35-13 count. It was the Vikings' largest victory margin in the series since a 32-6 win at Green Bay on December 7, 1986, and Green Bay's most lopsided setback overall since a 36-14 pasting at the hands of Dallas on October 3, 1993.

Former Wisconsin Badger tailback and Vikings' No. 1 draft pick Michael Bennett missed the game, but Daunte Culpepper and reserve running back Doug Chapman ran roughshod over the Packers' defense, a unit that entered the contest fourth in the league against the rush, third overall and first in fewest points allowed (50).

However, the Vikings dominated with 377 yards, including 196 rushing. Culpepper ran for 71 yards, including a 14-yard score, and Chapman led the ground attack with 90 yards on 22 attempts. To add to Green Bay's miseries, defensive leader LeRoy Butler suffered a bruised sternum and left in the second quarter.

Randy Moss entered the contest with gaudy career stats against Green Bay: 30 catches for 753 yards (25.1 average) with seven touchdowns in six games, in five of which he'd surpassed the 100-yard plateau. He hauled in eight of Culpepper's 18 completions, but he had a long of only 17 and absorbed two vicious hits from Green Bay safety Darren Sharper.

Cris Carter grabbed only three aerials, but a 43-yard score gave Minnesota a 7-0 advantage as the hosts never looked back. Culpepper had been sacked 17 times through five games but hit the turf only once on this day.

Green Bay's offense entered ranked third in yards gained, but the visitors couldn't take advantage of several early opportunities to jump ahead and take the boisterous crowd out of the game.

Ryan Longwell missed 51- and 42-yard field goals in the first half, center Mike Flanagan unleashed two terrible snaps in the shotgun formation, and Packers' leading ball carrier Ahman Green was stuffed for a loss on a fourth-and-one play from the Minnesota 7-yard line with 5:56 remaining in the first quarter to end a drive that could have given Green Bay the first score and the momentum.

Green finished with 73 yards on 11 carries for a 6.6 average, but 61 of them came on a third-quarter scamper. That meant he gained only 12 yards on his other 10 tries, showing how much the Vikings controlled action in the trenches.

Brett Favre completed 21 of 35 passes, but they went for only 169 yards as he and the offense missed starting receiver Bill Schroeder, who was out with a sprained ankle. Favre tossed two TD passes, but one came at garbage time in the final minute, and his only interception resulted in Kailee Wong's 27-yard TD jaunt that gave Minnesota a 14-0 lead during a 20-0 second-quarter blitz.

"We'll find out if we're as good as we think we are," Favre said in *Packer Plus*. "If we play like today, we'll be home for the playoffs. It was apparent they wanted the football game more than we did."

That was obvious from the get-go, but it proved to be another unusual trip to the House of Horrors for Green Bay, evidenced by the incident in which Packers' special teams coach Frank Novak was injured when long snapper Rob Davis drilled him in the chest with a ball while warming up on the sidelines.

Mike Sherman summed it up best in a *Packer Plus* article.

"There was a time where the game was anybody's to grab, we didn't grab it when we should have, they did grab it and they took advantage of it. That whole day was like something out of the 'Twilight Zone.' Everything that could go wrong went wrong."

DEC. 30 AT GREEN BAY: The outcome was much the same in game two, statistically speaking, anyway, with the struggling Vikings dominating the playoff-bound Packers until the fourth quarter.

Minnesota had lost six of eight outings since their meeting at the Metrodome, including Detroit's lone victory through 15 games and a 33-3 thrashing at home to Jacksonville.

So, most prognosticators and those in attendance thought the prohibitively favored Packers would roll, especially considering how Minnesota seemingly had its bags packed and the hosts were still entertaining hopes of earning home-field advantage to open the postseason.

The Vikings grabbed a 13-10 lead when starting and third-string quarterback Spergon Wynn hooked up with tight end Byron Chamberlain with 10:03 remaining. However, Brett Favre cranked up his usual late-game, cold-weather magic again, throwing for 72 of the 79 yards in Green Bay's ensuing seven-play drive to regain the lead and a sense of sanity for most of the crowd of 59,870.

Then cornerback Mike McKenzie bolted 38 yards with a perfectly timed interception to sew up Green Bay's 11th victory of the season, 24-13, with 5:25 left. That left the Vikings at 5-10, their most defeats since 1990, while assuring themselves of a top-10 draft pick for the first time since 1985.

Wynn finished 11 of 30 for 114 yards with three interceptions that could have been much worse had Darren Sharper not dropped a couple more chances. However, most of Wynn's ups and downs occurred in the final quarter because Dennis Green's strategy coming in was to run the ball, and run the Vikings did.

With a game-time temperature of 19 degrees, a wind-chill factor of 5, an inexperienced man behind center, and a banged up Green Bay defense, Minnesota ran 44 times for 199 yards, including rushes on its first 12 plays from scrimmage.

With Daunte Culpepper and number-two quarterback Todd Bouman out with injuries, Wynn didn't complete a pass until late in the second quarter.

The situation worked surprisingly well, though, with former Badger Michael Bennett gaining 104 yards on 25 carries. But that meant the visitors' vaunted receiving duo of Randy Moss and Cris Carter combined for only three catches for 21 yards.

Despite almost constant double coverage from McKenzie and Sharper, Moss was expected to be more of a factor, considering he had burned Green Bay for 38 receptions and 826 yards in his previous seven matchups vs. the Packers. But it wasn't meant to be, as he and Carter spent as much time pleading with their coaching staff to open up the offensive playbook as they did trying to latch onto the pigskin on the frozen field.

Meanwhile, Green Bay couldn't do much of anything against a rejuvenated Minnesota defense, which allowed a season-low 213 yards to the high-powered Packers, including just 56 on the ground, which included Donald Driver's 31-yard wide receiver reverse for a TD. The Vikings sacked Favre twice and limited the Packers to only 2 of 11 on third-down conversion attempts.

But the only number that always matters is the final score, and for that Green Bay headed into the postponed season finale (because of the September 11 terrorist attacks) with a much-needed win and not a demoralizing setback, improving its NFL-best December mark to 31-10 during the past decade.

"I thought we'd be more productive on offense," said Favre in *Packer Plus* after improving to 20-2 overall at home in December and 8-2 at Lambeau vs. the Vikings. "But I knew this team wouldn't lay down for us. They might do that against other teams, but not against the Green Bay Packers."

Dennis Green said Mother Nature dictated much of what happened in the frigid slugfest.

"I don't think either team threw the ball well today," he said to a *Packer Plus* reporter. "Winter football. Take out [the Packers'] last drive and how many yards did [Brett Favre] get? It was that kind of day, and both teams were trying to run the ball. A lot of almost catches, which don't count because of the wind, because of the way the ball moved. It was that kind of day."

Bennett told *Packer Plus* that he relished his shot of playing in front of family and friends.

"I think our offensive line did a great job today. It got me in a rhythm. I just appreciate the opportunity that I had to play here and look forward to playing again."

Minnesota failed to capitalize on its rushing dominance, and McKenzie's first professional touchdown made up for his unit's often inept performance.

"We had seen the play all week," McKenzie said in a *Packer Plus* interview. We knew he (Wynn) was a young quarterback. He seemed to want to make up his mind early where he wanted to go with the ball. I think most of the guys in the secondary got a pretty good bead on him. It was a great feeling to catch the ball, secure it, and finally get to do the Lambeau Leap."

CHAPTER SIX

TOP TEN GAMES

Minnesota quarterback and holder Fran Tarkenton can't catch Green Bay cornerback Hank Gremminger, who galloped 80 yards with a blocked field-goal attempt to clinch Green Bay's 37-28 victory in October 1963 at Bloomington.

THIRTY OF THE Green Bay–Minnesota meetings have been decided by seven points or less, including six overtime contests in which the Vikings hold a 4-1-1 advantage.

While that means plenty of suspense, not all of those close encounters could be included in a list of most memorable games. Legitimate arguments probably exist for numerous battles that were left on the cutting room floor.

Not all of these matchups came down to the closing moments or decided the division championship. But every one proved significant in its own way, so here is one author's top 10 games, not in any specific order, that describe what this series is all about.

1. BETWEEN THEATRICS, A FOOTBALL GAME ERUPTED
DEC. 1, 1997, AT THE METRODOME
GREEN BAY 27, MINNESOTA 11

Twenty seconds can be a long time in a football game, especially when it involves Green Bay quarterback Brett Favre. Unfortunately, Favre probably felt like he was in a scene from the movie "Groundhog Day" after the events of this bizarre stay in the Twin Cities.

Minneapolis morning radio personality Lee Mroszak, better known to KQRS listeners as "The Cabe," aired a spot throughout the day of the game claiming that Favre had been in a hotel room with a woman who was not his wife. Mroszak pretended to be an employee of the Marriott City Center where the Packers were staying, he said. He knocked on a door he said was Favre's and a woman answered, saying the All-Pro was in the shower. She then slammed the door. The broadcaster admitted the fabrication the next day and was fired. The station apologized to Favre, his family, and the hotel for the hoax.

Said Favre later, "He got what he deserved. It never ceases to amaze me what people will do."

Sixty-four thousand fans inside the Metrodome and millions more during a "Monday Night Football" telecast were amazed again hours later.

Less than five minutes remained in the crucial tilt, and the Packers held a comfortable 20-3 cushion when the audience saw Green Bay Coach Mike Holmgren's emotions of several frustrating setbacks at Minnesota erupt.

On a Vikings punt, then backup wide receiver Bill Schroeder was penalized 15 yards for unnecessary roughness, which put the hosts at the Green Bay 47. As Schroeder reached the Packers' sideline, Holmgren grabbed him by the jersey and chewed him out.

"We talked about not getting goaded into things, and I was just reminding him of what he needed to do in that situation," Holmgren said in the *Journal-Sentinel's Packer Plus* magazine. "You've never seen me do it, and I probably shouldn't have done it. But this was a very important game, and I wanted to impress upon Bill and the rest of the team that you can't do that in that situation."

In-between all of the shenanigans, the Packers played a good football game against a quality opponent without suffering turf toe as they had done repeatedly during the past five visits to Minnesota.

Green Bay earned its first win for Holmgren at the unfriendly confines of the Metrodome, 27-11, as strong safety LeRoy Butler made 10 total tackles and defensive end Reggie White dominated with 2 1/2 sacks to lead the defense, and halfback Dorsey Levens led the offense with 108 yards rushing and two touchdowns.

The Packers improved to 10-3 and knocked the Vikings to 8-5 a week after trouncing the Cowboys to end their nightmarish losing skid against Dallas. Green Bay had lost five straight, the last four by a combined 17 points on the carpet to the Vikings, mainly because of a turnover deficit of 17-9. However, they turned the turnover tables this time, 2-0.

The visitors led 10-3 at halftime and 17-3 after three quarters. Favre connected with wide receiver Robert Brooks on an 18-yard strike to cap an 11-play, 86-yard drive late in the second quarter, one play after Minnesota's Corey Fuller dropped an apparent interception in the end zone.

Regardless, the Vikings never got going offensively. They entered the contest with the No. 1 unit in the league, but quarterback Brad Johnson left injured and ineffective, completing 15 of 30 attempts with an interception and 117 yards. Minnesota gained 99 yards rushing, but 39 came from reserve QB Randall Cunningham in mop-up duty.

The hosts, who entered the contest after consecutive road losses to

Detroit and the New York Jets, converted only 4 of 16 third-down plays and gave up six sacks.

Favre didn't really light it up but was an efficient 15 of 29 for 196 yards. He also didn't turn the ball over, and the offensive line allowed just one sack.

Green Bay then clinched their third straight Central Division title a week later with another big road victory, 17-6, at Tampa Bay.

2. MOSS, VIKINGS BURY PACKERS, WINNING STREAK
OCT. 5, 1998, AT GREEN BAY
MINNESOTA 37, GREEN BAY 24

A national television audience also witnessed this "Monday Night Football" game in which the Vikings smashed the Packers, snapping the hosts' 25-game home winning streak after both teams had entered with 4-0 records.

Green Bay was a seven-point favorite on a rainy night at Lambeau Field, but the cloudburst that drenched the Packers came in the form of rookie wide receiver Randy Moss from Marshall and veteran quarterback Randall Cunningham.

Moss caught only five passes, but he turned them into 190 yards, including touchdowns of 52 and 44 yards and gains of 41 and 46 against a bewildered, shorter, and less athletic Green Bay secondary.

Cunningham was hardly touched in the pocket, never sacked, as the Vikings offensive line did a stellar job against Reggie White and the Pack's defensive front. The former Philadelphia Eagle signal caller riddled the three-time defending Central Division champions for 20 completions in 32 attempts for four scores and 442 yards, the most ever against a Packer team.

Moss wasn't the only beneficiary: Cris Carter hauled in eight catches for 119 yards, and Jake Reed chipped in four receptions for 89 yards, topped by a 56-yard TD for Minnesota's first score.

Meanwhile, Green Bay's three-time MVP, Brett Favre, suffered one of his worst and most disappointing outings of his banner career. He completed 13 of 23 attempts for only 114 yards. He was intercepted three times, twice by strong safety Robert Griffith. Favre's 21-game streak of at least one touchdown pass also was broken (regular and postseason).

Minnesota outgained the Packers 545-319 and held the ball almost nine minutes longer as halfback Robert Smith contributed 78 yards rushing on 25 carries and scampered in from 24 yards out on a swing pass in the second quarter.

"I've learned that this team expects to win," Moss said in *Packer Plus*. "That's the atmosphere around here. Tonight we did what we were supposed to do."

Defensive leader LeRoy Butler registered 11 total tackles for the porous Packers. "It's embarrassing," Green Bay cornerback Tyrone Williams, toasted twice by Moss for scores, said in *Packer Plus*. "It's frustrating. When you get beat, you got to take it like a man, and tonight they beat us."

Packer wide receiver Antonio Freeman saw it the same way in his interview with *Packer Plus*.

"We lost the game. We lost at home. We lost in front of a huge national audience. We got whipped. It all hurts, but the great teams bounce back."

The Vikings went on to finish a great season, setting an NFL record for most points scored (556), while going 15-1 before losing to Atlanta in the NFC Championship game.

But on this night, they dominated their rivals on the road.

"This was the greatest night in my football career," said a rejuvenated Cunningham in *Packer Plus*. He went on to lead the league in passer rating while earning Player of the Year laurels. "They don't get beat here. Against the No. 1 defense in the league, to do what we did here is just a blessing."

Carter couldn't have agreed more, saying in *Packer Plus*, "To beat our No. 1 rivals on 'Monday Night Football' at Lambeau, it's great."

In a game that was 37-10 until backup quarterback Doug Pederson threw two late touchdown passes to somewhat mask Minnesota's dominance, the often forgotten Vikings defense held Favre without a TD toss for the fifth time in the series.

It was the most points the Vikings have scored on the road against Green Bay and their second-highest total in any game against the Packers.

The last game an opponent had scored more than the Vikings' 37 points at Lambeau Field was back in 1983, when Green Bay defeated the Washington Redskins, 48-47, in what's still the highest-scoring "MNF" game.

3. ERIC WHO? BLOWN COVERAGE SINKS PACKERS
SEPT. 26, 1993, AT THE METRODOME
MINNESOTA 15, GREEN BAY 13

Vikings quarterback Jim McMahon improved to 9-1 as a starter against Green Bay as the hosts claimed a victory after second-year cornerback Terrell Buckley's inexcusable blown coverage in the waning seconds.

Minnesota faced a third-and-10 situation from midfield with 14 seconds left on the clock and no timeouts remaining.

Anthony Carter lined up wide to the left side, Cris Carter was in the slot on the right, and little-known rookie Eric Guliford was on the far right. The play was designed for Anthony Carter to run 10 yards down field and then across the middle. Cris Carter ran a 20-yard down-and-out pattern to the right, while the 5-foot-8 Guliford, seeing his first action of the season, went straight down the right sideline as an anticipated decoy.

What was so amazing was that the Vikings had called the same thing two plays earlier. Green Bay, in a 4-2-5 defense and playing a four-deep zone, had stopped it perfectly. Buckley had followed Qadry Ismail on the deep route, while nickel back Corey Harris and safety Butler had blanketed Cris Carter, who caught the pass out of bounds.

Ismail said later that he had told McMahon after the play that Buckley didn't think the aging Brigham Young alumnus could throw deep. McMahon proved Buckley wrong, sort of, anyway.

Sprinting out to his right, the former Bear wobbled a pass down field. Guliford came back to the 10 to catch it and was knocked out of bounds by free safety Mike Prior at the 5 with six seconds left. Kicker Fuad Reveiz booted a 22-yard field goal as the stunned Packers looked on.

The unbelievable final seconds were made possible by earlier heroics from McMahon and Cris Carter. Minnesota started at its 17 and still faced a fourth-and-8 from its 19, having used up its timeouts. But the tandem hooked up for 19 yards to keep their faint hopes alive. Two completions and three incompletions set up the deciding play.

Buckley later said he just guessed wrong, afraid to give up a gain to Carter and set up Reveiz for what he thought would be a sure field goal; Reveiz had nailed one from 51 yards and just missed from 49.

He said that his comments about McMahon didn't happen like Ismail had reportedly remembered them. Buckley said in a *Packer Plus* story that the Vikings were still on their 20 and Ismail was standing at the Packer 10 waving his arms.

"I said, 'What you got your arm up for, he can't throw it that far. [McMahon] is on the 20. You show me a quarterback who can throw it 80 yards on the run."

It didn't matter because Green Bay fans, who never warmed up to the Florida State product after his rookie holdout the year before and his sometimes brash attitude, wanted Buckley's head on a platter after this one.

Minnesota had outgained the Packers by a modest 272-256 (including 107-106 rushing) before the McMahon-Guliford connection. Two Favre interceptions, 50 yards in penalties, and a dropped pass by tight end Jackie Harris in the end zone helped seal the Packers' fate as they lost to McMahon for the third time in the final seconds.

The Packers were numb to say the least.

"I've never had anything like that happen before, at least not a long pass like that," Reggie White said in *Packer Plus*.

"I thought we had the game won from the getty-up," Butler added. "You've just got to win those games. It's very frustrating. I don't know what you do."

"It's hard to describe the feeling you have when that happens," Holmgren told *Packer Plus*. "Every coach has it. All your energy is focused into the game. When it ends, there's not words to describe the feeling."

Disbelief also reigned on the other sideline, only it was the good kind.

"We got in a tough situation, but nobody panicked," stated McMahon, who told a *Packer Plus* reporter he played like an old woman up to that point. "I just heard a lot of screaming. Our guys were jumping around. Pretty good sign."

"All we needed was one big play," Cris Carter said in *Packer Plus*. "We kept telling each other in the huddle, we just needed one play."

They couldn't have asked for and gotten a better and more unpredictable one.

4. WHAT THE HELL'S GOING ON AROUND HERE?
NOV. 5, 1995, AT THE METRODOME
MINNESOTA 27, GREEN BAY 24

The Vikings' triumph was their fifth victory of four points or less in the series since 1992, including their third consecutive such win at the Metrodome, Mike Holmgren's annual nightmare.

Despite shuffling through three quarterbacks because of injuries, Green Bay still had an opportunity to give Holmgren his first win on the road against the Vikings. But third-stringer T.J. Rubley, subbing for the already sidelined Brett Favre and Ty Detmer, put his name right next to Terrell Buckley's among the Packers list of biggest gaffes in history.

With the score knotted at 24, the Packers faced third down and less than a yard to go from the Minnesota 38. Holmgren had called for a quarterback sneak, if for no other reason than to line up a potential game-winning field-goal attempt.

But Rubley audibled a pass play, effectively signing his own walking papers out of Green Bay. Under heavy pressure, he rolled right and threw a wounded duck that was tipped and eventually intercepted by former Packer linebacker Jeff Brady. The hosts then drove down field and Fuad Reveiz's 39-yard field goal won it as time expired on the Packers, and on Rubley.

The Packers were in a four-receiver set with one running back. But when Minnesota lined up with six men in the box against Green Bay's five blockers, Rubley thought the quarterback sneak wouldn't work despite center Frank Winters' pleading for him to stick with the call.

"The audible, I would do that again time after time," Rubley said in a *Packer Plus* article. "It was only third and a foot, but I felt it would be blocked. The audible doesn't bother me. It was the decision once I audibled that really bothers me."

"I'm not a bad quarterback," he added. "I made a bad decision. There is a difference there. I'm anxious to get a chance to redeem myself."

That never happened, at least not in Green Bay.

Rubley gained the spotlight because Favre had badly sprained his left ankle, and Detmer, who was lost for the season, tore ligaments in his right thumb while landing hard on the turf.

It was a fitting end to a wild contest in which Green Bay left with other injuries to worry about, namely defensive ends Reggie White and Sean Jones. They collided while rushing Minnesota quarterback Warren Moon, White spraining a knee ligament and Jones suffering a concussion.

Favre completed 14 of 20 pass attempts before his injury in the second quarter. Unfortunately for him and the Packers, he tried to play on it and went 3-for-10 for 21 yards and two costly interceptions in the third quarter before giving way to Detmer again. One of Favre's interceptions set the Vikings up at the Green Bay 9-yard line, and the other was picked off in the end zone when he overthrew Mark Chmura, which proved to be a swing of 10 to 14 points on back-to-back series.

Favre finished 17 of 30 for 177 yards. Detmer completed 8 of 15 tries for 81 yards, hooking up with Chmura for a touchdown and two-point conversion to tie things at 24 before his season ended.

Then Rubley fumbled his first snap from center at Green Bay's 20. However, the Vikings returned the favor on the next play as Butler forced James Stewart to cough it up, which fellow safety George Teague recovered.

Minnesota blew another chance at victory when Reveiz's 42-yard boot was nullified by a penalty, thus forcing him to try again from 47 yards, which he missed.

Robert Brooks finished with nine catches for 120 yards for the Packers, while Cris Carter equaled his reception total for 91 yards to lead the Vikings. Defensively, LeRoy Butler led the Packers with 10 tackles, and linebacker Ed McDaniel recorded 14 for Minnesota.

The loss dropped Green Bay to 5-4 and into second place behind Chicago, but the Packers rebounded to win six of their final seven games to win the division for the first time since 1972. Meanwhile, the Vikings improved to 4-5 after the victory but floundered down the stretch to finish 8-8 and out of the playoffs.

5. PACKERS ALMOST BLOW 20-POINT, SECOND-HALF LEAD
OCT. 13, 1963, AT MINNESOTA
GREEN BAY 37, MINNESOTA 28

Green Bay won a thriller in its first road game after going 3-1 at home to start the campaign.

Minnesota scored two defensive touchdowns, one on a 47-yard interception return by cornerback Ed Sharockman and the other a 26-yard fumble return by linebacker Roy Winston.

Green Bay had outscored the Vikings 143-45 in their first four meetings, but it needed Hank Gremminger's 80-yard TD return of Herb Adderley's blocked field goal to secure the triumph with 1:48 remaining in a game that saw the Vikings rally from 24-7 halftime and 27-7 third-quarter deficits.

Bart Starr passed for 253 yards, including TDs to tight end Ron Kramer and running back Elijah Pitts, but the Packers lost four of seven fumbles and threw two interceptions. Three of Green Bay's scores were set up by turnovers in Minnesota territory.

The clubs combined for 773 yards of offense, 522 of them through the air. But the game wasn't decided until Herb Adderley's maneuver in which he switched from the left to the right side of the formation. The Vikings' end blocker took Willie Davis, leaving Adderley to get around the corner unscathed, blocking the kick with his facemask.

As for the low-key Gremminger, it proved to be his only NFL touchdown in 10 years with Green Bay (1956–65).

"I was just in the right spot," Gremminger said afterward to a Green Bay *Press-Gazette* reporter. "I'm not the primary rusher in that situation. I'm just there to see that they kick and don't pass."

Adderley said his role was vindication for what he called a poor game.

"I had the worst day I've had on pass defense since I've been playing regular," the former Michigan State star said in a *Press-Gazette* story. "I felt real bad about it and I was hoping I could do something to make up for it."

"The man who holds the ball (Fran Tarkenton) had his back to me, so I changed to the right side, Adderley continued. "I wanted him to see me . . . hoped it would rattle him. I actually thought Willie Davis, who was next to me, was going to go in. I thought the corner man would block me, but he didn't, he took Willie, so I went right around him. He never touched me. The ball hit me right across the faceguard. I didn't see Hank running with it until he was 50 yards downfield. I was on the ground when he got the ball."

The decisive play was only the last of many fireworks that day.

Tom Moore connected with Max McGee on a 19-yard halfback option pass for the first score, Starr combined with Ron Kramer from 9 yards and Jerry Kramer booted the first of his three field goals for a 17-0 margin.

Sharockman's theft and return trimmed it to 17-7, but Elijah Pitts' 7-yard catch and Jerry Kramer's second field goal increased the Packers' seemingly comfortable cushion to 27-7. Winston's score made it 27-14 after three quarters, and Jerry Kramer's final boot made it 30-14 before the Vikings made things interesting.

Tarkenton, who finished 14 for 23 for 282 yards, combined with Paul Flatley on a 29-yard score and led Minnesota on a 60-yard TD drive after a McGee fumble to trim the hosts' deficit to 30-28.

Minnesota got the ball again at its 42 after a 24-yard punt return by Billy Butler. Tarkenton and Flatley hooked up for a huge 45-yard gain to the Green Bay 10. However, three running plays netted 7 yards, forcing Fred Cox to try the deciding field goal. Ray Nitschke then thwarted any heroics in the final seconds with an interception.

"That was a great play by Herb Adderley," said Vince Lombardi in the Green Bay paper. "I was thinking if they were going to score, I hope they score right now. Then there would still be time for us to come back.

"I'm not taking anything away from the Vikings, but we gave them the game," Lombardi added. "And they're a darned scrappy bunch. They don't need much."

His counterpart, Norm Van Brocklin, also lamented his team's generosity.

"We gave them 24 points in the first half, but the kids just wouldn't quit," he said in the *Press-Gazette*.

Both teams squandered scoring opportunities. Safety Chuck Lamson, who also had a fumble recovery for the Vikings, picked off Starr at the Minnesota 2. Cox missed a 28-yard field goal.

The teams combined to complete 34 of 58 passes, with the Packers' Boyd Dowler latching onto seven for 93 yards. Meanwhile, Green Bay won the rushing battle 153-98, led by second-year back Earl Gros' 15 carries for 67 yards. He was subbing for Jim Taylor, who injured his leg in the second quarter.

The victory kept the 4-1 Packers one game behind the undefeated Bears in the Western Conference standings.

6. SO CLOSE, AND YET SO FAR
DEC. 27, 1992, AT MINNESOTA
MINNESOTA 27, GREEN BAY 7

Mike Holmgren's surprising Packers entered the season finale with a six-game winning streak, which started with a thrilling 27-24 verdict over the Reggie White–led Philadelphia Eagles.

The Los Angeles Raiders upset the Redskins a day earlier, so all Green Bay had to do was defeat Minnesota to gain a playoff berth. Despite driving 56 yards to take a 7-0 advantage in the first quarter, the visiting Packers suffered their first of many disheartening losses on the Metrodome turf during Holmgren's regime.

Current ESPN football analyst Sean Salisbury passed for a career-high 292 yards without star receiver Cris Carter as the Vikings, who clinched the Central Division crown with an 11-5 mark in Dennis Green's first season, won going away.

Green Bay allowed a season-high 447 yards, including 165 on the ground, as it finished with only its second winning record since the strike year of 1982. But the Packers' offense was even more dismal, accumulating season lows in plays (49), net yards (211), first downs (13), and rushing yards (29).

Favre threw three interceptions, while the visitors managed only 11 yards in 11 carries until the final 20 seconds of the game. Favre failed to reach 200 yards passing for a third straight outing after shattering a team record with 11 in a row before that.

One bright spot for the Packers was wide receiver Sterling Sharpe, who broke Art Monk's National Football League season record for receptions with 108 (he surpassed that mark with 112 the next year). But his six catches gained only 45 yards.

Tight end Steve Jordan hauled in a 13-yard strike from Salisbury to tie the score at 7 after one quarter, then Reveiz booted two field goals and reserve tight end Mike Tice scampered down the sideline virtually uncovered for a score and a 20-7 halftime cushion.

Minnesota put the game out of reach in the third quarter when Terry Allen plunged in from 1 yard out to cap a 65-yard drive that was highlighted by Salisbury's 51-yard pitch to Reed.

Allen finished with 20 carries for 100 yards, and former San Francisco great Roger Craig chipped in 54 yards on 17 attempts.

Apparently some Vikings had extra motivation despite sewing up the division crown the week before, mostly courtesy of Chicago coach Mike Ditka.

"Our guys were a little ticked off because everyone from Mike Ditka on down seemed to think that Green Bay was the best team in our division," said then Minnesota defensive coordinator Tony Dungy in *Packer Plus*. "They wanted to demonstrate something different."

"I'm surprised that Ditka, being a former player, a guy who's been in the league as long as he has, would make a comment like that," Vikings middle linebacker Jack Del Rio added. "He knows that the games are won on the field, and I've never known him to be a Packer fan, so that kind of surprises me, even though I think the hidden message was to try and put us down."

The game also set the tone for the rest of the 1990s: lots of pushing and shoving and trash talking.

Green Bay players were upset and said that Minnesota tried to show them up late in the game, using a halfback option pass with seven minutes left and then throwing deep with 35 seconds remaining.

Vikings' offensive coordinator Jack Burns said he kept calling pass plays because the Packers continued to blitz.

"I think this rivalry that already existed just intensified a little more after today," Green Bay tight end Jackie Harris said in *Packer Plus*.

Packer middle linebacker Brian Noble agreed: "In my eyes, that doesn't show a whole lot of class, to go up top [leading] 27-7," he told *Packer Plus*. "But like I said, what goes around comes around. We'll have our day."

However, this wasn't one of them, said Green Bay nose tackle John Jurkovic.

"Minnesota came out and played a better ball game," he said in *Packer Plus*. "They were the better team on this particular Sunday."

7. COREY'S CATCH CAPS LAST-MINUTE HEROICS
SEPT. 26, 1999, AT GREEN BAY
GREEN BAY 23, MINNESOTA 20

This was the eighth time since Dennis Green took over the Vikings in '92 that the matchup was decided by a touchdown or less.

The contest was tied at 10 at halftime and at 13 after three quarters before Favre and his receivers pulled out another last-minute miracle.

Green Bay and Minnesota entered with 1-1 marks, but the Packers and a crowd of 59,868 wanted to avenge the 1998 debacle at Lambeau that featured Moss' national coming-out party. They weren't disappointed.

The decisive drive started with 1:51 left, the Packers trailing 20-16 and 77 yards from paydirt. Favre drilled a 22-yard strike to wide receiver Corey Bradford on the first play and then hit halfback Dorsey Levens for 10 more and another first down.

Three more completions moved the Packers to Minnesota's 23, but they had no timeouts remaining and faced a fourth-and-one play. Favre aligned his weapons and took the snap from Winters with 17 seconds left, looking to his right and then lofting a pass to the streaking Bradford in the end zone on the left side to give the Packers another heart-stopping win in the final seconds, after opening the year with a 28-24 win over Oakland.

Favre completed 24 of 39 attempts for 304 yards, but more important had no interceptions while being sacked only twice.

Levens gained 49 yards on 18 carries, but his skills out of the backfield made the big difference. He caught nine passes for 84 yards, and Schroeder pulled in five more for 85 yards.

Minnesota's offense contributed a few big plays as Jake Reed and Cris Carter combined for 10 catches and 193 yards, 108 by Reed. However, Cunningham didn't have the same magic as in 1998. He threw for 244 yards on 18 of 32, but he had two interceptions, both by rookie cornerback Antuan Edwards, one of which he returned 26 yards for a touchdown.

Green Bay doubled Moss most of the game, forcing Minnesota to run 29 times compared to 34 passes. Robert Smith churned out 85 yards on 21 attempts, but Moss was limited to two grabs for 13 yards, and 10 of them came on his TD that gave the Vikings a 20-16 lead to cap an 80-yard drive with 1:56 left.

The Vikings chugged away for drives of 14, 15, and 13 plays, but the last two yielded only field goals and the first was stopped when Cunningham was thrown for a 4-yard loss on a third-and-goal play from the Green Bay 1. However, Packers' linebacker George Koonce was flagged for unsportsmanlike conduct, giving the visitors another set of downs that led to a 7-0 margin.

As for the game-ending fireworks, Moss said it wasn't like No. 4 hadn't turned defeat into victory before.

"I wasn't jumping up and down," Moss said in *Packer Plus* after the Vikings lost for the first time in a game in which he had scored. "I was happy we had gone 80-some yards to score, but I knew we had to give it back to the magician, and he worked his magic."

Minnesota cornerback Jimmy Hitchcock didn't see anything magical about the play; he was the one Bradford blew by on the winning play. And despite the disappointment and being chastised by teammates, Hitchcock didn't avoid the microphone after the game.

"I dug up underneath him," Hitchcock said in *Packer Plus*. "I was up in his face, and then I saw the ball in the air. It's a big loss. I take responsibility for it. I'm a corner. It happens."

Bradford, who finished with four catches for 72 yards, got to enjoy a Lambeau Leap after his shining moment.

"I thought he was going to check the out route or something, catch it and then get right out of bounds," Bradford told *Packer Plus*. "I never thought we were running that audible."

As for his part, Favre said in *Packer Plus* that it was a storybook ending.

"I'm just a big kid out there," Favre said. "That touchdown pass, I've dreamed about that a million times when I was a kid. But I don't think Corey was in that dream."

It was the first time the Vikings had been knocked below the .500 mark during the regular season since October 22, 1995, when Green Bay whipped them, 38-21, to leave Minnesota at 3-4.

8. THE MAD SCRAMBLER DOES IT AGAIN
OCT. 4, 1964, AT GREEN BAY
MINNESOTA 24, GREEN BAY 23

A blurb in the *Green Bay Press-Gazette* the day before this showdown made this prediction: "Perfect weather is on tap, but punters, passers, kickers and ladies wearing fancy hats are hereby warned that there may be fresh northeasterly winds."

Something much more unusual would blow through because, even though the Metrodome wouldn't open for another 18 years, the Packers found a way to lose another bizarre contest to their rivals with the clock winding down and victory in their grasp.

Minnesota rallied for its first win in the series and its only triumph in the teams' initial 10 meetings.

Fran Tarkenton used his scrambling feet and right arm to do in the Packers, a win that helped Norm Van Brocklin's expansion franchise to its first winning season (8-5-1), which tied the Packers for second in the Western Conference.

Tarkenton and his teammates faced a fourth-and-22 from their 35-yard line. No. 10 couldn't have drawn up what ensued any better had he been scratching it out in the sand on the old playground.

Tarkenton eluded future Hall of Fame defensive end Willie Davis more than once, finally spotting an open Tom Hall. He let loose and thought he had a completion, but his tight end, Gordy Smith, leaped to grab the aerial. Smith gained another 10 yards and got out of bounds to stop the clock.

Fred Cox turned what would have been a 23-21 setback into a victory with a 27-yard field goal, evening both teams' records at 2-2.

Tarkenton explained what happened in the huddle and during the amazing play in his 1976 book *Tarkenton*.

"I could see them peeling back toward the end zone as I was about to call the play," he wrote. "We just didn't have anything in our playbook that can cover a fourth-and-22 against a three-man line. Nobody does. So I just said, 'All the receivers go down about 25 yards. Pick a spot and turn around. I'm going to run around until I find somebody. Good luck. On two, break.' Just like that. Can you imagine? Super sophisticated professional football.

"I got the ball and pretended to drop back, but I was really looking which way I should break, right or left," Tarkenton continued. "I headed right. Willie Davis was chasing me. When I got to the sidelines nobody was open, so I turned and went the other way. I got someplace near the center of the field, way back, and I started diagonaling back toward the right sideline. I could feel Davis. I actually could because on one swipe he got a piece of my heel.

"I looked downfield and Lord, there was Tom Hall open on the sidelines at about the Packer 25. I had a lot of momentum coming upfield and I just threw the hell out of the ball. It was right on the money to Hall. It was zooming in on him right at the numbers. But just before it got to him I saw a form come flailing into the line of flight. I just groaned. I said, 'No, Gordy, no.' But up he went and he made a sensational leaping catch, ran another 10 yards and out of bounds. Freddie Cox came in and kicked a field goal and we won. Vince Lombardi just stood there. It was as though somebody just told him the pope was Presbyterian."

"Amazing little fellow, isn't he?" Lombardi said in a *Press-Gazette* article. "We chased him out of the pocket every time. You can't do any more than that. He threw the ball when an ordinary quarterback wouldn't. He's a great scrambler."

Linebacker Lee Roy Caffey wholeheartedly agreed.

"You couldn't get hold of him. We played him twice when I was with the Eagles last year, and he wasn't the ballplayer he is now," he said in the *Press-Gazette*.

Tarkenton rushed six times for 49 yards, but Bill Brown's two one-yard dives provided the Vikings' scores in the second quarter. However, Starr connected with Dowler for a 50-yard pass and then Paul Hornung scooted in from a yard out to cut the visitors' deficit to 14-13. Linebacker Rip Hawkins had blocked Hornung's first extra-point attempt, which proved to be the difference for the second time in four games for Green Bay (it had lost 21-20 to Baltimore two weeks earlier under similar circumstances).

Starr and Dowler again worked their magic, this time a 32-yarder for Green Bay's first lead, 20-14. But Tarkenton found Hall from 6 yards out for a 21-20 Minnesota margin after three quarters.

Hornung drilled a 20-yard field goal for a 23-21 Packer advantage with 4:52 remaining to set up Tarkenton's Houdini act.

Taylor and Jerry Kramer missed the contest, and the battle of attrition knocked Adderley and Henry Jordan out of Green Bay's defensive arsenal, while the Vikings played without top ball toter Tommy Mason.

The teams combined for 663 yards, 38 first downs, and the usual number of fisticuffs.

Minnesota ran 68 plays compared to Green Bay's 50, including a 48-24 margin in running plays. Hall caught seven passes for 103 yards, while Dowler led Green Bay with 96 yards on five receptions.

On defense, Berlin, Wisconsin, native and former Packer Billy Butler received a $500 bonus from Van Brocklin for his performance.

But those in attendance should have known the game would come down to something extraordinary: Acrobats and clowns from the Ringling Bros. & Barnum and Bailey Circus had performed before the contest.

All-Pro Davis said in the *Press-Gazette*, "I don't know what you do against the guy [Tarkenton]. He's the best I've seen at scrambling. The best I've seen in my life."

9. TITLETOWN ENJOYS ANOTHER TITLE

DEC. 10, 1972, AT MINNESOTA

GREEN BAY 23, MINNESOTA 7

Talk of jinxes in this series didn't start with the Packers' sad plight in the Metrodome of the 1990s, as comments in the *Press-Gazette* before this important showdown attest. Minnesota had won eight of the past nine encounters.

"I definitely don't think there's a jinx involved," said Green Bay safety Al Matthews. "The strange part of it is, they have always played well at Green Bay and we've always played well in Minnesota. Since I joined the team in '70 we've only beaten them once, but every game we've played could have gone the other way."

Wide receiver Carroll Dale said the Vikings have had success because, like all quality teams, they usually find ways to win close games.

"There is no mystique about it," Dale said. "They're a good football team that tries to get the other team to make a mistake. That has been their winning formula."

The Packers had made a statement in a three-team title race with a 33-7 home victory over one contender, the Detroit Lions, a week earlier. They claimed the top prize for themselves with a dominating second half during this victory at the frigid Met against the third prospective playoff participant, ending the jinx label for one game.

The bruising tandem of 1,000-yard rusher John Brockington and his backfield mate MacArthur Lane did most of the damage as Green Bay's win clinched its only division crown between 1967 and 1995.

Almost 50,000 fans braved a game-time temperature of zero and wind-chill factor of minus 18 degrees.

Minnesota had kept the Packers' offense in the deep freeze in the first half. Green Bay was stymied for -1 yard in the first quarter and trailed 7-0 at the break when former Wisconsin Badger tight end Stu Voigt scored on a reverse in the second quarter.

But Lane's 37-yard rumble ignited Green Bay's second-half surge, which led to Chester Marcol's first field goal. The battering Lane finished with 19 carries for 99 yards and a touchdown as 214 of Green Bay's 270 yards came on the ground.

Green Bay, which entered as a four- to six-point underdog, held a plus 13 margin in giveaway-takeaway ratio coming in, and the Packers used several turnovers to turn the tide in their favor.

Outside linebacker Fred Carr returned a fumble 26 yards to the Vikings' 28 to set up quarterback Scott Hunter's one-yard dive and a 10-7 Green Bay lead. Then cornerback Willie Buchanon, later named the league's defensive rookie of the year, put the Packers 24 yards away on the final play of the third quarter with one of his two interceptions, which led to Lane's 3-yard TD run and a 17-7 cushion.

Three Minnesota penalties helped the Packers put the game out of reach: Punter Ron Widby was roughed, and then defensive tackle Alan Page was whistled twice for being off sides. Those miscues set up Marcol's second of three field goals, a 42-yarder with 5:42 remaining.

Buchanon's partner at cornerback, Ken Ellis, then returned an interception to the Minnesota 34. That led to another Lane scoring run, which was nullified by a penalty, setting up Marcol's 10-yarder with only 46 seconds left for the final margin and the division championship.

Veteran linebacker Dave Robinson knew one big reason why Green Bay's defense controlled most of this game.

"I've been in Green Bay for 10 years and never seen anybody tackle Fran Tarkenton three times in one game, but Big Cat [Clarence Williams] did it today," he told the *Press-Gazette*.

On the other side of the ball, the Packers' bread and butter, a strong offensive line and their vaunted running game, dominated the final 30 minutes.

"The championship overshadows my getting 1,000 yards for the second year in a row," said Brockington in the *Press-Gazette* after surpassing the coveted rushing plateau with 114 yards. "I wasn't aware of 1,000. I was thinking of getting first downs, eating up the clock and getting closer to that goal line."

Lane used the same approach, and that's why Green Bay earned its spot atop the Central.

"The atmosphere has to be right to have a winning ball club," Lane said in the Green Bay paper. "I'm convinced of that. These cats love each other here. That's what it takes. We started jelling right there in the second half. We knew what we had to do. We knew we had to get some points to take pressure off the defense."

Lane added that the title meant so much because only a few of the players, such as Ray Nitschke and Dave Robinson, had had previous chances to appreciate what the team had just accomplished.

Green Bay head coach Dan Devine, whose nightmarish rookie season in 1971 included a broken leg he suffered when players bowled him over on the sidelines in the first game, told the *Press-Gazette* that it was a fitting victory in a special year.

"We deserve the championship," he said. "There's been a heck of a lot of heartaches and hard work poured into the success of this season."

10. IMPROBABLE BOBBLE TURNS INTO IMMACULATE RECEPTION
NOV. 6, 2000, AT GREEN BAY
GREEN BAY 26, MINNESOTA 20 (OT)

It won an ESPY Award as most spectacular sports play of the year, and deservedly so. And only through modern replay technology could fans across America see how special and improbable it was.

Although they had to wait for replay officials to confirm it, Antonio Freeman's "immaculate deflection" catch and run gave the flailing Packers, 3-5 entering the "Monday Night Football" showdown, hope for a playoff run with the overtime victory.

Green Bay's offense approached the line of scrimmage with a third-and-4 situation from the Viking 43. The call was a slant, but Freeman signaled Brett Favre for a slant-and-go.

In the rain and swirling wind, the play appeared doomed. But pennies from heaven splashed down on the Packers. Minnesota cornerback

Cris Dishman tipped the ball with his right hand, it bounced off his shoulder and grazed off a sliding Freeman before the latter pulled it into his arms just inches above the ground.

He got up, dodged another Minnesota defender and scooted into the end zone, setting off a delirious Lambeau Field celebration despite the fact most people in attendance hadn't seen what actually happened.

It also eased some of the pain for Freeman, who had endured a troubling chain of events off the field and hadn't performed to his usual standards on the field.

"I have never been carried off the field before, but those guys know that I have been going through tough times and I needed a break," Freeman said in *Packer Plus*. "I got it tonight.

"I got an early Christmas gift, I guess," he added. "It fell in my hands. Who said football was all skill? Sometimes you need a little luck, and tonight we got our lucky bounces."

Lucky or not, it was a classic, even though the Vikings, who entered 7-1, dominated the statistical sheets. Minnesota finished with a 407-216 margin in total yards through four quarters. Robert Smith rushed for 122 yards on 24 carries, and Randy Moss, usually the receiving star when these rivals square off, took a back seat despite six catches for 130 yards.

The Vikings lost because of five turnovers, including three interceptions thrown by Daunte Culpepper, and 11 penalties for 129 yards. And don't forget the catch.

"Anytime you get into one of these rivalry games, you're going to have unusual plays like that," Vikings coach Dennis Green said in the next week's edition of *Packer Plus*. "And usually those unusual plays affect the outcome of the game."

Just a few minutes earlier, it appeared Minnesota had locked up the game as Gary Anderson lined up for a 33-yard field goal with eight seconds remaining. But holder Mitch Berger couldn't handle the wet ball, instead trying to throw for a score. Cornerback Tyrone Williams intercepted on the first-down play and forced the extra period.

Berger said he asked for a dry ball but didn't get one, which he should have expected on the road, especially against Green Bay.

The Packers, who turned the Vikings' generosity into only three points all game, took advantage of their final shot. Bill Schroeder hauled in a 22-yard gain on a third-and-10 play to put the ball at the Minnesota 49. Three plays later, Favre, Dishman, and Freeman became forever linked in one of the most incredible events in the league's history.

However, fans probably forgot most of what led up to the final exhilarating series.

Anderson and Green Bay's Ryan Longwell exchanged field goals, and then the action kicked into high gear later in the second quarter—literally. Minnesota wide receiver Cris Carter kicked Packer cornerback Mike McKenzie after an incompletion on a third-and-19 play. McKenzie and several other Green Bay defenders surrounded the All-Pro, who was still sprawled out on the soggy grass. McKenzie was whistled for an unsportsmanlike conduct penalty.

The Vikings gladly accepted the 15 yards and an automatic first down. They used a 22-yard run from Robert Smith and a 42-yard pass from Culpepper to Moss to set up Carter's 12-yard TD and a 10-3 lead.

The NFL kicked back at Carter, slapping him with a $5,000 fine a few days later.

"It [the fine] was justified," Carter said in the *Minneapolis Star-Tribune*. "It was just something that happened, that's all."

Green Bay responded with a six-play, 87-yard march. Freeman found a crease for a 33-yard reception before Dishman was flagged for pass interference, setting the Packers up at the 6. Then Favre, about to be sacked, zipped an underhanded pass to halfback Ahman Green for a 5-yard score to tie it again. Culpepper completed passes of 33 and 22 yards to Moss and Smith, respectively, to move Anderson within range for a 48-yard field goal as time expired in the first half.

McKenzie's 26-yard interception return was the only turnover the hosts capitalized on as Longwell knotted things at 13 with a 31-yard field goal. But Smith broke feeble tackle attempts by Tod McBride and LeRoy Butler, turning a 3-yard flat pass into a 45-yard TD and a 20-13 lead.

But the wild third quarter wasn't over yet. Allen Rossum sprinted 90 yards with the ensuing kickoff return, and Green bulled in from 2 yards out to force the fourth tie before a scoreless final quarter.

Still, all of the players' attention was focused on the game-winner, and who could blame them.

"I saw it on the field, and I couldn't believe he caught it," Ahman Green said in *Packer Plus*. "I saw the replay, and it was obvious he did catch it. It's one of those things that can happen but is still hard to believe."

As for Favre, the gunslinger had shot mostly blanks during the second half but came up with a bull's-eye when it counted. He was just lucky he was using buckshot on the last play the way his bullet bounced around.

"I was standing there waiting and I hear, 'Brett'" he said in the *Packer Plus* article. "I knew it was Free. When I looked out he kind of gave me the signal, and I kind of nodded my head. Your star player wants the ball, give it to him. He made the play. I don't even know if you can call it a play. That was remarkable, unbelievable.

"I run down there and jumped on him, and during all of the mayhem I kind of whispered to him, 'Hey, did you catch it?' When he responded, it was actually Donald Driver I was asking. I had the wrong guy. Donald said, 'I don't know if he caught it.' We were hugging and kissing and everything else. It felt good for a while. I was just hoping they didn't overturn it."

CHAPTER SEVEN

CHEESEHEADS AND PURPLE FANATICS

Sharing the same last name means nothing in this rivalry,
as family feuds break out two weekends every year.

"THE FUNNIEST THING I've ever seen was about four or five years ago," said Larry Primeau, "when this guy comes walking through the parking lot wearing this huge gorilla suit and carrying a cage with a Viking inside it with the gold locks and helmet. It's hard to explain, but the upper part of the gorilla and the Viking guy's legs were fake, but this man was the upper torso inside the cage and his legs were the gorilla's legs. It looked about seven feet tall. I had to get some pictures of that. I haven't seen it since. That was the most creative Packer-Viking thing I've ever seen."

That's saying something for Primeau, a guy known as "The Packalope" because he wears a vintage Green Bay football helmet mounted with antlers from a 10-point buck that he bagged.

The De Pere resident is a mechanical engineer at Kimberly-Clark Corporation in Neenah, but he's become famous for his Packer van topped with a huge chunk of Wisconsin cheese and tailgating festivities before home games in the Lambeau Field parking lot.

"I don't know how this all started, I think I did it as a joke," said Primeau of his most recognizable apparel besides the No. 64 jersey he always dons as a personal campaign to get former Green Bay great Jerry Kramer elected to the NFL Hall of Fame. "People kept coming up and asking to take pictures and it kinda evolved and snowballed from there. It's been a fixture at my tailgate parties ever since."

Primeau got his moniker in 1990 after his wife, Sue (Mrs. Lope), watched an episode of "America's Funniest Home Videos" that featured a regular skit about a creature that was half jack rabbit and half antelope, thus jackalope and Packalope.

The original piece of work sported six points, but that one is sitting in the Hall of Fame in Canton, Ohio, where he also was named a member in January 1999, one of 31 fans representing each of the league's franchises.

"As the Packers marched to the Super Bowl in 1996, I figured a championship team needed a championship rack, so I converted another helmet with the 10-pointer," Primeau said of an ensemble that was completed with Mardi Gras beads, fitting for the victory in New Orleans, and a small wedge of you know what.

His late father, Lawrence, was a big Packers fan before the Primeaus moved from their native Wisconsin Rapids to Washington State for 10 years. But at age 16 they returned, and Larry moved to Green Bay. He says he'll never leave again.

"It's 10 minutes from my front door to my parking spot at Lambeau," Primeau said.

Speaking of homes, the affable 45-year-old has created a Packer shrine of sorts in his basement: lights, books, photographs, footballs, helmets, carpeting, anything and everything green and gold.

"I don't think there's an inch of space that isn't covered," Primeau said. "I'm constantly moving stuff around because I'm out of room already. I have a lot of things from the 1960s players because I respect them so much. This is where I go to get away. It's like heaven."

That fervor is displayed throughout the community and the Fox Valley because Primeau attends live radio and television talk shows throughout the season.

"I attend annual Alumni Association dinners, the Fantasy Camp luncheons, and our big tailgate cookout for work," he said. "I get all of these pictures taken with the players and get them autographed. Then I donate a bunch of my memorabilia to the telethon for St. Jude's Children's Hospital [in Tennessee] and to local charities. My wife had cancer, so I try to give back what I can."

Primeau's contributions are obvious because his tailgating gatherings are among the most popular places to be and fashion trendsetters whether it's Packer green or deer hunting orange.

"I bought the van and painted it green and gold, and then a friend of mine painted a mural of Lambeau Field on one wall inside," he said. "I've got a home stereo hooked up to a 1,000-watt generator and customized five or six CDs on my home computer with all kinds of Packer tunes. That way I don't have to keep going in and out of the van. Besides, I can't fit my helmet in the door to change them."

Such is life for this die-hard fan. Primeau, who attended his first game at Lambeau in 1974, was on the waiting list for season tickets since 1973. He's lucky because he was about No. 3,500 out of more than 50,000 before moving up considerably when renovations are done and the seating capacity at the venerable stadium increases.

"I would buy my tickets from an older couple who didn't use them, so I got to every game, the Milwaukee and Green Bay packages," he said. "My dad was always a huge Packers fan and went to games, and I guess it got in my blood from watching them on TV as a kid."

The Packers recruited Primeau as one of the leading players during their Team Lambeau campaign for the $295 million stadium project. Brown County residents voted yes, by a 53 to 47 percent margin, for a sales tax to help build the project in a referendum held September 12, 2000.

Primeau is glad that battle is over. However, the twice-annual confrontations against Minnesota put him in the fighting mood all over again.

"I remember back in the '60s, watching Dave Robinson chasing Fran Tarkenton and wondering why in the heck can't they catch him," Primeau said. "It was so frustrating to watch our linebackers and defensive linemen running all over the field. I wanted to jump into the TV set and get my hands on him.

"And in the last seven or eight years the Vikings have had incredible luck," Primeau added. "I don't know why that is, but they just throw the ball up in the air and come down with it every time, or they seem to come up with every fumble. And Cris Cater, it was so irritating to watch him whine about wanting to get every call against our DBs, and that's what added to the rivalry for me."

However, Primeau and his other Green Bay faithful enjoyed the 2000 season because the pigskin bounced their way twice as the Packers swept the Vikings for only the second time since 1988.

"That year's Monday night game was the most unbelievable, with Freeman's catch, which we call the 'immaculate deflection,'" he said. "It used to be the Packers and Bears because Mike Ditka was in Chicago and Forrest Gregg was here, but this has taken over. And to beat them twice . . ."

Primeau said it goes with the territory, but he knows good and bad fans from both sides of the fence.

"A guy at work is a huge Vikings fan, but after last year [2000] he didn't dish out much because he knew it would come back at him tenfold," Primeau said. "I couldn't believe after they lost to the Giants in the NFC Championship game, all of the e-mails picking on the Vikings. We were up at the Mayo Clinic for Sue's surgery, and all of the nurses were dressed up in purple smocks and everything. But when Minnesota got beat it was like nobody was around. We saw signs in people's yards to [Coach] Dennis Green that said, 'Thanks for nothing.'

"Man, we waited 30 years [between Super Bowls]," he added. "They're not all that way because I know some great Vikings fans, but some of them are so obnoxious and arrogant. They come over here thinking they're going to win all of the time. That's why it was so nice to beat them twice that year."

One person who had to swallow those setbacks was Jerrod Valley, a Pulaski native and Vikings fan who lives in New Franken, east of Green Bay.

"Some years are harder to live around here than others, and those two losses were tough," said Valley, a science teacher at Green Bay Preble High, whose school colors are, you guessed it, green and gold. "I have a Vikings helmet on my desk, and when my students first came in they'd ask what that's all about. The first seven games [in 2000] the Packers weren't doing so well, so I kept razzing them. I know when Minnesota loses I'll have 120 kids who won't keep their mouths shut, but I have a fun time rooting for the Vikings, even in Packer country."

Like most football fans, Valley's genes and environment gave him little choice as to which team he'd cheer for.

"I was born in 1969 and was growing up when Minnesota had lots of talent and was going to Super Bowls and the Packers were down," Valley said. "I got a Fran Tarkenton jersey when I was a kid and always loved watching him throw deep to Ahmad Rashad and Sammy White, which was very similar to [Cris] Carter and [Randy] Moss today. I remember Matt Blair, Alan Page, and Carl Eller, and their success hooked me.

"Then in the late '80s, I was a big Tommy Kramer fan, and the Vikings had the great defenses with Keith Millard and Chris Doleman," Valley added. "I was going to college at the University of Wisconsin and lived with a bunch of die-hard Packer fans from the Milwaukee area, so it was a big rivalry for us."

Valley said his wife, Joan, tries to remain neutral whenever possible, but he's not going to hold his breath about their two sons.

"I still have one of those little old Viking helmets that's full of green and gold scars from playing with the neighborhood kids," Valley said. "It took quite a beating. But our son, Noah, will be a Packer fan because I can't put him through what I went through. He cheers for Brett Favre, so we got him a No. 4 jersey. And then we've got Carter, so . . .

"I used to teach at Green Bay West, and one time I bet the students that if the Vikings lost I'd wear a Favre jersey for a day," Valley added. "So I had to buy one; it's still hanging in my closet."

Just in case it comes in handy down the road.

However, Valley has had his share of victorious moments of late, especially when the Vikings roared into a soggy Lambeau Field in 1998 with the teams tied for first place at 4-0 and atop the Central Division.

"Not too many Packer fans expected them to lose, so I took some ribbing during the tailgate party and stuff," he said. "I really enjoyed it because they all look at us Viking fans as being fair-weather, but Randy Moss had a great game, it was outside and it was miserable and raining. There were a lot of Packer fans who cleared out early, and that made it the most memorable game because I never expected to see something like that."

Valley said he's accepted the fact he's a minority in the land of Curly Lambeau and Vince Lombardi. He says it's OK for fans to agree to disagree, which he does occasionally.

"I went to two games in Minnesota in the late '80s, both nonconference games because they were easier to get tickets for," Valley said. "The Metrodome is a terrible place to watch a game. My seats were high up and awful. I wish I would have had the chance to see the old Met. I think the majority of Viking fans would like to see them playing outside.

"But I hate it when people complain about how guys like Cris Carter whine to get their way," he said. "I think he's absolutely wonderful and that what he does is 100 percent competing. You also see Favre doing the same thing when he's missing a bunch of his passes. That's like anybody else. I think a lot of the antics you've seen in more recent years are because they have respect for each other and it has only increased the rivalry."

Valley takes solace in knowing that he's lonely, but not alone.

"I run into Viking fans once in awhile, most of them transplants who grew up in Minnesota, or kids in my classes whose parents are fans and they moved to this area," he said. "And Joan teaches with a big Vikings fan."

You could have said that about Cheryl Hobbs, but not anymore.

She and her husband, Walter, have retired to her native Tomahawk after spending 23 years in the Twin Cities and five more in Green Bay. When it comes to which football flag she waves proudly every fall, she no longer has any doubts.

That became apparent after her stay in Titletown, which she proved while writing a story that she submitted to the *Minneapolis Star-Tribune*. Here are some of her observations that were published in the Sunday, November 5, 2000, edition, one day before the Vikings and Packers squared off on "Monday Night Football" at Lambeau Field.

"I knew Green Bay was a football town, but I didn't know it was crazed until I moved there from Minnesota in 1995," she wrote. "When I moved to Green Bay I was a Viking fan. It wasn't long before I changed my allegiance. As a Viking fan I'd been tolerated, but as a new Packer fan, I was accepted. The Packers were the only common denominator. I could have been a madam or a swindler; whatever else I might be was not important.

"I knew I had transformed when I went to the paint store to buy stain for the screen porch," her article continued. "All they had were shades of brown and gray. 'I need green,' I said. 'Not just any green, but Packer Stadium green.' The clerk knew exactly what I meant."

Hobbs said she wasn't always a football fan, but she got caught up in the game and a city's love for its team.

"I was a Viking fan but found myself rooting for them except when they played the Packers, and I didn't quite know what to do as far as my loyalties," she said in a telephone interview. "But I switched when I saw the spirit during the 1996 season and the Super Bowl. It was quite a phenomenon. It was the food, the clothes, the cars, people decorating their houses. My granddaughter was 2 years old, and you should have seen the day care center. It was such a contrast. I didn't see that in Minnesota, at least not like in Green Bay."

So Hobbs jumped on the Packers bandwagon and hasn't left.

"My sister-in-law was a Viking fan, so we started getting into the rivalry and decorating our home and making a big deal about it," Hobbs said. "We had all of our family over, and they've all become Packer fans."

You won't find Brian Maas jumping on anything, unless it's ridiculing a Green Bay player who's warming up nearest his front-row seats in the Metrodome.

"I enjoy engaging the opposing team's players in friendly discussions about their play, mothers, lack of certain chromosomes, etc.," the Minnesota season ticketholder said.

A good example was the November 22, 1998, contest in Minneapolis in which the Vikings virtually sewed up the division crown with a 28-

14 triumph. One Packer became the center of Maas' attention, as in veteran center Frank Winters.

"Jimmy Hitchcock intercepted a Favre pass and returned it 58 yards for a score in the first quarter, and Randy Moss caught eight passes for 153 yards, including a 49-yarder," Maas said. "But the game was memorable for another reason. I got into it with Winters by telling him he, of all the cheap shots in the NFL today, he is the king. As two officials walk by, I tell them to watch Winters as he tends to hold, chop-block and hit players in the back after the whistle because he's too much of a girl to take them on face-to-face.

"Winters hears this and starts mouthing off to me," Maas continued. "I successfully got into his head, so I sit down, my work done. Winters went on to have numerous false starts and holding calls in the game. At one point he had two false starts in a row."

Like most of the players, Maas is more subdued when it's not game day. He is a pharmacist for Merck-Medco. He grew up in Jamestown, North Dakota, and graduated from North Dakota State University in 1984. Maas then worked in greater Washington D.C. and in Texas before settling in the Minneapolis suburb of Plymouth in 1990.

But his love for the Norsemen was kindled long before that.

"One of my earliest memories comes from when the Vikings won the National Football League championship in January 1970 by beating the Cleveland Browns, 27-7," Maas said. "I remember quarterback Joe Kapp running out of the pocket on a pass play. Browns linebacker Jim Houston charged forward to try and sack Kapp. Unlike QBs of today, Kapp didn't try to slide. He didn't try to run out of bounds. Kapp headed straight for Houston and tried to hurdle him. Kapp's knee hit Houston square on the chin and knocked him out of the game. I can still picture Kapp on the sidelines laughing. I've been a die-hard fan ever since."

That zeal was recognized in January 1999 when Maas joined Primeau in the Hall of Fame as the Vikings top fanatic. Maas' notoriety earned him a guest visit on Bill Maher's "Politically Incorrect" show.

Maas said that Minnesota has enjoyed awesome rivalries against Detroit and Chicago and in more recent years against the Tony Dungy–led Tampa Bay Buccaneers. However, he agreed that none have enjoyed the consistency of the Vikings vs. the Packers.

"The Packer rivalry certainly heated up during the '90s," he said. "That can really be accounted to both teams battling for divisional crowns and being at the top of their games. The only thing missing was a Vikings-Packers playoff game. Everyone thought Green Bay would be making a trip to Minnesota for a divisional playoff game in 1998 before Steve Young made a dramatic touchdown pass to take the rug out from under the Packers. I'll never forgot the 'deer-in-the-headlights' look of Brett Favre on the sidelines.

"But the intensity also heated up for players on the field," Maas added. "Corey Fuller's vicious, yet legal, hit on Antonio Freeman in the 1996 season has been rated by many Vikings fans as the hit of the decade. But Fuller's illegal poking of Winters' eye set the stage for several blood feud games where late hits from both sides were rampant."

Maas said he favors many of the older Viking players such as Kapp and Dave Osborn, a fellow North Dakotan. But the most memorable Green Bay-Minnesota skirmishes have come in the last 10 years.

"I don't remember any of the games from the '60s or '70s, and because I was in Washington D.C. or Texas during the '80s I didn't get any Vikings-Packers games on TV. So my most memorable games occurred during the '90s."

Two in particular stand out. September 26, 1993, the Vikings' 15-13 improbable victory after Jim McMahon's heave to little-known Eric Guliford:

"I remember the chant '94 East' being yelled through the dome as Packers fans departed for the exits."

And October 5, 1998, the 37-24 Monday night massacre at Lambeau that ended the Packers' 25-game home winning streak: "This was the first time I went to the airport to greet the team upon its return. I was so pumped that even when I got home about 2 a.m. I still couldn't sleep. Instead, I got online and talked about the game on several Vikings discussion boards. I went to work on 30 minutes of sleep. The whole day was spent terrorizing the only two Packers fans in my office. One went home early complaining of stomach pains."

Maas has been a major instigator in resuming the traditional tailgating that has helped put Green Bay on the map and used to be a fixture before the Vikings moved indoors.

"I have been hosting tailgates since 1996," he said. "Before that there was no legal tailgating allowed at Metrodome games, mostly due to all the parking lots being indoor ramps. I worked with then Vikings marketing director, Stew Widdess, to allow two outdoor lots along Washington Avenue to become official tailgate lots. It's been a huge success.

"For a noon game, I'm usually up by 4:45 a.m. and down to the lot setting up by 6:30. I've had Vikings fans join us from 37 states, as well as from Norway, Great Britain, Germany, Mexico, and Japan.

"My largest tailgate was actually for a road game," he said. "I had an estimated 245 Viking fans show for my tailgate at Atlanta for the 1999 season opener. This road trip was made into a documentary by the Travel Channel for the television show 'American Journey.'"

Maas said geography has a lot to do with this series.

"It boils down to the proximity of the two teams," he said. "I also know that there are Minnesota natives working in Wisconsin and Wisconsin natives working in the Twin Cities, so that during Viking-Packer weeks you'll see a lot of workplace bragging rights being staked out around the water cooler.

"And then there are the mixed families. I have a close friend who lives in Milwaukee who is a huge Vikings fan. His Wisconsin license plate reads 'Go Vikes.' Yet his entire family is Packers fans. I have a married couple that regularly tailgates with us. He is a Vikings fan, she a Packers fan. And it's always fun to see those two go at it after the games.

"And six seats from me in the dome is a Vikings season ticket holder who is a Packers fan. He wears his green and yellow for that one game each year and for all the others he wears the colors of the team the Vikings are playing that week. This last year I was able to grab his hat and throw it onto the field to [Vikings mascot] Ragnar, who promptly rubbed his armpit with it. We all laughed. It's always good-natured ribbing between Packers and Vikings fans. I think each side realizes that the bragging rights only last as long as the very next game."

That's not exactly how it works for Jan Kuchenbecker, an ardent Packer fan from De Pere. She makes no bones about her disdain for Green Bay's neighbor to the west.

"I think my dislike of the Vikings started back when they were going to the Super Bowl and my aunt saved an article in which a St. Paul writer ripped the people of Green Bay," Kuchenbecker said. "I know I'd rather see Chicago, Dallas, or anybody else win before the Vikings. I always hope they lose.

"I remember back when the Vikings were winning and the Packers were down, and we went over there on a bus trip. We all wore shirts that said, 'I'd rather be a has-been than a never-will-be.'

"I think Lynn Dickey was hurt and so David Whitehurst was our quarterback," she said. "The Minnesota fans thought they had it made, but we beat them and by the third quarter they were starting to leave."

Kuchenbecker's roots as a Packer fan run pretty deep on her family tree.

"I was a Packers fan before I understood what it was about, before I knew that you got three tries to get a first down," she said. "My father's uncle was there for games at all of the stadiums since the beginning, so he saw all of the good and the bad. I think he's why we got interested, and now we're all Packer fans. I bought stock for all of my nieces and nephews. It didn't pay to put your name in before [on the waiting list], but I signed up for the lottery to get tickets when they expand the stadium."

Kuchenbecker works in sales for a local cheese company and runs into dozens of Green Bay's faithful followers during business trips around the country.

"I've been in Packer bars in Dallas, D.C., Denver," said Kuchenbecker, whose favorite players have included Bart Starr, Reggie White, and Brett Favre, for their talent and what they've meant to the community. "I go through withdrawal in July and August, so I have to throw in a tape from the Super Bowl, NFC Championship game [against Carolina], beating Dallas (45-17 in 1997) or Vikings games.

"I went to the [2000] Monday night game and didn't get home until 1:30 a.m., but a friend who couldn't go taped it for me and I watched it after I got home. You see stuff you miss while at the game. Then I had to be to work by 8."

Losing sleep appears to be part of the job description when it comes to fans of the Packers and Vikings, and not far down the list of prerequisites is patience, especially for Green Bay backers who've waited decades to get firsthand glimpses of these football gladiators.

Rainy and Hal Knutson of Janesville moved up an estimated 20,000 spots on the season ticket list from the time they signed up in the mid-1960s until they got the call they thought might never come in 1997.

Hal, a retired General Motors worker who does furniture upholstery and tinkers with classic cars, said the couple attend quite a few of the games at Lambeau and usually donate one to a raffle at St. William Catholic Church.

"We had an opportunity to get a package when they left Milwaukee [after the 1994 season], which is two home games and one preseason game, but we decided to wait. Rainy was always bugging the ticket office, and finally we got them."

The Minnesota game that he most remembers is the "Monday Night Football" game that most of the country witnessed in 1998.

"We sat through that and watched Randy Moss slaughter them [the Packers]."

Rainy is an even more rabid Green Bay fan. She and several fellow nurses from Mercy Health System and their husbands have thrown Super Bowl parties for about 25 years.

"We have always followed the team," Rainy said. "It was sometime before their first two Super Bowls that we, just out of a whim, signed up for season tickets. We were at a scrimmage or preseason game or something. But I never thought it would take that long."

Although he doesn't enjoy the same luxury of owning season tickets, Otto Raster finds other ways to stay in touch with his team.

Raster, 84, is a Medford, Wisconsin, native who moved to the Twin Cities in the 1950s. He lived in Medford and worked in Wausau but lives in the St. Paul suburb of White Bear Lake.

Otto goes by the Metrodome at least a couple of times every week, but his heart has been with Green Bay since the early 1930s. He watched some of his favorite stars from that era, such as Don Hutson, Arnie Herber, Clarke Hinkle, Tony Canadeo, and Cecil Isbell. He also attended the 1939 championship game in Milwaukee in which the Packers avenged their 1938 title contest loss to the New York Giants, posting a 27-0 victory in front of 32,279 at the State Fairgrounds as Herber and Isbell threw touchdown passes.

He keeps up with his beloved team through a subscription to *Packer Report* and watches games on TV. He's such an avid rooter that he attended three consecutive legends fantasy camps from 1996 to 1998 and has a photo gallery of sorts in his house.

"I believe I was the oldest guy to ever do that. Here I am, 81 years old, and I'm catching passes from Bart Starr and Lynn Dickey. And I caught every one, too."

That kind of support is what separates Cheeseheads from most others, said Raster, who had Viking season tickets in their early years.

"Fans over here are very different in that they want a winner, and when their team loses they desert them," he said. "I think it started way back when the Gophers were good and well-known nationally. Packer fans hang in there win or lose. But people over here respect my allegiance."

Raster said things have changed since the Vikings moved indoors.

"I hated it when they moved into the Metrodome. Parking is a heck of a problem. I just don't like the atmosphere. But I loved it back when they played at Metropolitan Stadium. I remember one of their playoff games, against Los Angeles. It was snowing like hell. They [the Rams] looked lost."

Raster has passed many of his football-following traits onto his son, Tom, who settled in Hugo, Minnesota, after attending the University of Minnesota.

Tom, 57, bounced around with his family in Wisconsin and Pennsylvania but has spent most of his life in Minnesota. However, his heart has always remained with the Green and Gold.

"With my dad, I was a Packer backer from the get-go. As a kid growing up around the Packers' first Super Bowl teams, you followed all of those guys, Paul Hornung, Jim Taylor, Fuzzy Thurston. In those days, you knew every car in town, and it was the same with football players. There weren't as many teams or players, so you knew all of their names and positions.

"After the Vikings showed up, a piece of my allegiance naturally went to them, but in the depths of my soul it was still the Packers. So with us, we would win no matter what."

Tom said living on foreign soil hasn't been too painful for him.

"The Chicago Bears were always the No. 1 team to beat; that series goes much further back. That was blood," he said. "But this has always been a good rivalry. Minnesota fans gravitated to Green Bay before the Vikings arrived, and then when the Vikings started they gained some of the old Packer fans."

Tom, who went to games at Metropolitan Stadium on his motorcycle because he could park much closer, accompanied his father to the 1998 fantasy camp in Green Bay.

"I wanted to do something special, and that was definitely exciting to be around those guys from the '50s and '60s," Tom said. "But to do that with your dad, that was special beyond belief. I spent more time watching him than worrying about what I was doing."

Rick Brantner understands that feeling all too well. His father, Matthew, brought him up a Packers fan.

Brantner lives near Eau Claire and owns a bar called The Welcome Matt, which is named after his father and is 2 1/2 miles off Interstate 94. He and family and friends have become famous for their tailgating parties at Lambeau that feature a casket and someone named Elroy, a remote-controlled guy who represents Packers fans and is the bar's mascot.

Brantner, who usually has a $100 bet with a Vikings fan every time the two rivals square off, usually takes bus trips to Green Bay games through You Make the Call out of Shawano.

"I didn't watch a lot until I got out of high school, mainly because there wasn't much to watch in those days," Brantner said of the Packers' mostly feeble performances. "The rivalry is pretty intense around here, but Viking fans in Wisconsin are pretty good. We get some Viking and Bear fans, but mostly it's Packers.

"Over in Minnesota, some of the Viking fans can be hateful. They throw beer and everything at Packers fans," said Brantner, who attended Green Bay's 27-11 victory at the dome on "Monday Night Football" in 1997, one of only two Packer wins there in the 1990s. "I must admit they've had a pretty tough time over there. While Lambeau is packed all of the time and you feel just fortunate to go to a game there, in the Twin Cities any Tom, Dick, or Harry can usually get in. But your view isn't very good, and sitting inside isn't football to me."

Most Minnesota fans would concur, especially transplants such as Rob Nelson of Janesville who's had an opportunity to watch from Lambeau's bleacher seating.

He became a Viking fan because when he was eight years old his family moved to Minnesota from North Dakota. They lived there for about 2 1/2 years, and that was when Nelson started to learn about football and began rooting for the team. He moved to southern Wisconsin when he was 10 but said he remained "pig-headed" when it came to cheering for the Purple and Gold.

Nelson gained notoriety in recent years from losing bets with one of his bosses, Butch Hanson, a Packers fan from Beloit. Nelson had to wear everything from boxer shorts, caps, and sweatshirt to a green and gold cape, mask, and cheesehead.

His favorite players over the years have been Fran Tarkenton, Anthony Carter, and Cris Carter.

"I take a lot of ribbing, and I give it out, too. But I don't take it to heart because it just boils down to people rooting for their two favorite football teams. I'm a Badger fan, but my dad is a big Vikings fan, so I've always hung onto the purple."

And Nelson has kept a tight grip on this storied series.

"This became more of a rivalry in the 1990s because both have had quality teams, which has made it easier for us Viking fans to come out of the closet around here," Nelson said. "But one thing about Green Bay that I can appreciate as a pure football fan is the Frozen Tundra, the mystique of Lambeau Field and the history of the Packers. They have a lot of pride in their hometown team, and you can feel it when you're there."

Nelson has attended several games at Lambeau in the past seven or eight years, but one incident he remembers is traveling to the Metrodome for the December 1 "MNF" game in which the Packers gave coach Mike Holmgren his first and only victory on the artificial turf.

"Lab Safety took a bus over, and I was the only Viking fan out of 54 people," Nelson painfully remembered. "They threatened to drag me behind the bus, and I think the fact that the Packers won is what saved my skin. I thought some of them might throw me off from the upper deck, but it was all in fun. They taunted me for five hours there and five hours back."

Tad Turek of Oregon, Wisconsin, can sympathize. He is a Faribault, Minnesota, native who's lived in the Madison area since 1988. He is a UW-Madison alumnus and Badger fan who works in the capital city.

He's attended quite a few Packers games, getting tickets through friends. Turek had his moment in the spotlight while at the 1998 Monday night game in which Randy Moss became a bona fide star in ripping through the Packers secondary.

"I was wearing a Vikings uniform, the helmet with horns and braids and the works, and I got on TV," he said.

Turek has never seen a Viking contest in the Metrodome but has attended Minnesota-Wisconsin football showdowns and Twins baseball games indoors. But he said nothing beats being outdoors at Lambeau Field.

"If you want to go to the dome, you might as well watch it on TV," Turek said. "The open air makes everything feel right. Lambeau is a fabulous place to watch a game. There's no comparison if you're a football fan. You have a much better time. And even though you get ribbed if you're wearing the opposing team's colors, I don't have anything bad to say about the Green Bay fans."

One visit didn't prove so happy, though. Turek, Matt Kussow from Waterloo, Wisconsin, and one of Turek's best friends from high school, Jeff Elstad, attended the Minnesota–Green Bay game in 1996.

"Jeff parked in a yard across from the stadium, and we got packed in up against somebody's house," Turek said. "Everybody else had Wisconsin plates; his was the only one from Minnesota. We had to wait around for three hours after the game to get out. I think some of the people were inside the house. My buddy wasn't too happy, especially because he still had a seven-hour drive back home."

Turek's house isn't covered in Minnesota memorabilia, but he defends his territory.

"You have to support your team."

His favorite players have been quarterback Fran Tarkenton, tight end Joe Senser, and Randall McDaniel, an All-Pro guard who left for Tampa Bay in free agency and recently retired.

"I was an offensive lineman when I played in high school, so I always pay attention to play in the lines."

Vic Haen knows those names, but he harkens back to the pre-Viking years, the 1940s and 1950s, when he tracked the feats of such Green Bay greats as Tony Canadeo, Billy Grimes, Tobin Rote, Jack Jacobs, and Ted Fritsch.

"Those were the days when you used to know the rosters by heart," said Haen, a Kaukauna, Wisconsin, native who's lived in the Twin Cities since 1976. "I remember Bart Starr when he was third-string behind LaMar McHan and Babe Parilli. My father went to games at City Stadium when I was a kid. That was back when you could even sneak in."

Haen, 63, doesn't try that anymore. He has season tickets but usually makes it across the Badger State for only one game per season. His brother, Jerry, two sisters, and his mom still reside near Kaukauna, so family members continue the Packers' rallying cry.

"My brother and I went to the Ice Bowl and froze, so I won't go to anything after November," said Haen, a semi-retired accountant who stays busy during tax time. "It has to be something in September or October and not a night game so I can drive back. That pretty much leaves a noon game on a Sunday." Regardless, Haen said he definitely sees differences between the teams' followers.

"As far as Viking fans go, the Packers are their biggest rival," he said. "For many Packer fans, it's still the Bears, although that has not been much of a rivalry recently. Packer fans stick with their team through thick and thin, but Viking fans jump off the bandwagon. They're great at following a winner, but with Green Bay, the Packers are the only thing."

Dan Frost would agree with some of Haen's observations, but he'd strongly take exception to others.

The 31-year-old is from a northern Minneapolis suburb and moved to Madison in the early fall of 1997, where he works in marketing and sales for Ameritech. He cheers for the Vikings no matter what their record is.

"Being born and raised up there, it was baptism under fire," Frost said. "My family was football fans, so we followed the local team. I had all of the posters and jerseys of Tarkenton and [Chuck] Foreman. I grew up idolizing Tarkenton, Sammy White, and [Ahmad] Rashad. The Vikings have always been number one."

Frost was among the Minnesota fans who frequented the Badger Bowl south of the Beltline in Madison when the establishment had an NFL Sunday Ticket contract during the 1999 season in which games that weren't televised locally could be viewed via satellite hookup.

That arrangement has ended, but Frost said his support for the Vikings and their rivalry against Green Bay will endure.

"It's been kinda fun the last couple of years," he said. "I don't think there's ever been an all-out hatred, but some fans dislike each other. I get razzed all of the time, but I give it back as much as I get it. I'm a black sheep in the hub of Packer country.

"Both teams have been so much more dominant in recent years, so it's been a nice, intense situation," Frost added. "I don't care for some of the things he does, but I'm glad Randy Moss is on our side. My friends and I didn't think the team would be higher than third or fourth [in the division] with Daunte Culpepper, but I think he surprised the whole league. And I don't like his cheap shots, but Cris Carter is a great player.

"I tease Craig [Thill] a lot," Frost said of one of the managers at the Badger Bowl who's a big Green Bay fan. "We golf together all of the time and bounce everything off each other. I was telling him that in two or three years the Vikings will sign Favre because he'll be an old retread or because they'll have salary cap problems."

Packer fans worldwide would shudder at the thought of such an outrageous development, but one place where the discussion would no doubt be heated is Gabe's By the Park.

Tim Weiss has run the sports bar for 13 years, carrying on a tradition established by previous owner and longtime bartender Bill Driscoll. It's not unusual that either sports fan ran the establishment in St. Paul. But the fact it's been a watering hole for Packers fans in enemy territory for 23 years makes it stand out.

"I was a big Packer fan even before buying Gabe's because my dad was a big fan," Weiss said. "We own 120 season tickets, but our business comes first, so I haven't been to many Viking games the last couple of years. But I try to get over to Lambeau at least once a year."

Weiss said Gabe's, which is a mile north of Interstate 94 on Lexington Parkway, is always packed on game days.

"We have a great clientele," Weiss said of crowds that range from 200 to 500. "It's usually about half Green Bay fans and half Minnesota fans, and there's a lot of bantering back and forth. We stop stuff before it gets too out of hand.

"We figure the more the merrier," Weiss added about allowing the dreaded people wearing purple to enter. "People come in wearing everything. Sometimes they bring in Viking candles and table settings and the whole works. This year we had two Dumpsters, one purple and gold and one green and gold. We have a lot of people from out of town show up. Some come from as far away as Eau Claire and Tomah."

Dave Timm, 43, and his wife, Mary, wouldn't have to travel that far. They are residents of New Richmond, just 15 miles from the Mississippi River.

He's a Packers fan who works at Anderson Windows in Bayport, Minnesota, and a native of Clayton, Wisconsin, about 30 minutes northeast of New Richmond in Polk County.

"We usually go down [to Green Bay] and get tickets through a travel agent or try to get them from scalpers at the games at Lambeau," Timm said. "My brother, Geoff, and his wife, Nancy, go over all of the time and tailgate and watch from one of the bars if they can't get tickets."

They haven't seen Minnesota play at Lambeau, but they've seen Tampa Bay twice in the first three games they attended.

"We see a lot of Packer and Viking stuff around here, but if Minnesota's losing, you don't see much purple," he said. "You see Packers fans with everything on their cars or at lots of house parties."

Timm said the competition can get fierce.

"At work, every week is a rivalry regardless of which team wins or loses or even if they're not playing each other," he said. "Most of the fans from both teams are pretty good-natured about it, but a lot more of the Viking fans are fair-weather."

Not unlike the aforementioned Rasters and many fans from both sides, the Timms' relationship with their favorite team is a family affair. Nancy and Geoff Timm attend as many games at Lambeau Field as they can, getting tickets through Event USA or from those dreaded scalpers.

Even though the longtime fans haven't seen their Packers play against Minnesota, they live in the middle of contested real estate.

"Sometimes it gets pretty vicious for my husband at work," Nancy said. "Most of them are good people and take the ribbing well. They have bulletin boards where fans from both teams can put up newspaper clippings, T-shirts, etc. I've heard stories about Packer fans who've gotten their license plates vandalized and stuff over there [Twin Cities]."

Nancy said she has a rather large memorabilia collection, which includes earrings, hats, scarves, Mardi Gras beads, jerseys, pants, shoes, pretty much anything green and gold.

"My family thinks I take things to an extreme," she admitted. "When we can, we take people over who've never been to a game at Lambeau before. We do the tailgating, but my favorite thing is when we first get into the stadium, and to watch people, especially the little kids. When they get to see their favorite players and how excited they get.

"At one game, I think it was against Detroit, I noticed this guy wearing a Minnesota jersey. I asked him about it, and he said he was having such a good time and that he was rooting for the Packers that day. I think a lot of Minnesota fans miss the atmosphere of an open stadium because it's not the same. They have such a positive thing going on in Green Bay."

That's not always the case in northwestern Wisconsin.

"The number of Viking fans has increased over the years, but they seem to be more fair-weather fans," she said. "I get so nervous whenever we play them because the rivalry is so strong. You have to live up here to really appreciate this rivalry."

Even though Tom Tibbetts was born in Bemidji, Minnesota, and has lived in Wisconsin since he was a youngster in 1955, he grew up a big Baltimore Colts fan.

"I remember Johnny Unitas, and then the Vikings joined in '61, so they became my second team," the Beloit resident said. "My favorite player for the Colts was tight end John Mackey. Back then it was always Green Bay winning, and everybody would tell you that Bart Starr was better than Unitas. I hated that. But then the Colts moved to Indianapolis, so I dumped them and have followed the Vikings ever since.

"I liked the Purple People Eaters and then the Orange Crush in Denver, back when all of the defenses had great nicknames," Tibbetts added. "I loved Keith Millard. He was such a tough defensive player."

Tibbetts said it gets frustrating living in Packer country, but part of that is his own fault. He has been co-owner of T&T Sports for 20 years; his partner, Glen "Snook" Thostenson, is a Green Bay fan, although both share a strong loyalty to the Wisconsin Badgers.

"I've gotten so I hate Packer fans, they're all sons of bitches," Tibbetts said with a hearty but needling laugh. "So, what better team to pick up and root for than the Vikings? The majority of Packer fans are the biggest whiners around. A friend of mine says the Vikings are low-lifes, but if it's something about Green Bay then it's a different story. Like in 1998, when Minnesota broke the record for scoring points, they're saying that the Vikings keep passing and are running up the scores. A couple weeks later the Packers are way up, by like 17 points, and they're doing the same thing. That irritates me. It's a bunch of bullshit."

However, the Vikings' season-ticket holder—he and his sister share four seats—says that the rivalry is still great.

"The Packers and Bears are a big deal to Bears fans, and I don't want to say it's not a good rivalry because of the history, but Chicago has been on such a downhill turn," Tibbetts said before the 2001 season. "So the Packers-Vikings is a much bigger game to win. It's a lot more important because the Vikings have been much better. I'm the type of person who would rather beat a good team than beat up on a poor team. It's like when I'm playing golf. I want you to have your best game and I want to have my best game and beat you. I think most sports fans would. That makes the win that much more satisfying."

Tibbetts said the 2000 Monday night contest that ended with Antonio Freeman's miraculous catch and a Green Bay victory was not a good example of that.

"I love being indoors because the team that plays the best will win," he said. "The Vikings outplayed them but bad luck, the rain and the bobbled snap on the field-goal attempt made the difference. All that talk about that's the way the game was meant to be played, which to me says you want more luck involved. Luck can go both ways, so I'd rather see it truly be decided on the field."

Still, Tibbetts said this series is worth the price of admission.

"There are thousands of people cheering all of the time, and that helps you get into each and every play," he said. "It's so fun because somebody's high-fiving it for everything. All of the Packer fans and their kids who've followed these teams since the early '60s, this game is unique."

Dean Johnson from Willmar, Minnesota, knows of what Tibbetts speaks. He's been a Minnesota state legislator for almost 25 years, while serving as a Lutheran pastor for 30 years.

"I don't totally dislike the Packers, but some people around here think they're married to the devil," Johnson said. "I used to love the Packers and watched them every Sunday afternoon. Men like Vince Lombardi and Bart Starr were my childhood idols, but when the Vikings came along I had to make a decision. Today, it's nice to take Cheeseheads' money and beat them, too."

That certainly wasn't the case at first.

"The first Packer-Viking game I went to was when I was 21, which is 32, 33 years ago, when they played each other at the University of Minnesota," Johnson said. "I was working with campus security and got assigned behind the Green Bay bench. I thought I had died and gone to heaven. I remember vividly the images, how big and fast those guys were.

"In the old days, you'd sit in the snowbank, drink beer, and eat hot dogs. That was just the way it was supposed to be," Johnson added. "All of the players that come to mind—Jim Taylor, Gale Gillingham, Fuzzy Thurston, and Max McGee. And Vince Lombardi, the person I admired most. He knew exactly what he wanted every day and took crap from no one."

Although Johnson said the ever-increasing price of and difficulty in getting tickets has forced him not to attend as many games as he used to, the rivalry is still big.

"I think it's intensified for both teams," he said. "When you're in that dome, you can't even talk to the person next to you. The energy from Packer and Viking fans is second to none."

CHAPTER EIGHT

FROZEN TUNDRA AND HOUSE OF HORRORS

Inclement weather is commonplace when Minnesota and
Green Bay tangled. This was a classic example, as the Vikings
claimed a 13-6 victory at Lambeau on November 27, 1977.

MINNESOTA AND PARTS OF Wisconsin were buried in a foot of snow, as the first major winter storm of 1970 hit the region November 21–22.

The Twin Cities suffered mostly wind, but it gusted out of the northwest at more than 40 mph when the Vikings and Packers took the field that Sunday afternoon. The temperature at game time was 16 degrees under clear skies, but it dropped during the day, creating a wind-chill of 25 below zero and worse. Clint Jones' short run in the third quarter was the only touchdown by either team as Minnesota prevailed, 10-3.

As was Viking head coach Bud Grant's edict, the Vikings didn't take advantage of any kind of heating contraption on the sidelines, and gloves were off limits. Meanwhile, Green Bay brought in a blast furnace or two for the bench, and Phil Bengtson's Packers were issued mittens.

Kicker Fred Cox, Minnesota's resident meteorologist, checked the conditions an hour before kickoff, trying to read the wind.

"I couldn't figure it," Cox said in the *Press-Gazette*. "I decided I'd just aim for the middle of the goal posts and drill it."

Cox was successful from 25 yards out but shanked one from 29. Green Bay's Dale Livingston missed attempts from 25 and 31 yards in the first half and then bounced a 13-yarder off the upright in the fourth.

"I talked to Cox before the game," Livingston said in the article. "He told me how tough it would be, but hey, from the 12-yard line you should be able to kick a field goal in a gale."

Green Bay punter Donny Anderson was equally troubled by the wind. Twice during the third quarter he had to kick against it from near his end zone, resulting in 28- and 34-yard efforts.

The 34-yarder gave Minnesota the ball on the Packers' 42, and Viking quarterback Gary Cuozzo threw a 37-yard pass to Gene Washington, who might have scored on the play, but the whipping wind played with the ball like an updraft catching a Frisbee. Washington came back and waited for the ball, enabling a Green Bay defender to bring him down at the 4-yard line.

"I feel terrible," Anderson told the *Green Bay Press-Gazette.* "The wind has a downward direction inside the 20. That and the Viking rush really made me hurry my kicks."

"You try not to think about the wind," said Green Bay quarterback Bart Starr, who completed 12 of 23 passes for 123 yards. "But it was the wind, not the cold, that affected the passing game. There were times when I threw the ball away rather than take any chance at all against the wind."

Almost 48,000 hearty souls braved Mother Nature's fury as the Vikings won their seventh straight game en route to their third consecutive Central Division title.

Even Grant said in the *Press-Gazette* that getting anything accomplished proved impossible at times.

"It won't be this bad in December. It can't get worse. It was like reaching into a grab bag every time you put the ball in the air."

Cox knew exactly what Grant was talking about.

"This was the toughest stadium in the league to kick field goals in because of the open spots in the stadium," he added.

According to Joe Soucheray's book, *Once There Was a Ballpark: The Seasons of the Met, 1956-1981,* it was the windiest game ever played at Metropolitan Stadium.

But as ESPN announcer Chris Berman would say, that was life in the NFC's Norris Division, where surviving the elements was second only to blocking and tackling in determining the outcome of many games.

So, playing in the Twin Cities, Green Bay, or Milwaukee before the Vikings and Lions built their fancy, temperature-controlled palaces in the early 1980s often meant playing, and winning, mind games as well as the physical ones, especially at Metropolitan Stadium in Bloomington, where the Vikings compiled a 97-59-4 record, including the playoffs.

"Bud Grant's philosophy was that it was all psychological," Cox said via phone interview. "Yes, it was cold, but if you made up your mind, it always came down to doing a better job than the other team. You had to turn it into your advantage.

"I remember one year over here it was 30-below wind chill. The bottom line is that the field was frozen. They took the balls out before the game, so you can imagine what they were like by the third quarter. It was like kicking ice chunks. The winds were always a problem here. If they were from the northwest it wasn't bad, but if they were coming out of the east, it was one miserable stadium. Kicking in Green Bay was much better from a wind standpoint because it was usually coming at or going with you."

Most players from the 1960s and '70s said the games were more special despite those limitations.

"Football was meant to be played outside, and the elements were supposed to be a factor," said Cox, who has four grown children and 11 grandchildren with wife Bonnie. "Playing in the dome is a kicker's paradise. Playing there says to me made-for-TV, not getting cold and dirty. But nobody said us football players were supposed to be smart."

Soucheray's 1981 book relates that the coldest game at the Met was played December 3, 1972, when the Vikings hosted the Bears.

The temperature at kickoff was 2 degrees below zero, with a north wind at 11 mph, creating a wind-chill factor of minus 26. A crowd of 49,784 shivering souls watched Chicago complete two passes, gaining only one net yard through the air in losing 23-10.

"You can't call this cold," Grant said in the book. "We played games in Winnipeg when it was 20 below."

Leave it to the austere one to put things in perspective.

But because of those factors, memories came easily for players from both teams.

Willard Harrell came to Green Bay via the University of the Pacific in Stockton, California, so naturally he was one of many who faced major transitions upon arriving in the Upper Midwest.

"I remember when Bart flew me in after getting drafted in the third round," Harrell said from his St. Louis office. "What the team and the aura of the Packers was all about. And then reality set in. I had never been in snow before. It was a shock. I don't know if I ever got used to it, but cold is cold. I remember guys in the locker room trying to figure out what to wear, whether they should use Vaseline or anything to keep warm.

"But football back then meant being outdoors, smelling the grass, the hot dogs and popcorn, and a lot of that is missing today. It was all about falling down and getting grass and mud stains, getting down and dirty."

Former Green Bay quarterback and assistant coach Zeke Bratkowski said he doesn't remember playing in a lot of snow, but the wind and field conditions provided much bigger obstacles in their tussles against Minnesota.

"It was important to know what areas were shaded, where the ground was frozen, so you could get your footing or know where to set the ball for placements," he said from his balmy Florida residence. "I always wanted to know if it was going to be sunny, if it would be windy and affect the flight of the ball, what the field would be like, to determine what kind of cleats to wear.

"At Metropolitan Stadium, with the open end and the wind, that would play into whether you wanted to receive the opening kickoff or how you wanted to start the second half. We both had good teams, so it was a matter of who held onto it. And special teams were a major factor."

Stu Voigt grew up in Madison and played at the University of Wisconsin, so the series and its accompanying conditions weren't news to him when he joined the Vikings in 1970.

"Three or four times I remember we played at the end of the year either at Lambeau or Metropolitan Stadium, and even though I don't remember having any zero degrees, much of the time the field was frozen and it was the Packers and the Vikings. As tough as it was on the players, it was even tougher for the fans that came out all bundled up.

"But that's the way the Packers and Vikings should do battle. The winds could be brutal at the Met, so we had a definite advantage against anybody other than the Packers. Both teams were used to cold weather and the elements."

All-Pro guard Gale Gillingham, who like Voigt was raised in Wisconsin, attended the University of Minnesota. He said the respective stadiums and fans stand out in his mind.

"We always seemed to play when it was cold and all froze up," he said from Little Falls, Minnesota. "I think the game belongs outside; playing indoors is ruining football. The stadiums were always packed. I can remember up there when it was extremely cold, that by the end of the game about half of their guys would be down on our side of the bench."

Hank Gremminger, an easy-going Texan, worked in construction for 26 years. The Fort Worth area resident knew his business, having built a solid career with the Green and Gold in which he recorded 28 interceptions, including five in both 1961 and 1962.

He didn't remember much about specific games against the Vikings, even the 37-28 barn-burner in 1963 in which his 80-yard touchdown scamper with a blocked field goal clinched the outcome.

The late Gremminger said Fran Tarkenton always gave the Packers fits but that he intercepted the Vikings' star just before halftime once and got another one or two during his career against No. 10.

"It was physical football, especially when Norm Van Brocklin was the coach up there," Gremminger said in 2001. "It got miserable, sometimes, but the thing I didn't like about playing at Metropolitan Stadium was that you couldn't get your traction on the infield. I always liked playing in Lambeau, our backyard, where I loved playing for the finest fans in the world."

Those people, who have filled all four playing venues for the past 40 years, have constantly amazed these gridiron greats with their patience and devotion. They were, and are, the centerpieces of what this rivalry boils down to: football played the way it should and an atmosphere seldom matched anywhere in sports.

That spirit has been evident in dozens of ways: music by polka bands and marching units; campers and vehicles of every make and model dressed up for game day; charcoal smoke filling the air as sizzling meat, soups, or any food imaginable cooking on grills; thousands of liquid imbibers; and such loony and lovable characters as Krazy George, Gang Green, and the Packer Priest drumming up support in the parking lots and stands.

And while the other three stadiums had/have their charm and history, Lambeau Field ranks as the true Mecca of the NFL.

Located on the southwest side of Green Bay, it was known as City Stadium until being renamed in honor of the team's founder and first coach, Curly Lambeau, who died in 1965.

Erected in 1957 and dedicated at the September 29 season opener against the Bears, such dignitaries as Vice President Richard Nixon, NFL commissioner Bert Bell, and Miss America Marilyn VanDerBur participated in activities that culminated with Green Bay's 21-17 victory over Chicago.

The stadium's original 32,500 capacity has steadily increased until the prerenovation setup which featured almost 200 luxury boxes and 2,000 club seats, a sound system, and end zone scoreboards with JumboTron replay systems accommodated seating for almost 60,000.

However, nostalgia and mystique still reign at the venerable site, and Packer players and their foes are reminded by the large gold letters that display names of the 19 Green Bay greats in the NFL Hall of Fame and the numerals for the years that represent the team's record 12 championship seasons.

Sold out on a season ticket basis since 1960, the Packers started playing all home contests there in 1995 after 61 years of sharing time with County Stadium. In 1998, *Sports Illustrated* named it the No. 8 venue in the world to watch sports, with no other NFL stadium making the magazine's top 20 list. So, it's easy to see why Viking and Packer players love strapping it on there.

Darrin Nelson, the seventh pick in the first round of the 1982 draft out of Stanford, provided the Vikings with many of those same qualities that Harrell did for the Packers.

"I loved Lambeau Field. It was my favorite place to play," said Nelson, an associate athletic director at his alma mater and the sixth-leading rusher in Minnesota history with 4,282 yards (4.8 average) who also retired as the team's No. 3 career kickoff returner. "Playing on the grass was one reason, and the intimacy of the stadium was another. The fans were so close to the field, and they knew their football.

"After the game in the parking lot they'd feed you bratwurst, steak, a beer or two," added Nelson. "We got invited into people's trailers, even after beating them a couple of times."

Nelson said that attitude made it easy to see why Green Bay fans were so loyal, which was also evident when they showed up in the Metrodome.

"We never got any special pep talks, but the rivalry was always intense," Nelson said of a series Green Bay won 12-7 during his tenure. "And it seemed like half the Viking fans turned into Packer fans when we played them. It was always a great atmosphere, and the games were always sold out. There was a lot of demand for tickets for that game in particular."

One of the rivalry's old-timers, defensive lineman Bob Lurtsema, wouldn't change anything about his experiences.

"The greatest thing about playing the Packers was that you knew you'd get to play at Lambeau Field. You can't say enough good things about it. With Lombardi and everything, it was like a cloud, a mystique hung over that place. It was pure football: being outdoors, on grass, not a bad seat in the house, the fans and the uniqueness of it all."

One of Nelson's teammates, All-Pro safety Joey Browner, felt it, too.

"We played many of our games in Milwaukee, so I didn't get to go to Lambeau a lot," he said. "But that first time I was almost floating on air.

It was very exciting to walk out there. I could remember seeing all those old games on TV with guys breathing and the steam coming off, and it was cold as the dickens. I guess I'm a purist, an old-school kinda guy."

Cornerback Carl Lee, one of Browner's running mates in the Minnesota secondary, said the atmosphere at Lambeau was something to behold.

"One of the amazing things to me was going in and out of Lambeau and all of the people cooking and offering you food. I had a steak sandwich I'll never forget. Being there was more than going to a football game.

"Guys in my generation didn't have the experience of playing at the old Met, and I don't know if that was a blessing or a curse," Lee added. "But that was the battle of the ice teams, the two coldest places. So, especially as a young player, being at Lambeau was a big deal, the mystique of playing there and being around that atmosphere. The first time out of the locker room there I couldn't fathom what it was like. They had something going on that I didn't know anything about. The Cheeseheads, they were a thorn in our side."

Green Bay had its share of dreadful games and seasons along Lombardi Avenue, but the Ron Wolf–Mike Holmgren era restored much of what had been lost, making Lambeau an intimidating place to visit for the rest of the league.

The Packers were 47-5 there from 1992–1998, including 5-0 in the playoffs, but Minnesota notched two of those victories, the season opener in 1992 and the "MNF" mugging in 1998.

County Stadium, like the Met in Bloomington, was a baseball field with both benches on the same sideline. And even though seating and many other amenities didn't compare to Lambeau, the Packers enjoyed a lot of success at the former home of the Braves and Brewers, finishing with a 105-61-3 mark (.630).

Despite complaints of the facility's shortcomings, veteran Packer players talked about having fond memories after their final game there, a 21-17, last-minute victory over Atlanta on December 18, 1994, that helped them reach the playoffs.

One of them was offensive tackle Ken Ruettgers, who played 40 regular and preseason games there.

"Sitting in the tape room, icing down, it was kind of, how should I say this, melancholy," he said in a *Packer Plus* article. "It was the last time I would be taped here, the last time I would shower here, the last time I would play here. It has been a nice 10 years of coming down here to the Milwaukee fans."

Ed West, a tight end who always brought his lunch bucket to work on Sundays, missed that game because of bad ankles. But that didn't mean it wasn't a special day and place.

"All of the years I've been coming down here, to end it off on a winning note is a great feeling," West also said in the *Packer Plus* article. "But it is kind of sad to end something that has been really good to us. I don't think a lot of the players feel the way I do about the change. It definitely hit me. It's an emotional feeling for me. I appreciate the fans here and all the cheers and handshakes that I've got from the people of Milwaukee."

The magnitude of the moment wasn't lost on Holmgren either, who let down his guard in the *Packers Plus* piece.

"I don't usually get an opportunity to do that during a game," he said of looking up into the stands. "To see those people and acknowledge our fans. It was very emotional for me. I'm a little corny that way. Just glancing around, every section I looked at the people jumped up and yelled. It was really something. I'll never forget it."

It was the site for Green Bay's first NFL championship won on Wisconsin soil in 1939, and the team also claimed the 1967 Western Conference title there.

Weather was occasionally a legitimate factor in Milwaukee, but Metropolitan Stadium, where Green Bay finished 11-10, always presented potential story lines.

Capacity surpassed 48,000, and the rural-like setting about 12 miles from the Metrodome was home for some of the best players and most memorable games in the series.

Green Bay fullback John Brockington recalled the ups and downs he witnessed there, including these comments from *The Glory of Titletown: The Classic Green Bay Packers Photography of Vernon Biever.*

"When we played that game in '72, you know, for the division championship. Man, that was like running on concrete," Brockington said. "You couldn't find a hole, you couldn't find a soft spot, you had to find cleat marks from previous games and stick your cleat in those to get some traction. It was the worst. And that wind would come hawking through there: when you hit it, oh my goodness. It was the pits, a baseball field. It was rough, man."

Rookie Green Bay cornerback Willie Buchanon was more than surprised by what he encountered that day.

"I remember the first time I walked out on that frigid field; I had never felt anything like that," he said from his San Diego office. "Some guy was driving something that looked like a big lawn mower, with flames shooting out to melt the field. Guys tried to wear tennis shoes and all kinds of things for the different conditions. We didn't have all of the Nikes and Adidas like they do today. But weather was always a factor."

Wisconsin native Larry Krause also suffered under those conditions.

"I remember playing up at Metropolitan Stadium, the frozen ground and [Minnesota fullback] Bill Brown running around in his short sleeves," Krause said from his Dane County, Wisconsin, home. "That was the coldest place to play, in November and December with the wind coming out of the north, which was open at that end."

Former Green Bay offensive tackle Karl Swanke recalled a comical afternoon in the Twin Cities.

"One time at the old Met, the grass and ground were all frozen, well, basically it was mostly dirt because it was late in the year," said Swanke via phone from Vermont, another less-than-tropical destination. "So they had painted it green. Here we are, in the NFL and playing on TV. You had green paint all over your pants. It was pretty funny and definitely interesting."

Ex-Packer center and current announcer Larry McCarren said there's no comparison about where he preferred playing the Vikings.

"We were considered the two real northern teams in the division and with Bud Grant's hard-nosed attitude, we shared that common trait," McCarren said. "So, I hated to see them go inside because it changed the whole personality of that team. The Met was a great place to play, and I enjoyed it. That was good, old-fashioned football. They also had all of the tailgating, and then you'd come out of the dugout onto the field and see your breath, the boisterous fans, the vapors coming off players' helmets."

Green Bay star receiver Boyd Dowler, who was selected for the 1965 and 1967 Pro Bowls, said the weather didn't dish out anything he couldn't handle.

"I was born and raised in Cheyenne, Wyoming, and played at Colorado, so I wasn't a stranger to the cold, wind, or snow," the Atlanta Falcons scout said. "You knew that in those two places, and in Chicago and Detroit, that when November and December rolled around, you could confront some bad weather."

Minnesota tackle Tim Irwin, a lawyer in Tennessee, said that didn't really matter to the players or fans.

"There were many cold games, but they always had great fans, win, lose, or draw," Irwin said of Green Bay. "They hung in with the Packers through thick and thin. They loved their football and made lots of noise."

That was and certainly is the case, but nothing compares to the ruckus these enemies have caused in the 62,212-seat Hubert H. Humphrey Metrodome since 1983.

Quarterback Brett Favre and Holmgren summed up their troubles in the reverberating complex after the Packers' 28-14 loss in 1998:

Favre, who's been known to start singing at the drop of a hat, didn't want to play the same old tune, but his team's uneven offensive display was mainly because of the noise inside the bubble.

"There ain't much you can say . . . I think that every team that's come in here and played against their crowd and their pressure defense is going to get false starts," Favre said in the *Minneapolis Star-Tribune*. "That's part of it. So, you can complain all you want about the crowd noise and all that stuff, but that's part of it, and you've just got to handle it. And we came back and got a fourth-down play, a big play for us. But as I watched film of it all week, everybody had false starts against them. Trying to get off quick, trying to beat them on the count, you can't hear, so you anticipate sometimes and you get beat to the punch. That's one of the things you have to contend with when you come in here and play against their defense."

Holmgren was slightly more perturbed after the rash of procedure penalties forced his squad into even worse predicaments.

"Well, it was pretty noisy," he told the *Star-Tribune*. "If you have five procedure penalties in a row like that, and the quarterback turns around and says, 'I can't hear,' and they [the officials] say, 'Go ahead and play'... They're supposed to, if I understand the rule correctly, give you some consideration. I thought we had pretty good proof. We couldn't snap the ball without something . . . We weren't being careless with it. It was five times. After that, shoot, we'd better tell 'em we can't hear."

Green Bay safety LeRoy Butler, the team's senior member, reiterated how tough it's been for the Packers to play in the Metrodome, where the Vikings were 116-59 through the 2000 season, leading up to their second meeting of that year.

Butler said the Vikings have had Green Bay's number there, where they hold a definitive home-field advantage. He said the crowd noise and piped-in music have always contributed to Green Bay committing way too many penalties, especially false starts on offense and stupid roughing penalties when defenders can't hear the whistle or after pushing and shoving lead to fights in which officials always catch the second guy.

As for lining up in the Metrodome, Swanke agreed that the noise played havoc.

"They had that big horn, and when that sounded you knew they were doing well," he said. "But once they moved into the dome, what stands out is when they did the wave. It was louder than if everybody was just cheering because when one side was doing it, it would bounce off the other side and echo all the way around."

Regardless of the score or situation, Carl Lee said the Packer faithful came in droves and made their presence felt.

"I could never figure out where all of those Wisconsin people came from. It was almost like playing at a neutral site. You could have households split, one wearing a Viking jersey and the other a Packer jersey. That was all new to me.

"I remember a huge eyesore, a billboard that somebody had put up above I-94 supporting the Packers," Lee added. "Everybody wondered who had the nerve, but every day you looked up and saw it. It was a great ploy. It was like in the old days when you'd steal the other team's mascot before the big game."

The first contest between the two rivals in the Metrodome was November 13, 1983, and, perhaps fittingly, the weather outside was 38 degrees at game time with a light coating of snow turning into slush and mush.

Fans may have longed for a return to the past, but that was then, and this is now. However, players and Minnesota team officials probably begrudge what Green Bay and its fans have, especially after Brown County residents passed a referendum in September 2000 for a renovation project at Lambeau Field as the Vikings continue to press for a stadium to replace the Metrodome.

Wisconsin voters approved a tax hike that will provide $160 million of the $295 million needed to complete the job. An additional 10,000 seats will be added, raising Lambeau's capacity to about 71,000, and luxury box adjustments are estimated to raise the Packers' revenues to the upper third of the league.

"It's a great decision for the community there," Vikings executive vice president Mike Kelly said in a *Star-Tribune* article. "Whether it's Miller Park [in Milwaukee] or Lambeau Field, Wisconsin has always been terrific in supporting its franchises. And they went about it the right way. The public didn't just reject every possibility out of hand. They looked at a number of different possibilities and settled on one."

Obviously, roof considerations weren't even a serious option at open-air Lambeau. Still, Kelly couldn't help but fuel the rivalry's fire, even if it added to the political wrangling going on in the Twin Cities.

"As a loyal Minnesotan, I hate to get beat by the Packers in anything," Kelly added. "The last thing I want to see is the Packers get any sort of edge over us. So, we certainly don't want to be outdone by the Cheeseheads."

Kelly and the rest of the Minnesota organization worked tediously during 2001 to present a vision for a future football home for the Vikings and the University of Minnesota, a retractable roof stadium with a capacity of 68,500 located on the Gophers' campus.

At least they got it half right, allowing for a return to the days of yore during nice fall conditions. And the proposal would allow for the return of tailgating, a must for hearty Minnesota and Green Bay fans win, lose, or draw. The project is expected to cost between $450 million and $500 million to construct. The Vikings have committed to chipping in $100 million, and the NFL's matching construction program was expected to throw in an additional $51.5 million.

No matter what happens with the stadium issues in the land of 10,000 lakes, members of the Purple and Gold fraternity said having played at Lambeau has been one of their career highlights.

That included wide receiver Cris Carter, a sure bet to make the Pro Football Hall of Fame. In 21 career games against the Packers heading into 2001, he had 101 receptions for 1,212 yards and 10 touchdowns. Carter hung up his cleats before the 2002 season to take a job with HBO.

He still calls Lambeau his favorite place to play on the road, as these statements before their first meeting in 2000 prove.

"I just love the history of it," he told *the Star-Tribune*. "I love the small community. It reminds me of when I was going to play my high school games on Friday night. You turn the corner, and there the stadium is.

"It's the same feeling there. You walk out of the same tunnel the Cowboys walked out of in the Ice Bowl. Everything is exactly the same, for the most part, given a few upgrades. But the history, and Lombardi, and the fans, and playing against a great team and a great franchise like the Packers, that's why it's my favorite."

Ex-Minnesota guard Terry Tausch was a second-round draft pick in 1982 after a stellar career at the University of Texas. He said from his home in the Lone Star State that conditions often mirrored those of the Winter Olympic games.

"One time it was like 20 degrees and they had the heaters on before the game to warm up the field, but then they turned them off and the ground froze," said Tausch, who ended his career with a Super Bowl ring with San Francisco in 1989. "It was like ice skating. We played with Astroturf shoes. We were the better team, but we couldn't do diddly on that ice. They played power football, and we were sliding all over the place. I think they had that planned."

However, Tausch said, there was no strategy involved with the Green Bay fans. They were always there, and thus a factor home and away.

"It was like Dr. Jeckyll and Mr. Hyde," said Tausch, who remains good friends with former Viking quarterback Wade Wilson and ex-Minnesota tight end Mike Mularkey, who's on the Pittsburgh Steelers' staff. "Going in, the fans would be rowdy as heck and flipping you off. Afterward, they were the nicest folks, offering you brats, big ol' steak sandwiches, and everything."

Dale Hackbart played for both organizations, so he had firsthand knowledge of Packer and Viking fanatics.

"Packer fans have been tailgating from Day One," he said via phone. "I can remember going to games and it's freezing outside and these people are half-naked at 10 a.m. for a 1 p.m. kickoff. I was totally amazed to see that kind of support in a small town.

"Then when I was in Minnesota, Karl Kassulke and I would go over to the stadium between 9:30 and 10:30 and it'd be the same thing. I think they picked up the tradition from Green Bay. Some of them in snowmobile suits, others half-naked and all painted up."

Regardless, former Viking offensive tackle Doug Davis (1966–72) summed up most players' feelings about indoor vs. outdoor, turf vs. grass.

"I played on artificial turf a couple of times, and I have no use for the stuff," Davis said from his Tampa area office. "If a cow can't eat it, I don't want to play on it, and that's how football should be."

CHAPTER NINE

MEDIA MUSINGS

Viking wide receiver Randy Moss has torched the Green Bay secondary since his rookie year of 1998. But Antuan Edwards blankets the Minnesota star in this 1999 contest at Lambeau, a game in which Edwards picked off two passes, including one he returned for a TD in the Packers' 23-20 victory.

S PORTS JOURNALISTS love making predictions, usually backing them up with reams of statistics and injury reports, while a few weather maps and astrological charts are thrown in for good measure.

Most professional football purveyors of prose have learned that figuring out what will happen next in the Minnesota–Green Bay series is fruitless, but that hasn't stopped them from doing it just the same.

And when you can throw in a few references about the opposing team's fans, such as the girth of their midsections, how many accessories adorn their headgear, and what their beverages of choice are, including the odors that accompany this consumption, the better yet.

Columnist Tom Powers of the *St. Paul Pioneer Press* unveiled his prognostication before the November 6, 2000, "Monday Night Football" showdown at Lambeau Field:

"Under other circumstances, it would be considered a clash of apocalyptic proportions," he wrote. "We have a white-hot rivalry, several bitter assistant coaches, a Monday night setting. There's just one little thing getting in the way of this being a battle for the ages: The Packers aren't any good."

Later in the piece he fires a couple of customary salvos—it wouldn't be Viking-Packer week without them—at Green and Gold supporters. He's talking people here, not their jock straps.

"Granted, tens of thousands of Packers fans already are three sheets to the wind as they gear for Monday's game. Folks, there won't be one ballot cast in Tuesday's elections in Green Bay. The entire town doesn't sober up until Wednesday after a Monday nighter.

"The Packers, spurred by probably the best fans in football—just don't light a match near them—could create some mayhem early. It won't last."

His call of the game was way off; Green Bay won, 26-20, in overtime in a contest that was arguably the most dramatic win in series history. As for what went on in the stands afterward and throughout the city for days, Powers was probably dead on.

Another long-time Twin Cities columnist, Patrick Reusse of the *Minneapolis Star-Tribune*, zeroed in on Packer backers in an article that was published in the *Milwaukee Journal-Sentinel's* September 26–October 2, 1996, edition of *Packer Plus* magazine. His lampoon came after the Vikings remained undefeated with a 4-0 record, while handing Green Bay's apparently weakened juggernaut its first setback of the season, 30-21, also ending Packer fans' constant chatter about the Super Bowl for at least one week.

"There always has been a hefty contingent of Packers types when Green Bay comes to the Metrodome," Reusse wrote. "Never previously had there been so much green and cheese inside the big, blue room. The level of Wisconsin loyalty was such that it smelled like Colby and Leinenkugel's."

A collective and hearty "prost" rumbled across Wisconsin and nearby parts as they finished reading the story and awaited the next round, 'er, meeting.

And although members of the fourth estate in the Dairy State haven't coined a real good equivalent to the Cheesehead in Minnesota, press from east of the Mississippi River take their pot shots at the Vikings and their failings, especially of the postseason variety, whenever possible.

For example, Mike Vandermause, executive editor of *Packer Plus*, took advantage of such an opportunity in his December 21–27, 2000, column after Green Bay had completed a season sweep with a 33-28 triumph at the Metrodome.

In his article, Vandermause asked whether the Packers were the NFC's best team, considering they had beaten Chicago at Soldier Field, Detroit at home, and Minnesota on the road in successive weeks heading into the season finale against Tampa Bay.

His rationale against the Vikings holding that lofty position was this: "Minnesota is engaging in its usual late-season swoon. After a torrid 11-2 start, the Vikings are on the verge of entering the playoffs with a three-game losing streak [which they did after falling at Indianapolis a few days later]. The Packers exposed Minnesota's fraudulent defense Sunday at the Metrodome, with Brett Favre carving it up like a Christmas turkey. No matter what the Vikings do in the playoffs, and don't bet the farm on their chances, let it be noted that they couldn't beat the Packers this season."

Don Langenkamp enjoyed the same pleasure in his Monday, December 12, 1988, column in the *Green Bay Press-Gazette* after the Packers' 18-6 victory over the Vikings at Lambeau Field.

He wrote: "The Green Bay Packers, almost inexplicably, have laid claim to football supremacy in the two-state territory of lofty balsams, etc., with a pair of resounding victories over the big, bad Vikings, who have been labeled bona fide Super Bowl material by many."

Langenkamp continued: "Many of the players admitted to deep satisfaction in beating the Vikings, who had talked earlier in the week of the total embarrassment after the first Green Bay win. It got to the point where the Vikings were acting like a supreme boxer fighting a bum and getting sucker punched."

All of the jousting aside, those who have covered the Central Division rivals during the past four decades know that many of the games have had postseason implications. The hullabaloo surrounding the series has only added to the fun, particularly during the past 10 years worth of games, several that belong in Ripley's.

Dennis Krause is a Hartford native who's been the sports director at WTMJ-TV in Milwaukee since 1994, where he anchors the 4:30, 5, and 6 p.m. weekday reports. The UW-Oshkosh graduate has been at the station since 1987 and rattled off a bunch of memorable Packer-Viking moments.

"I remember standing on the sideline a few feet from where Terrell Buckley got burned for the long pass in 1993 at the Metrodome," Krause said. "The Packers seemingly had that game won until that play. I remember going into the Packers' locker room to do interviews, and you could just feel the anger and frustration. The players bit their tongues, but they were livid about the blown coverage.

"I wasn't at this game, but the T.J. Rubley nightmare in 1995 has to rank up there with some of the most infamous plays in Packer history. It just seemed to sum up the Packers' futility at that time at the Metrodome.

"The Randy Moss 'Monday Night' game in 1998. I recall the stunned disbelief at Lambeau Field as the Vikings embarrassed the Packers. It was like a basketball game of alley-oop as Randall Cunningham just served up deep passes over the Packers' secondary. And the 1998 rematch at the Metrodome wasn't necessarily a great game, but it was the loudest crowd I can ever remember. Between the blaring music and the fans, it was hard to even breathe or think.

"The 1999 game at Lambeau when the Packers won in the final seconds was a magnificent effort by Favre and the offense, and I remember the frustration of the Vikings offensive players as they watched their defense get torn apart when it mattered most."

Krause also has hosted various Green Bay pregame and postgame shows on the Packers Radio Network. He said the 2000 games may have topped them in excitement.

"The Freeman catch has to go down as one of the greatest and most memorable plays in Packers history, certainly in the Packers-Vikings rivalry," he said. "I was in the press box and looked away after I saw the ball deflected, figuring the play was over. I look up and Freeman is running into the end zone. We all watched the replay and were stunned that he actually caught the ball without it hitting the ground.

"What's easily forgotten is how Mitch Berger could have prevented all of that if he hadn't panicked on the fumbled field-goal snap. The Vikings had more downs to play with.

"I was not at the game in Minnesota, but my reaction was that the Packers dominated the line of scrimmage," added Krause, who also is an analyst for Milwaukee Bucks games. "I was surprised the Vikings didn't play with more fire considering home-field advantage was on the line. The future is tricky to predict. The Vikings' salary cap cuts would seem to weaken them, but you never know."

Len Kasper would definitely concur. The Michigan native and Marquette University graduate joined WTMJ radio in 1994. He was the sports anchor on "Wisconsin Morning News" after a run on "The Green House" in the afternoon.

"The Freeman catch will stand as one of the most incredible plays in the history of the NFL," Kasper said. "It was a regular-season game, but it was on 'MNF' and it was in a rivalry game. Plus, when you consider what a disappointing year Freeman had, this will probably be remembered a long time from now, more than him missing the finale vs. Tampa Bay.

"The second game was very surprising," Kasper added. "Yes, the Packers were streaking at the time, but I didn't think they'd walk into the dome and win. They made the Vikings look old and very overrated. It was also one of those wins that made Packer fans say to themselves, 'If only the Packers could get in the playoffs, they can do some damage.'

"I guess we found out how overrated the Vikings were in the NFC title game. My guess is that maybe 2000 signaled a changing of the guard in this rivalry. Sweeping the Vikings has never been easy for the Packers. And as long as Dennis Green was there, it continued to be very difficult. But while the Packers appear to be getting a little stronger again, the Vikes look to be disintegrating, slowly but surely. Another part of me thinks that no matter how good or bad these teams are in any given year, those two games will always be competitive."

Like Krause, Kasper said recent history is dominated by such examples.

"The few games that stand out to me are actually Packer losses. The Terrell Buckley game in '93 when he blew the late coverage and the inimitable Eric Guliford burned him for the game-winning TD stands out because it really signaled the end of Buckley's career in Green Bay and continued the Metrodome curse. I think of T.J. Rubley audibling into an interception there and a heartbreaking loss. Rubley was such a nice guy, it made for a tough post-mortem because all you could say was, 'What a boneheaded play.' The Metrodome truly was a house of horrors for Mike Holmgren, and those games stood out.

"But I think 'the' game that stands out the most is the Monday night game in 1998 that really signaled the end of the Packers' dynasty. After two Super Bowl appearances, they were embarrassed by Randy Moss at home, which seemed unthinkable. It was at that point that the '98 season turned for the worst in terms of the fans. Many began to wonder, 'Are we now seeing this team on the decline?' I really think Denny Green cherished that win as much as any in this series because he did it in Mike Holmgren's backyard, a place that was so sacred for so many years.

"I hate to admit that the games that stand out are Packer losses, but the fact that the Vikings have had so much success against the Packers says a lot about this rivalry. Because the Bears, up until '99, just could not beat the Packers for so long, I believe that rivalry lost a lot of luster. Sure, the rivalry always will be strong because of the history, but the Vikings became a more hated rival because of the competitiveness of the matchups.

"I hope the Vikings and Lions never leave their horrible domes because they have such a bizarre aura that has played into those rivalries," added Kasper, who now holds a broadcasting job with the Florida Marlins. "Just like cold, blustery Lambeau Field from the other perspective. Yes, they crank the music and crowd noise too loudly through the speakers at the Metrodome. Yes, it's distracting to the Packers. But it's also those things that make winning there so great if you're the road team. It's the ultimate challenge.

"So, as a radio guy on the flagship station of the Packers, I loved this rivalry. Four times a year, two vs. the Vikings, two vs. the Bears, I knew the callers would be charged up whether the Packers won or lost, and it made great radio."

Wayne Larrivee knows all about the Vikings and Packers from his 14-year stint as radio voice of the Chicago Bears. He's gotten an up-close look at the teams the past three seasons upon taking over for Jim Irwin on the Packer Radio Network.

His first two games in the series just happened to be during Ray Rhodes' first and only season as Green Bay's head coach. Regardless of how ill-prepared his team was or how sporadically it performed, Green Bay turned in respectable efforts against the Vikings.

"The Packers were the underdog coming into that first game [of 1999] because of what the Vikings had done to them the year before and the kind of season Minnesota had in '98," Larrivee said. "Everybody was holding their breath to see what would happen. But Antuan Edwards got his first interceptions and the game turned into a defensive struggle and had a lot of the old Black and Blue Division feel to it.

"The Vikings scored to take the lead again, and then Brett moved them down the field. And then [Corey] Bradford popped open for the TD, an incredible moment, especially because the Vikings looked like they were loaded again."

Green Bay pulled that one out, 23-20, but fell just short in the follow-up contest by an almost identical tally, 24-20.

"Then, in the second game, [Matt] Hasselbeck's TD pass on the fake field goal was a great play, and they had a chance to win it at the end, but unfortunately they didn't get it."

Larrivee also couldn't believe what he saw—and didn't see—on that gloomy November evening during the 2000 season.

"Before the catch, obviously you think about the Vikings setting up for the chip-shot field goal to win it, it starting to pour and them messing up the opportunity, sending the game into overtime," Larrivee said. "They had been inconsistent all game, but the Packers started moving the ball. It seemed like an ordinary play. And I'm thinking, 'What in the hell is Freeman wasting his time running to the end zone?' But you have to give him credit for not giving up. It was hard to see, but I reacted more to [Minnesota cornerback Cris] Dishman waving his arms and everything.

"It was a miracle finish, one of the greatest in Lambeau Field history, and you can go back and check this out, but all of these have occurred in the south end zone. The Ice Bowl, Bradford's catch, and this one. It's without a doubt the most hallowed ground in Packers history."

Larrivee knows a lot about that history, having grown up a Green Bay fan in his native Lee, Massachusetts.

"The Packers of the 1960s were great teams, and that was a once-in-a-lifetime run because I don't think anybody will ever win three [titles] in a row again," Larrivee said. "They weren't always the best team, but it was the way they won it, like in the Ice Bowl. They were a big-play, big-game team. Like in '67, they weren't the best, but they still won the championship."

And ever since Bud Grant took over in the Twin Cities, Larrivee said the Vikings have been at or near the top.

"Dennis Green and Mike Holmgren were part of it," Larrivee said. "Green had Holmgren's number. Almost every year somebody wrote him off, but you had to give Green and his staff a lot of credit. Nine out of 10 times he was right on, including the latest move with Daunte Culpepper. Even if you've got a good personnel department, it's the coach who puts the team together. And as much as I hate the Vikings, Green's the one who did the job.

"Even when the Bears had their run during the mid-'80s, it was the Vikings they had to get past," he added. "That goes back to 1968 when Minnesota won its first division title. That said to people that they had to go through them. It's been that way with both teams, especially in the last decade. This has been the biggest rivalry, more so for Minnesota, because the Packers and Bears weren't competitive together for so long. You'd have to go back to 1963 to find when the Chicago–Green Bay games really decided a championship."

Langenkamp said many of his experiences from covering the games for the *Green Bay Press-Gazette* have lost their sharp edges, but the former newspaperman still recalled a few colorful images from "the old days."

"I covered a few games at the old Met and always felt the Vikings fans of those days more closely mirrored those here," he said. "The Viking mascot was more real. The cheerleaders wore mukluks. The fans were bulked up in parkas and snowmobile suits. And, of course, there was Bud Grant, who never allowed heaters on the sidelines. In many ways, the scene was similar to County Stadium with both benches on the same side of the field. Once they moved into the dome and became more successful, the crowd became more upscale and certainly more refined."

As for the former Viking players and Grant, Langenkamp recalls some fleeting scenes.

"I remember interviewing Fran Tarkenton and being startled about how small in physical stature he was. He claimed to be six-foot, and was thusly listed that way. He was lucky if he was 5-10.

"Carl Eller, I believe, weighed only 240 or so, but he seemed much bigger. He carried the biggest wad of bills I have ever seen in a locker room. When the trainer handed him his valuables after the game, he dug down into a sock and came out with a bankroll even his large paw could not encircle. Conversely, Alan Page was almost thin, storklike. In today's NFL, I don't see how he could've played defensive line. But Simeon Rice [of the Tampa Bay Buccaneers] reminds me a bit of Page.

"And Grant, who has become far more entertaining in retirement, was the most taciturn coach I can recall," Langenkamp said. "Before one game at the Met, I was standing in the parking lot talking with some friends who had made the trek from Green Bay. One, a trivia buff, spied Grant making his way into the stadium. 'Who was the leading receiver for the Philadelphia Eagles in 1952?' he yelled. 'Would it have been Harry P. . . .'

"For just a split second, Grant turned his head. He never acknowledged the question, never slowed down. But for just a millisecond, I swear the faint semblance of a grin crossed his face."

Chuck Ramsey can relate to that, having worked in Titletown since the Vikings came into the league. The longtime but retired WBAY television newsman started in the sports department after attending Brown Institute in the Twin Cities.

He covered the Packers and put together the coaches' shows with Phil Bengtson and Dan Devine. One blustery afternoon stands out at Metropolitan Stadium.

"I was filming the game for the show. I forget what game or year, but it was December," Ramsey said. "It was the coldest and worst day of my life. The wind was just terrible. There weren't any spots left, so some of us had to go up on top of the press box. It was so windy that we put lag bolts into a 4-by-8-foot piece of plywood to anchor our tripods and camera down. I told Rex Marx, who was the top gun at ABC, that I thought I was going to freeze to death. He used some kind of infrared spotlights to keep the film from breaking.

"Because it was so cold, the rubber viewfinder got so hard that it made my eye all purple and bruised," Ramsey added. "My wife asked me about it and then I realized what had happened. It was a terrible day.

"And then their GM [Jim Finks]. He didn't impress me at all. He said, 'You gotta move.' And I said. 'I'm shooting for the coaches' show, I'm anchored down and I'm staying right here.'"

Ramsey said the rivalry heated up once the Vikings started winning in the late 1960s.

"In those days, it was always Chicago," Ramsey said. "They were our big rival, and we were theirs. And then you had the annual Thanksgiving Day games at Detroit. I know Lombardi hated going up there every year, but it was preordained or something.

"I think the Packers and Vikings started to become a rivalry when Bud Grant became the coach. He was such a neat guy and a great football coach. Things really got energized when they starting having that big Viking mascot and everything."

Ramsey said the three-hour grudge matches weren't enough. Sometimes the rivalry extended past the final gun, although that could be the case with many Minnesota opponents.

"I remember one game over there when Joe Kapp was Minnesota's quarterback. He threw his body around like Favre does today. It was a real close game, and he threw himself into the end zone for the winning score.

"There were only a couple of us media guys who went over there in those days, so we rode on the team bus. Well, I was sitting on the same side near Bart Starr, and you know Bart, he was such a nice guy. It just so happens that Kapp is out there waiting out on the curb for a ride or something. Bart waves to him, and Kapp gives him the finger! Well, one of the Packers next to me goes crazy. He says, 'Stop the bus, I'm going to kill him. Nobody gives Bart Starr the finger.'"

Although he wasn't around the series as long, Ramsey's former WBAY counterpart Bill Jartz knows all about the gamesmanship involved.

He was the station's sports anchor before joining the news side in October 1998. The Clintonville High School graduate worked in Wausau and used to do play-by-play for Packers preseason games.

"The thing with the Packers and Chicago was always small vs. big, and it centered on the coaches," Jartz said. "You had Halas and Lambeau or Lombardi, some of the biggest names in the history of the game. Then came Mike Ditka vs. Forrest Gregg, which was very emotional and smash-mouth stuff. But when the Bears went into a funk after winning the Super Bowl [in 1986], the series lost a lot of its luster. You know, the Bears still suck.

"The Vikings have been on the rise and they've been pretty equal with the Packers, and that's what makes a rivalry, when one team wins one or two and then the other does it. When it gets to be four, five or six in a row by one team . . .

"When Green and Holmgren took over, you had two guys brought up in the West Coast offense, and it was more of a cerebral thing in which they matched Xs and Os. It was competitive, but in a different way.

"I think some people want to manufacture it into a rivalry. Old Packers would still say the Bears, but some of the contemporary guys would say the Cowboys or 49ers. But the Packers-Vikings has had its moments, like when Frank Winters got poked in the eye [by Corey Fuller in 1996] and the Favre-John Randle TV commercials."

Jartz said that fans provide a good barometer, his case in point being the electricity in the air surrounding the 1998 "Monday Night Football" game at Lambeau.

"We had to move our pregame show inside because of the rain. But there were Viking fans in their Nordic wear. It was very, very high-energy. You could feel it in the city and in the stadium. But the Vikings spanked them and fed the Packers a pretty good piece of humble pie. After being to the Super Bowl twice, the Packers should have had more of the swagger, but Cris Carter and Randy Moss gave Minnesota the upper hand in the psychological battle. I'm sure it's been tremendously frustrating for the Packers, especially up in the dome on that turf.

"But Dennis Green's tenure reminds me of when Bart Starr was coaching in Green Bay in that they didn't enjoy the success I think they thought they would," Jartz added. "They should have beaten Atlanta a couple of years ago. That window [of opportunity] doesn't stay open for very long."

Joe Schmit has heard those grumblings of discontent in the Twin Cities for a long time as sports director at KSTP-TV in St. Paul.

"Viking fans really give Packer fans hell if Green Bay loses. Just take

Interstate 94 and you'll see all of the signs and things on the overpasses," Schmit said. "This rivalry is a Super Bowl twice a year for many fans, and the series has been so close it's phenomenal. It's one of the oldest cliches in the book, but you can throw the records out when these two get together, and that's true."

Schmit knows, having grown up in the Badger State. He moved to Seymour, Wisconsin, when he was five, graduated from UW-LaCrosse in 1979, and then joined WBAY-TV in his native Green Bay in 1981 for a five-year stint before heading to the Twin Cities.

"I grew up a major league Packers fan, with Bart Starr, Paul Hornung, and Jim Taylor, so I was die-hard to the core," said Schmit. "So when I moved to Minnesota, it was tough not to root for the Packers. But we all know it's a lot easier to cover teams or players when you build allegiances with them, so I've become pretty purple over the years. Especially with many of the older Viking players who've stayed around the Twin Cities, like Bill Brown, Bob Lurtsema, Mick Tingelhoff, Paul Krause, and those guys. But it's hard to give up that green and gold altogether.

"They took buses over to the games and always had extra tickets, so I went to a lot of games when I was growing up," said Schmit, whose father ran the American Legion hall in Seymour. "I remember my parents going to the airport to welcome the team back after big games and getting lots of autographs."

He did the Green Bay preseason games with Hornung during 1982-84, which marked the end of Starr's coaching run and the beginning of Gregg's.

"These Viking-Packer games are the hardest ones to do every year because I have a lot of family and friends over there who know I work here, and there are people here who know I'm from the Green Bay area, so I can't win.

"I remember the first game that I covered at the Metrodome while in Green Bay. We had celebrated our Christmas party and the after-party party the night before. Needless to say, I imbibed too much, and then we took a small, twin-prop plane over to the game the next day. We hit turbulence and were bouncing all over the place. I was sitting next to [Packers President] Bob Harlan and remember asking everybody if they had anything that would help. I didn't remember three-fourths of that game."

However, Schmit knows that these two teams have provided many special moments over the years.

"From getting to know many of the old players, the legends of the Vikings, almost to a person they'll tell you how much they loved playing against the Packers and playing at Lambeau Field."

He remembers running back Darrell Thompson, a University of Minnesota graduate and one of Green Bay's two first-round draft picks in 1990, scoring his first NFL touchdown against the Vikings at County Stadium.

"I was standing down near the end zone and he ran right toward me. It was a good, soggy, muddy field that day."

And the broadcaster said he doesn't have to go very far to see just how much Packer fans care about their team.

"Just go down to Gabe's By the Park in St. Paul," Schmit said. "There are so many Packer transplants over here you can't believe it. They're much more vocal and loyal than Viking fans. There will be huge lines to get into this place when the Packers are on. It's jammed every Sunday. It gets pretty colorful; they hang a Randy Moss jersey in effigy and everything."

Former Packer great Larry McCarren has covered the team since the late 1980s with WFRV-TV in Green Bay and since 1995 as one of WTMJ's radio voices. He said he's not so sure that the Minnesota–Green Bay series hasn't been a more heated rivalry than the Packers–Bears for longer than fans want to admit.

"I think people assume that [about the Chicago rivalry]," he said. "I'm not sure that's been the case inside the locker room. I think we're a little closer to Chicago mileage-wise, but we always used to bump into the Viking players more in the off-season. And when they were really good and going to Super Bowls, we always played them tough.

"I feel they've been our biggest rival, to be honest," McCarren added. "Guys care about the emotion of the moment, and both games have been super, but you can only drive up so much of this rivalry stuff. For so long you just knew the Packers or Bears were the better team, but with the Vikings you never knew who would win, and that makes for the best rivalry."

One of McCarren's sidekicks in the WTMJ booth was former Packer great Max McGee, who also became a fan favorite while providing most of the slapstick to Jim Irwin's play-by-play for almost 20 years.

McGee has been a Twin Cities resident since his playing days ended and he started making a name for himself—and lots of money to boot—in the restaurant business. He said the Central Division title almost always comes down to the Vikings and Packers.

"These two teams have been contenders for many years, now," McGee said, "so they usually have been the representative from the division. I've watched the Packers go to the bottom and come all the way back up to the top. And a lot of times that depended on how they did against the Vikings.

"For the fans over here and the Vikings, for them to get so close and not win the big one, pretty soon you get labeled. When Bud Grant was here, they didn't do it. And even though [Dennis] Green had one of the best records in the league, they haven't done it. And when you don't, you know your time has run out. It comes down to taking home the bacon and the rings."

He may not know anything about bacon or rings, but a person who's also had a keen eye on things has been Todd Korth.

The Oconomowoc native attended the University of Wisconsin and worked at the *Kenosha News* before taking the editorial reins of Green Bay's team publication, *Packer Report*, eight years ago.

"I think this rivalry has intensified, especially the last couple of years, as both teams have been more competitive," Korth said. "The Bears and Packers will always be a chief rivalry in most fans' minds, even when the Bears are down. But the Packers–Vikings is right up there, and that's made it pretty exciting here and in Minnesota."

Korth said the sights and sounds tell the story.

"We've done polls on our Web site and people still favor the Bears, but in the past couple of years the games at the Metrodome have been as loud as ever," Korth said. "Being in the press room, my computer would be vibrating from the noise. It's very intense, the fans screaming, and the crowds being so mixed, and that makes it even more exciting for Packers fans to win over there.

"Green Bay fans really get involved when the Packers play over in Minnesota, and they haven't been very successful over there, so Viking fans put up posters on the bridges along the highways, razzing the Packer fans to 'Go home, Cheeseheads.'"

"And you know that the Vikings purposely crank up the noise levels, under NFL guidelines, of course," Korth said with a hint of sarcasm. "I've talked to Viking personnel people who've admitted they do it. I know Mike Holmgren complained about it, and the league had them move the speakers to the end zone. But the next year they were back behind the Green Bay bench; they weren't hooked up. They said they were for the halftime show. It was a psychological thing, a tactic on their part."

Kevin Seifert has worked at the *Minneapolis Star-Tribune* for three years, but already knows what this series represents, especially to the people who pack the stands.

"Inside the locker room, to me, Tampa Bay has been the biggest rival for the Vikings, and that is based on the fact that Tony Dungy coached the Buccaneers after working with Dennis Green," Seifert said. "They had success down there, the coaches knew each other, so since the Packers went to the Super Bowl, this was the big game.

"But clearly for the fans, they see the Packers as the major rivalry," Seifert added. "I know there are more Packer fans than any other team that comes over here. I wondered how they got all of their tickets or who would sell them to Green Bay fans."

But Seifert got just as big a taste of what the rivalry means when he covered the "MNF" game in November 2000 at Lambeau.

"That was the headline, 'The Immaculate Deflection,'" Seifert said of Freeman's catch and heads-up TD run. "You had to stand up in the press box because even watching it live you couldn't tell what really happened. So you had to check the [replay] monitors. The people turned around and were banging on the glass. It was like being at a hockey game. Trying to write on deadline and all you could hear was the screaming and banging."

Another veteran of such on- and off-the-field occurrences is Bob Berghaus, sports editor of the *Press-Gazette*, who also covered the Packers while in Milwaukee.

"Back in the '60s, the Vikings early years, Fran Tarkenton drove Lombardi nuts," Berghaus said. "The Vikings dominated the Central during the 1970s, while the Packers weren't very good. But in the '90s both teams were perennial playoff teams and some of the fights on the field show how the games have been intense and meant something."

Berghaus, a Milwaukee native, said the 1998 game on Monday night was memorable for the game itself and for what happened in the locker room afterward.

"I was the only one to pick the Vikings to win that game," Berghaus said of the five *Packer Plus* panelists at the time. "Most of the Minnesota writers had also picked the Packers, so after the game I'm in the Vikings locker room and [John] Randle's in there holding court, swearing and saying, 'Screw you guys.' Then he noticed me and says, 'Hey, you're that dude who picked us to win.' He said it really pissed him off when their writers went against the Vikings, especially against the Packers. He spent four or five minutes talking to me. It was a funny deal.

"There have been some real characters along the way, and Randle was one of them. You add in the fact that Favre is colorful. He just laughed Randle off, and he would get on his offensive linemen not to listen to him and let him get under their skin. Randle's mouth was going all of the time, and once [Ross] Verba told me that Randle was talking to one of Green Bay's guys about his wife, but the guy wasn't even married, so it was actually pretty funny."

Berghaus said that even though Green Bay has struggled in the Pontiac Silverdome against the Lions, he senses much more hatred in the locker room when the Packers suit up to face the Vikings, especially because of the trouble they've had in the Metrodome.

"That 1998 Monday night game stands out," he said. "The stories [Ron] Wolf had to read about how he had the chance to draft Randy Moss, who had such a great game against them that night. It was really the changing of the guard in the NFC. It told the Packers that if they wanted to get back on top they'd really have to play offensive football."

However, that wasn't the first time the Vikings dashed Green Bay's hopes.

"In 1966, the Packers went 12-2 and lost, 20-17, to Minnesota, and I remember Lombardi was really ticked off," Berghaus said. "Through the years I've done interviews with guys like Jerry Kramer, and they always got fired up for the Bears. But I know the Vikings drove Lombardi up the wall at times and that he had a lot of respect for Bud Grant.

"And then in the final game of 1992, when Green Bay went over there with a six-game winning streak, they were 9-6 and needed a win to get into the playoffs. It was Favre's first year. But the Vikings won, 27-7. It was a big letdown to end the season, especially losing to the Vikings."

Stu Voigt has been in the thick of these clashes as a player and as one of the voices of the Vikings on WCCO radio with Dan Rowe. Voigt said a lot has changed since his playing days, but fans' love for these two teams remains as strong as ever.

"This has been a real healthy rivalry," Voigt said. "The fans have always been rabid, but they haven't gotten overzealous like some around the country. And for the most part, they have been respectful of each other.

There are a lot of Green Bay fans in the Twin Cities and a lot of Viking fans right over the border in Wisconsin.

"It's always been intense, but there's just much more media coverage today. We're in the Brett Favre era, and ever since the league expanded the playoffs to include wildcard teams, there's been power swings back and forth. And there's a lot more offense and wild scoring games and endings these days, which I think the fans enjoy."

CHAPTER TEN

BET YOU DIDN'T KNOW

Halfback Dave Osborn looks for yardage against Green Bay
in 1972. He played 11 seasons in Minnesota and then joined
the Packers during his final NFL campaign in 1976.

E ven though the Vikings didn't take the field until 1961, Green Bay has a history with teams from the Gopher State.

Green Bay's first season in the National Football League, 1921, included a 7-6 triumph over the Minneapolis Marines, a successful semi-pro squad, at Hagemeister Park in Green Bay. An estimated 6,000 fans witnessed the first gridiron contest between teams from the Midwest neighbors in the October 23 contest.

In 1922, the Marines fell by a 14-6 count in Green Bay on November 12 in front of 2,000 folks. The Packers followed with a 10-0 victory over the Duluth Kelleys in a nonleague tilt November 30.

Minneapolis came calling for the September 30 season opener in 1923, with the Packers again winning on their home field, 12-0. Green Bay downed the Kelleys by the same score as the previous season November 25.

Duluth earned Minnesota's first triumph over the Packers to open the 1924 campaign with a 6-3 home win in front of 2,000 fans. Green Bay avenged that setback with a 13-0 victory November 9 and downed Minneapolis 19-0 on October 26, the last time the two franchises faced each other until 1929.

The Duluth team changed hands in 1925 and dotted Green Bay's schedule again in 1926 as the Eskimos. The teams battled to a 0-0 deadlock October 3 in their only meeting.

Green Bay whipped the Eskimos, 20-0, on October 9, 1927, in their final confrontation.

Future Packer and NFL Hall of Famer Johnny "Blood" McNally suited up for the Eskimos during 1926–27. Oluf "Ole" Haugsrud was co-owner of the team that featured two other eventual Canton members, Ernie Nevers and Walt Kiesling, the latter who donned a Green Bay uniform from 1935–36.

Minneapolis resurfaced as the Redjackets in 1929, with the Packers claiming 24-0 and 16-6 wins at home and away, respectively, en route to a 12-0-1 record and their first NFL championship.

The Redjackets failed to score in the teams' two 1930 meetings, 13-0 and 19-0 in back-to-back skirmishes October 19 and 26. Green Bay went on to its second of three consecutive league titles, while that was the last heard from Minnesota until preseason games were played there in the late 1940s and throughout the 1950s.

* * *

After the Packers' 23-7 victory at Minnesota to clinch the 1972 Central Division crown, Packer middle linebacker Jim Carter recalled in a *Green Bay Press-Gazette* story a conversation he had with Minnesota great Alan Page.

"It was a little blue. When he was called offside the first time, he told the referee, "I was not offside, you blankety-blank. And I said to the umpire, he can't call you a blankety-blank. Then Page called me that. On the very next play, the umpire called the same thing on Page. I think he was still mad about what Page said to him on the previous play."

* * *

Two players with Green Bay ties helped Minnesota kick off its inaugural season of 1961 with an upset victory over Chicago, 37-13, in becoming the only expansion team in league history to win its first regular-season outing. Kicker Mike Mercer scored the first points in team annals with a field goal. He stayed with the Vikings for two seasons and bounced around the AFL before joining the Packers in 1968–69.

Tight end Bob Schnelker tallied Minnesota's first touchdown, hauling in Fran Tarkenton's first scoring pass for a 9-0 lead in the second quarter. Schnelker finished with only five more catches before being shipped to Pittsburgh. He later served two coaching stints with the Packers (1966–71 and 1982–85) before finding a job as Jerry Burns' offensive coordinator in Minnesota during 1986–1990.

* * *

Before the November 1, 1964, contest at Metropolitan Stadium, Father Francis Fleming of St. Olaf's Catholic Church in Minneapolis was quoted in the *Press-Gazette* as saying, "'It was suggested that I put a tag on the bulletin today saying that any visitors from Green Bay may receive communion even if they are going out to the stadium to root for the Packers; it isn't a mortal sin. That is theologically questionable."

* * *

One of the easiest scores in this series was the first touchdown, which occurred October 22, 1961, at Metropolitan Stadium. This account is from the book *Tarkenton* with Jim Klobuchar:

"The Vikings had an explosive offense, featuring Tarkenton, Hugh McElhenny, and receivers Jerry Reichow and Dave Middleton in the 1961 season, but their defense was very suspect at best.

"The Vikings' roster of defensive backs was constantly changing, the names and faces seldom known to the fans and not always to the coaches. At one stage the defense was being mangled so badly that Van Brocklin considered releasing the names only to the next of kin.

"One of the defensive backs was Rick Mostardi, a youngster from Kent State who was fast but fragile, bright but eminently beatable. In that game against Green Bay he established a rarely threatened NFL record by being beaten by 40 yards on a routine pass to Boyd Dowler.

"It was one of those play-action passes," Mostardi said. "Starr sends a back into the line pretending to hand off. Unless the defensive back is careful, this may make him forget all about covering Dowler and go for the fake.

"I'm covering Dowler. Starr sends Taylor into the line. I'm damned if I don't take the fake and come up on Taylor. Then Starr sends Hornung into the line, and I'm damned if I don't get faked by Hornung, too. I'm trying to sort them out, but neither one has got the ball.

"By deductive reasoning I figured there is only one place the ball can be at that exact moment. Right. It is floating high overhead. Dowler was standing there so long by himself he got impatient and started tapping his foot waiting for the ball to come down."

* * *

Injuries are a major and unfortunate part of pro football, and nobody knew that side of the game better than former Green Bay trainer Domenic Gentile. He related a story about Packers' defensive tackle Bob Brown's tolerance for pain in his 1995 book *The Packer Tapes*.

"Bob was never into conditioning or weightlifting. He felt he had God-given strength and that was all he needed. And he was one rough, tough son of a gun.

"Once he took himself out of a game in Minnesota and came over to me on the sideline. 'Domenic, check my leg. I have a little bit of a knot in there or something.'

"I examined his leg but couldn't find anything wrong. 'No problem,' he said. 'Don't worry about it. We'll get by somehow.'

"He went back in and played the rest of the game. The next morning, his leg was swollen, so we sent him to get some X-rays. Sure enough, it was broken. He had played the entire game against the Vikings on a broken leg."

* * *

Linebacker Dave Robinson said he and a handful of Packers had another good reason to beat the Vikings every fall.

"For several years it seemed like we always played the Vikings the first week of deer season, so you never wanted to get hurt because then you'd have to spend Monday in the training room instead of going hunting," Robinson said in a phone interview. "Jerry Kramer would take a carload of us up to some place up by Rhinelander.

"If you won, the fans would give you tenderloins, but if we lost we usually were served hamburger. I remember one year we only had one doe between all of us and were heading back. Well, all of a sudden a big buck runs out in front of Jerry, and he's driving his big four-door Continental, ya know, and he hits it. So we quick put a tag on and haul it back to camp."

* * *

The amiable Robinson became an All-Pro, but even he said his first couple of seasons were definitely learning experiences, much of it occurring on special teams.

"I was the fourth linebacker behind Bill Forester, Dan Currie, and Ray Nitschke," Robinson said, "so I played on all of the kicking teams. I even kicked off some my first two years because Paul [Hornung] was hurt and Jerry [Kramer] wasn't very strong on kickoffs. I remember saying I could do it and they told Vince. He comes up to me and I tell him I just want to work on being the best linebacker I can. And Vince says to me, 'Son, your best chance of making this team is as a kicker.'

"And then he tells me that because I get a head start after kicking it that I should get down first and bust up the wedge," Robinson added, still chuckling. "Well, that one time I got nailed by my own guy down there, and Dominic Gentile says he thinks I tore cartilage in my knee. But Vince comes over and tells me that I should get up and jog up and down the sidelines to loosen up and be ready to go back in just in case somebody gets hurt. I asked somebody to tell him somebody already was hurt, me. Luckily nobody else did, but that was just the way Vince was."

* * *

Minnesota defensive back Ed Sharockman also received a rude awakening to the NFL game, only his career hadn't even really started.

"I was drafted in 1961 [fifth round] but broke my leg in the annual College All-Star game against the defending world champion Philadelphia Eagles and missed my first year," Sharockman said. "Norm Van Brocklin was their quarterback, and then he retired and ended up coaching us."

* * *

Ron VanderKelen, the former University of Wisconsin star, landed a job as a backup quarterback with the Vikings in his rookie season of 1963.

He served in that capacity most of his career, completing 107 of 252 attempts for 1,375 yards, six touchdowns and 11 interceptions after leading the College All-Stars to a 20-17 victory over the defending champion Packers after his senior season. Robinson and University of Wisconsin athletic director Pat Richter were two of his all-star teammates.

* * *

After the November 27, 1966, game at Minnesota, a 28-16 Green Bay victory, the Packers' chartered United Airlines flight was forced to circle a second time because of strong winds at Austin Straubel Field.

Robinson said that the pilot deserved one of the game balls.

* * *

The Packers watched films of Travis Williams' four kickoff returns for touchdowns from 1967 before the October 4, 1970, contest against Minnesota at Milwaukee's County Stadium.

All-Pro tackle and future head man Forrest Gregg was an assistant coach and one of the four members of Green Bay's blocking wedge. He was joined by Robinson, defensive tackle Mike McCoy, and guard Gale Gillingham.

Gregg said it wasn't really anything mechanical, just determination that allowed running back Dave Hampton to rumble 101 yards for a score to give the Packers a 13-3 lead in the fourth quarter as they held off the Vikings, 13-10.

* * *

Speaking of Gregg, he established what was then an NFL record with his 183rd consecutive game played during the Packers' 10-3 loss November 22, 1970, at Minnesota. He broke a tie with former teammate and fellow Hall of Famer Jim Ringo, who had 182 straight.

"At last, I'm in that old record book," Gregg told the *Press-Gazette.*

* * *

Rough-and-tumble secondary player Dale Hackbart was a big hitter, but even he almost got dizzy trying to figure out where his NFL career would start.

"1960 was when the AFL started, and I was the first pick of the Minnesota franchise," he said from his Boulder, Colorado, office. "But they never played and all of their draft picks were transferred to the Oakland Raiders. I called them up and say, 'I'm your No. 1 draft pick,' and they say, 'Who?'

"Interestingly, Minnesota ended up getting an NFL team within a couple of months. But I signed with the Packers for $12,000 and got a $3,000 bonus; the Raiders offered me $7,500 and no bonus."

At one point, Hackbart was under contract with Green Bay, the Winnipeg Blue Bombers of the Canadian Football League and Coach Bud Grant, and the Pittsburgh Pirates of Major League Baseball.

* * *

Minnesota kicker Fred Cox was a teacher early in his career and then became a chiropractor. But a little known fact about him is that he invented the Nerf football, a foam rubber ball that remains a seller more than 25 years after he came up with it.

* * *

Former Minnesota defensive tackle Brad Culpepper (1992–93), a University of Florida product, was nicknamed "Caveman" by his Viking teammates.

* * *

Don Hasselbeck played seven seasons in the NFL, including the 1984 campaign with Minnesota in which he caught one pass while playing mostly on special teams and as a third tight end.

His son, Matt, was a backup quarterback behind Brett Favre in Green Bay during 1998–2000.

* * *

Linebacker Noel Jenke, a University of Minnesota product, was captain of the Gophers' football team and a three-sport star. He opted for professional baseball, playing two years in the Boston Red Sox farm system as an outfielder. The Vikings' 12th-round pick played on special teams and as a backup with Minnesota in 1971 before heading to Atlanta for one year and then to Green Bay in 1973–74.

* * *

Wide receiver Leo Lewis (1981–91) had been with the Calgary Stampeders of the Canadian Football League when he got a tryout from Vikings' head coach Bud Grant. Grant had played with and coached Lewis' father, Leo II, in the CFL.

* * *

When it comes to families, the Browners were at or near the top in NFL annals. Four brothers suited up.

Jim Browner was a defensive back with the Cincinnati Bengals during 1979–80 and Keith played linebacker with Tampa Bay, San Francisco, the Raiders and San Diego from 1984 to 1988.

However, the two most famous participated in the Minnesota-Green Bay rivalry. Joey patrolled the Viking secondary from 1983 to 1991 and finished his career with Tampa Bay in 1992, while Ross, a defensive end, played with the Packers in 1987 after stops in Cincinnati (1978–84 and '85–86) and the USFL (1985).

* * *

Two other brother combos battled in these border wars.

Grant Feasel was a Viking from 1984–86, while Greg, also an offensive lineman, wore the Green and Gold in 1986.

And the Huffmans also battled in the trenches. The late David Huffman, who died in a car accident in 1998, played two stints with the Vikings (1979–83 and '85–89) sandwiched around two seasons in the USFL. Tim Huffman was in Green Bay from 1981–85.

* * *

Two of the most rugged players to participate in this series were linebacker Lonnie Warwick (1965–72) and quarterback Joe Kapp (1967–69).

They were two big reasons for the Vikings' rise to prominence in the late 1960s, but they took their frustrations out on each other after a 30-27 home setback to Green Bay on December 3, 1967.

Kapp blamed his fumble, while Warwick was frustrated with his performance. The result: Kapp had two shiners and Warwick's nose was reconfigured.

* * *

While coaching in Winnipeg, Bud Grant wanted a fullback named Roger Hagberg, a University of Minnesota player who had been selected by Green Bay in the 10th round of the 1961 draft.

"He was ready to sign, but he wouldn't do it until he'd talked to the Green Bay people," Grant said in *Bud: The Other Side of the Glacier*, by Bill McGrane (1986). "We sat there in a motel room all night, calling the Green Bay guy every half hour. We finally got him early in the morning."

* * *

Minnesota swept the Packers in 1968. It won three of its final five games after beating Green Bay, 14-10, on November 10, to cap an 8-6 campaign. But the Vikings needed help from the Packers to win the division title and the playoff berth that went with it.

The Vikings had lost twice to Chicago, so they were rooting for the 5-7-1 Packers in the season finale at Wrigley Field. Green Bay held a 28-27 lead in the final minutes, but Chicago was driving and one or two plays within field-goal range.

Twin Cities sports columnist Sid Hartman did his play-by-play rendition, talking long distance to the Windy City, from the Minnesota locker room at Franklin Field in Philadelphia, where the Vikings had defeated the Eagles. When Green Bay middle linebacker Ray Nitschke intercepted a pass to secure the Packers' victory, the Vikings celebrated their first postseason appearance.

* * *

Grant and Vince Lombardi battled to sign the same players several times during their careers, including over Altoona, Wisconsin, native Fuzzy Thurston.

"I didn't know Lombardi well, but I had talked to him several times while I was at Winnipeg," Grant said in *Glacier*. "The first conversation was about Fuzzy Thurston. He'd been cut by Baltimore, and we brought him to Canada because we needed a guard. He'd been there a day or two when Lombardi got hold of him. Fuzzy came in to see me. He said he realized he had signed a contract with us, but his heart was still in the NFL. He said he would really appreciate it if we would let him go so he could get a chance with the Packers. We let him go, and he went on to become All-Pro at Green Bay."

* * *

Randy Scott played linebacker for the Packers for six years, 1981–86, before logging two games for the Vikings replacement team during the strike-marred 1987 campaign. He registered nine tackles during a 27-7 setback at Chicago.

* * *

Offensive lineman Karl Swanke remembers one harrowing experience surrounding Minnesota week, and it was just getting to the airport.

"We were flying into Minneapolis. It was one of the closest calls. We were banking to our left for the landing, and we see this small plane going in the other direction. It seemed like he was only a couple hundred feet away because we were close enough to see the person."

* * *

Dick Pesonen, a Minnesota-Duluth graduate who spent the 1960 season in Green Bay, started at right cornerback for the Vikings in their franchise opener against the Bears. He started 11 games that year, his only season in Minnesota.

Green Bay had lost Pesonen to the Vikings along with defensive tackle Ken Beck and running back Paul Winslow in the 1961 expansion draft. He went on to play with the New York Giants during 1962–64.

* * *

Minnesota cornerback Carl Lee eagerly anticipated the skirmishes against Green Bay, especially his one-on-one bouts against friend and foe, Sterling Sharpe.

His talents were recognized with Pro Bowl and All-Pro honors. However, he said being in the spotlight isn't always everything it's cracked up to be. That was especially true after the 1992 and 1993 campaigns when Sharpe set and broke his own NFL record for receptions in a season with 108 and 112, respectively.

"Unfortunately, he made the record catch in front of me, on one of those little short passes," Lee said with a chuckle. "I was close enough to be in the picture, so that was my claim to fame."

BIBLIOGRAPHY

Ballew, Bill. 1999. *Tough Enough to be Vikings: Minnesota's Purple Pride From A to Z.*

Bengtson, Phil. 1969. *Packer Dynasty.*

Cameron, Steve. 1993. *The Packers: 75 Seasons of Memories and Mystique in Green Bay.*

Carroll, Bob. 1993. *When the Grass Was Real.*

Daley, Art, and Jack Yuenger. 1968. *The Lombardi Era and the Green Bay Packers.*

Daly, Dan, and Bob O'Donnell. 1990. *The Pro Football Chronicle.*

Everson, Jeff. 1997. *This Day in Green Bay Packers History.*

Gentile, Domenic, with Gary D'Amato. 1995. *The Packer Tapes: My 32 Years with the Green Bay Packers.*

Goska, Eric. 1991 & 1993. *Packer Legends in Facts.*

Green, Dennis, with Gene McGivern. 1997: *No Room for Crybabies.*

Green Bay Packers media guides and yearbooks.

Green Bay Press-Gazette (newspaper and Internet site).

Klobuchar, Jim. 2000. *Knights and Knaves of Autumn: 40 Years of Pro Football and the Minnesota Vikings.*

Klobuchar, Jim. 1995. *Purple Hearts and Golden Memories: 35 Years With the Minnesota Vikings.*

Klobuchar, Jim, and Fran Tarkenton. 1976. *Tarkenton.*

Klobuchar, Jim, and Jeff Siemon. *Will the Vikings Ever Win the Super Bowl? An Inside Look at the Minnesota Vikings of 1977.*

Korth, Todd. 1998. *Greatest Moments in Green Bay Packers Football History.*

Kramer, Jerry, and Dick Schaap. 1968. *Instant Replay.*

Kramer, Jerry, and Dick Schaap 1985. *Distant Replay.*

Lombardi, Vince. 1963. *Run to Daylight.*

McGrane. 1986. *Bud: The Other Side of the Glacier.*

Milwaukee Journal-Sentinel (newspapers and Internet site).

Minneapolis Star-Tribune (Internet site).

Minnesota Vikings media guides.

Neft, David S., and Richard M. Cohen. *The Sports Encyclopedia of Pro Football.*

Packer Plus magazine, 1992-2002.

Poling, Jerry. 1996. *Downfield: Untold Stories of the Green Bay Packers.*

Rose, Steve. 1996. *Leap of Faith: God Must Be a Packer Fan.*

Rose, Steve. 1998. *Leap of Faith 3.*

Schaap, Dick. 1997. *Green Bay Replay: The Packers' Return to Glory.*

Smith, Don R. 1988. *Pro Football Hall of Fame's All-Time Greats.*

Soucheray, Joe. 1981. *Once There Was a Ballpark: The Seasons of the Met, 1956-1981.*

Time-Life Books. 1993. *Vikings: Raiders From the North.*

Torinus, John B. 1985. *The Packer Legend: An Inside Look.*

Wells, Robert W. 1971. *Lombardi: His Life and Times.*

INDEX